THE NORDIC WORLD

CASS SERIES: SPORT IN THE GLOBAL SOCIETY
General Editor: J.A. Mangan
ISSN 1368-9789

The interest in sports studies around the world is growing and will continue to do so. This unique series combines aspects of the expanding study of sport in the global society, providing comprehensiveness and comparison under one editorial umbrella. It is particularly timely, with studies in the political, cultural, social, economic, geographical and aesthetic elements of sport proliferating in institutions of higher education.

Eric Hobsbawm once called sport one of the most significant practices of the late nineteenth century. Its significance is even more marked in the late twentieth century and will continue to grow in importance into the next millennium as the world develops into a 'global village' sharing the English language, technology and sport.

Other Titles in the Series

Tribal Identities
Nationalism, Europe, Sport
edited by J.A. Mangan

European Heroes
Myth, Identity, Sport
edited by Richard Holt, J.A. Mangan and Pierre Lanfranchi

The Games Ethic and Imperialism
Aspects of the Diffusion of an Ideal
J.A. Mangan

Rugby's Great Split
Class, Culture and the Origins of Rugby League Football
Tony Collins

Footbinding, Feminism and Freedom
The Liberation of Women's Bodies in Modern China
Fan Hong

The Race Game
Sport and Politics in South Africa
Douglas Booth

The Nordic World

Sport in Society

Edited by

HENRIK MEINANDER

University of Helsinki

and

J. A. MANGAN

University of Strathclyde

FRANK CASS
LONDON • PORTLAND, OR

First published in 1998 in Great Britain by
FRANK CASS PUBLISHERS
Newbury House, 900 Eastern Avenue
London, IG2 7HH

and in the United States of America by
FRANK CASS PUBLISHERS
c/o ISBS, 5804 N.E. Hassalo Street
Portland, Oregon 97213-3644

Copyright © 1998 Frank Cass & Co. Ltd.

Website: http://www.frankcass.com

British Library Cataloguing in Publication Data

The Nordic world : sport in society. – (Cass series : sport
  in the global society)
  1. sports – Social aspects – Scandinavia
  I. Meinander, Henrik   II. Mangan, J. A. (James Anthony), 1939–
  306.4'83'0948

ISBN 0-7146-4825-6 (cloth)
ISBN 0-7146-4391-2 (paper)
ISSN 1368-9789

Library of Congress Cataloging-in-Publication Data

The Nordic world : sport in society / edited by Henrik Meinander and
  J.A. Mangan.
      p.   cm. – (Sport in the global society)
    "This group of studies first appeared as a special issue of The
  International journal of the history of sport, vol. 14, no. 3,
  December 1997" – T.p. verso.
    Includes bibliographical references and index.
    ISBN 0-7146-4825-6 (cloth). – ISBN 0-7146-4391-2 (paper)
    1. Sports–Scandinavia–Sociological aspects–History.
  I. Meinander, Henrik. II. Mangan, J.A. III. International journal
  of the history of sport. Vol. 14, no. 3. IV. Series: Cass series–
  - sport in the global society.
  GV706.5.N66   1997   97-43918
  306.4'83'0948–dc21   CIP

This group of studies first appeared as a special issue of
The International Journal of the History of Sport (ISSN 0952-3367),
Vol.14, No.3, December 1997 published by Frank Cass.

Printed in Great Britain by Antony Rowe Ltd.

Contents

Acknowledgements

Once again, without the meticulous and considerable effort of Doris Mangan this volume would not have met its publication deadline. The thanks of all the contributors and both editors are warmly extended to her.

Thanks are also extended to Dr Niels Kayser Nielsen for his assistance in locating Danish contributors, to Sara Donner for the initial translations of all Nordic contributors except for Per Jørgensen and Else Trangbæk, and to the Nordic Cultural Fund for funding these translations.

Series Editor's Foreword

In Norman Davies' recent and acclaimed *Europe: A History* there is no reference to 'the Nordic World'. It is with special satisfaction, therefore, that I applaud the contributors to this volume for adding a missing dimension to his mammoth historical enterprise.

Similarly, sport is considered by Davies in a most pedestrian way with specific references only to specific activities: athletics, football, mountaineering and the Tour de France. His chapters and chapter notes make only passing and parsimonious reference to sport as a European cultural phenomenon. He has certainly missed an opportunity; he has certainly dealt inadequately with a political and social manifestation of massive significance to modern Europe. Disappointing.

The contributors to this volume suffer from no such intellectual myopia and it has been a pleasure to work with them and to admire and assist their sterling efforts to express their evidence, ideas and arguments in a foreign language and to bring the culture of 'the Nordic World' within a European context, to a global audience through the medium of the English language. My appreciative thanks are warmly extended to them all.

J. A. MANGAN

Prologue: Nordic History, Society and Sport

HENRIK MEINANDER

'I am eating apples, smoking, missing Europe and composing,' wrote the 26-year-old Jean Sibelius to his fiancée one October day in 1891 from the little town of Lovisa on the coast of the Gulf of Finland.[1] The composer, who was later to become world famous, expressed a common view of the interaction between Central Europe and the continent's northern territories. Since ancient times there has been a strong tendency to accept the northern limit of the Roman Empire as the boundary of Europe despite the fact that numerous contacts were established with northern Europe beyond this later border during the Bronze Age. Cultural conventions are sometimes very tenacious! Nordic people today still talk about travelling to Europe when they cross the Baltic or North Sea, to more central parts of the Continent.

The dichotomy between the Nordic countries and Europe is in many ways an anachronism. Typically enough, the growing awareness of this has coincided with Sweden and Finland following in the footsteps of Denmark, though twenty years later, and joining the European Union in 1995. Nevertheless, underlying historic convention is a more long-standing feeling of irritation that Northern Europe is only thought of as at the margin of European civilization. A more polite and yet historically correct way of describing the relationship between the Nordic nations and other parts of Europe might be to describe the Nordic region as on the geographical fringe, but 'still an integrated part of a European network of economical, political and cultural communications with many centres and peripheries'.[2]

Continuous cultural interaction with Central Europe can be illustrated with another vignette from Sibelius's life. In the late autumn of 1891 he was in Vienna absorbing the intoxicating atmosphere of the diverse ethnic elements of the Habsburg metropolis. Exhilarated by the cosmopolitan environment of Vienna, paradoxically Sibelius suddenly found new inspiration from the Finnish national epic *Kalevala*, that would result in a music that was appreciated for its intense national charge.[3]

In the Nordic countries there are similar examples in the fields of literature and learning. Common to innovators was their ability to extract something from the larger European context that could also be used in a national and Nordic setting. The same capacity can be observed on the social level. Much of what we today think of as being typically Nordic is just the fruit of many centuries of close contact between the Nordic countries and 'Europe'. Protestantism, social democracy and the welfare state are all successful variations on common European trends. The same applies to the political, social and cultural evolution of modern sport in the Nordic nations, which is the theme of this volume.

What should actually be included in the all-embracing concept of 'Norden', 'the Nordic nations' or to use the precise translation 'the North'? In the mid-eighteenth century northern Germany, the whole of Russia, Scandinavia and some regions of the Arctic Ocean were included in the definition. In Central Europe and other parts of the western world, this sweeping definition still seems to hold good. Look at how the meteorologist on CNN waves his hand over the whole of the northern half of Europe when forecasting a new low pressure nearing 'Scandinavia'! However, the terms 'the Nordic nations' and 'Scandinavia' are strictly speaking not synonymous. By the Nordic countries is generally meant Denmark, Finland, Iceland, Norway and Sweden. In a strict geographical sense Scandinavia includes Sweden, Denmark and Norway, without Finland or Iceland. Since the 1950s the five countries have therefore officially used the term 'the Nordic nations', but in central Europe, and indeed the world, this distinction is rarely maintained. These elastic definitions accord with the fact that the history of the Nordic nations is not well known.

The five Nordic languages are similar, with the exception of Finnish, which is one of the few non-Indo-European languages on the continent. The other Nordic languages in all their dialect variants belong to a branch of the Germanic group of languages. Most of them are mutually understandable, even if Danish can often cause great problems for the other Nordic people. This is even more the case with Icelandic, which has kept much of Old Scandinavian that is not easily understood outside Iceland. Even Finnish with its over 400 Germanic loan words and a thousand-year-old cultural co-existence with the Swedish language has a strong connotative connection with the Scandinavian languages.

Politically, evolution has been less straightforward.[4] During the Viking Age (800–1050 AD) the first larger kingdoms and unions were formed in central and southern Scandinavia. At their strongest the Vikings, with their raiding sorties and trading voyages, came to dominate large parts of northern Europe – including both Russia and the British Isles. The Vikings retreated when the rest of Europe consolidated politically, when in the thirteenth century the power of the Roman Catholic Church increased and when the position of the German traders became stronger throughout the Nordic world. The integration of the church continued, but in the political arena there was already during the fourteenth century a strong reaction against the German domination of trade via the Nordic Hansa towns.

Animosity against the Hansa League petered out at the beginning of the sixteenth century with the birth of two strong monarchies in Denmark and Sweden, both of which broke with the Hansa, renounced the Catholic faith and converted to Protestantism in its Lutheran form. The Swedish kingdom had included Finland since the thirteenth century, while Norway and Iceland were joined to the Danish kingdom during the fifteenth century. Denmark and Sweden were rarely on good terms with each other and fought many internal battles up until the 1810s. With the exception of the Swedish victories in the Thirty Years War (1618–48) in central Europe, Swedish foreign policy to a great extent consisted of wars and confrontations with the great neighbour to the east, Russia. The period when Sweden was a great power, 1617–1718, was mainly due to Russia's weakness. When the Russian bear had regained its strength, the roles were reversed. The eastern part of the Swedish kingdom was occupied twice during the eighteenth century and when this happened for a third time in 1808–9 the whole of Finland was annexed to the Russian empire as a Grand Duchy.

In central Europe dynasties and national frontiers were restored after the Napoleonic wars, but in the Nordic countries there was a lasting change in the balance of power. Sweden's loss of Finland was compensated to a certain degree by the annexation of the Norwegian parts of the Danish empire in 1814. The result was stability in the Nordic countries, which has prevailed until today despite various political changes. Sweden's eastern policy became definitely defensive and its former rivalry with Denmark gave way to some political co-operation – *inter alia* the Swedish government supported the Danes during their wars against the Germans in 1848 and 1864. Stable relationships in the Nordic countries made it possible for Norway to gain independence peacefully in 1905 and even indirectly made it easier for Finland to liberate itself from Russia in 1917–18. Iceland got its independence in practice in 1918, although the Danish king was the official head of state until 1944.

The Second World War also changed the Nordic anthill. Sweden remained neutral, Denmark and Norway were occupied by Germany and Finland fought twice against the Soviet Union. The result was that these countries were on different sides when the Cold War set in. Finland signed a Treaty of Friendship and Co-operation with the Soviet Union that forbade an alliance with the West, Denmark and Norway quickly joined NATO, while Sweden clung to its neutrality. A common security policy was thus out of the question, but in other fields co-operation was intensified. In 1952 the Nordiska Rådet (Nordic Council) was established, a common forum for the countries' parliamentarians, and in 1973 a new form of co-operation was established in the Nordiska ministerrådet (the Nordic Council of Ministers). Passport control between the countries was abolished and during the 1960s a legal framework was created for a free Nordic labour market.

The break-up of the Soviet Union at the beginning of the 1990s created a new security policy constellation in northern Europe. Sweden and Finland had hardly had time to join the EU when the debate about the possibility of their joining NATO began. In Sweden's case there is questioning of the need to formalize and consolidate further a co-operation, that in reality has functioned for a long time. In Finland the NATO question has so far been taken up very cautiously, which is understandable due to its long eastern frontier with Russia. It is easy to understand that possible Finnish NATO membership will depend first and foremost on developments in Russia.

Nordic political stability after 1814 thus never led to military integration. But in the cultural sphere the internal balance was of the utmost importance, in that during the nineteenth century it slowly ripened into a practically oriented and deeply rooted interaction between the countries. Nordic artists and writers more than previously sought inspiration from each other. The countries' leading engineers, educationalists and physicians usually chose to develop their nations following the same guidelines as their Nordic colleagues. The expansion of popular movements – such as the 'Grundtvig', the workers' and women's movements – was seen as important to the state in the Nordic countries. Nostalgic references to the golden age of the Vikings were normal during the nineteenth century, but at the beginning of this century the vision of Nordic nations at the forefront of Europe replaced nostalgia.

Nordic self-reliance has not subsided during the twentieth century, even though two world wars have demonstrated in a concrete way how dependent the Nordic countries are on the rest of Europe and the United States. The confirmed 'Nordics' often refer to the resistance shown by the Nordic countries both to communism and fascism. Many of them also raise a warning finger against current European integration, which according to them, will lead to a gradual dismantling of the Nordic welfare state and to a reversion to a more open class society of a Central European type. These arguments prevailed when the majority of the Norwegian people voted against joining the EU in the autumn of 1994. But at the same time the majority votes in favour of the EU in the referenda in Finland and Sweden showed that most of the Nordic people see the EU more as a challenge than as a threat.

Parallel with the frantic search for a European identity, in each Nordic country there is a public debate about national cultural characteristics and the living conditions inside and outside the EU. What moral values are typically Norwegian? Is there a special Swedish attitude towards nature? Is the Finn really more stubborn than the Belgian? Why do the Danes smoke more than their neighbours? These kinds of question have certainly been asked down the ages, but today an increasing number of scientists and governments have become interested in such matters. The discussion goes back to the habit, mentioned earlier, of talking about the Nordic countries as something outside Europe. It is a question of whether we have our own past and our own future.

Academic research on the matter cannot provide a clear-cut answer. On the one hand, historians and theologians point out that European feudalism did not fully reach the Nordic countries and the rapid spread of Protestantism throughout the Nordic countries demonstrates a strong reliance on our own values. On the other hand, art critics and ethnologists stress that it is almost impossible to point to something in the material culture or social relations that would clearly separate the Nordic countries as a whole from the rest of Europe. Many sociologists and political scientists can be counted among those sceptics who stress that the borderlines actually cut across the Nordic world; between urban centres and rural peripheries, between the rich and the poor, between men and women. Most therefore now stress that, essentially, they are looking only for Nordic nuances and for regional characteristics.

This is the case in the present book. Its Nordic setting, however, has many practical reasons. The contributors have – typically enough in line with the ideal of 'Nordism' – for over a decade arranged seminars and joint publications with the consequent mutual references to and comment on each others' publications. Like many other Nordic research collaborations the language fellowship has been a natural driving force in the co-operation.

The general purpose of this volume is to show why sport came to play such an important part in the twentieth century in Nordic society. The breakthrough of modern competitive sports in Europe and the United States at the end of the last century coincided with the calculated establishment of collective rituals on a national scale. As Eric Hobsbawm points out, sport became an important tool in this mass production of invented traditions. In the Nordic nations special stress was laid on this function of sport because of the absence of ambitions in imperial and great power politics. Military and royal spectacles as a part of popular culture have not been lacking, but typically enough the visibility, energy and vigour of the countries' heads of state during this century have usually been connected with sport.

In Norway and Finland sport has become a crucial dimension of national self-definition. Norwegians still see skiing as the foremost manifestation of patriotism. Finns are supposed to show special interest in athletics because of the numerous Olympic victories of the long distance runner Paavo Nurmi. Although older and thus more self-confident nations, similar strongly positive correlations between sport and national identity are common also in Sweden and Denmark. As far as top level sporting performance is concerned, this kind of 'sports nationalism' does not differ from expectations in other parts of the world, but on the level of everyday

outdoor activities it is obvious that sport in the Nordic world is understood
to establish a decisive part of a special spirit of community. The people,
human body and nature constitute thereby a unity in the Nordic mind; it is
almost as if our national *and* Nordic existence is confirmed and embodied
only through a physical pilgrimage back to nature.[5]

Sport, culture and nature have gradually begun to entice academic
research in the Nordic countries. In his extensive studies on the origins and
expansion of the Swedish sports movements, Jan Lindroth has shown how
closely they are connected with the emerging civic society and, its economic
partner, expanding industrialization. Lindroth's thesis (1974) formed a solid
base for comparisons.[6] During the 1980s similar research on the other
Nordic sports cultures was published; in Finland by Seppo Hentilä and
Leena Laine, in Norway by Finn Olstad and in Denmark mainly by Ove
Korsgaard, whose book *Kampen om kroppen* (The Fight for the Body;
1982) has been quoted almost as much as Lindroth's work.

The attraction of Korsgaard's work lay mainly in his bold
characterizations. Influenced by Jürgen Habermas and Michel Foucault,
Korsgaard drew special attention to the body as a social means of expression
and instrument of power. He stressed the social dimension of the body
encapsulating this emphasis in his statement that modern sport embodies the
values of industrialized society. In his view, the spread of competitive sports
has revealed how a completely new view of mankind and nature is becoming
accepted. Similar conclusions had been reached already during the 1970s by
the German, Henning Eichberg, who has been an active participant during the
1980s and 1990s in Nordic research. Eichberg's sources have not been
Nordic, but through a number of well-documented surveys of the research of
others, his theses on the body as a contact surface between the individual and
the collective has been tested on Nordic material.

However, Matti Goksøyr objects to the body-centred paradigm. He
argues that it is unsatisfactory to describe the spread of a certain form of
sport as a kind of cultural transplantation of certain values from one place
to another. The spread of modern sports in northern Europe should to be
seen as a result of interaction between two dynamic systems. British rules
and equipment were willingly adopted, for example, in the Norwegian town
of Bergen, but their Anglo-Saxon symbolic values and social functions were
fundamentally altered by the local indigenous Norwegian society.[7]

Issues related to organizational structure and physical appearance in
sport were dominant in one or another way in the research until the late
1980s. Since then, though, the field of inquiry has expanded greatly. One of
the most important gains has been an increasing number of inquiries
involving social history and the history of ideas. This is in marked contrast
to the older historical research; a current ambition is clearly to get closer to

the sportsman and his social world. An indication of this can be seen in a special Nordic edition of the German sports history journal *Stadion* (1993/94). The Nordic tendency is the same as in the rest of the western world. The focus is more and more on questions that are topical in historical research in general; on cultural history, on microhistory, on gender history, on the social history of ideas and even on psychohistory.[8]

In short, academic research demonstrates an important shift in emphasis, namely, a greater interest in investigating the development of modern sports as one of many dimensions of the modernization of society. The consequence has been that the attempts to define what research in sports history and social science is, or should be, has lost much of its value. More and more scholars are beginning to think that definitions only give support to a restrictive academic attitude which seldom benefits research as a whole.

The contributions to this volume have been written by academics with very different standpoints. The aim is to present new research and show how varied it is. At the same time there is both a chronological and a thematic structure. The chapters cover a period of 400 years, starting with Mats Hellspong's analysis of the writings of the Swedish chronicler Olaus Magnus in 1555 and finishing with Else Trangbæk's discussion of gender roles in Nordic sports today. Most chapters span longer periods and overlap one another. Jørn Hansen's description of the symbolic value of gymnastics on the Danish–German border during the years 1848–1920 coincides, for example, both chronologically with Per Jørgensen's review of Nordic organizations prior to 1928 and Henrik Meinander's contribution on the sports rhetoric of the early twentieth century. This is intentional. The chapters in this way support and complement one other.

The thematic approach also has its own logic. The task of the authors was to choose as starting point a key word that was already important in their own current research and was seen as being an important aspect in Nordic sports culture. Mats Hellspong's key word was 'Time'. Hellspong has published surveys on everything from medieval to modern social phenomena. His ethnological education has made him, however, especially suited to take up the time element and the importance of space in the development and spread of modern sports. Hellspong has chosen to approach the question from a 'pre-historical' angle and after an analysis of the games of Sweden's agrarian society he turns to the much debated question of continuity between these and modern competitive sports. Hellspong notes, *inter alia*, the continuity thesis of Richard Holt, but finds it irrelevant in a Nordic context.

Jørn Hansen's starting point was 'Border' as key word, which usefully coincides with his having grown up near the Danish–German border. The border area has stimulated Hansen to undertake an analysis of the political functions of gymnastics. He touches on a central aspect of the ever continuous debate on the meaning of a Danish identity. From the 1840s the closeness to and dependence on Germany has led to nationalistic assertions and to definitions of Danes as completely different from Germans.

The Nordic countries' role in international sport is the subject of Per Jørgensen's contribution. His key word is 'Olympic'. Jørgensen shows how exclusive the selection of the national Olympic committees has been, even in the Nordic countries. Basing his views on substantial archive research, he argues that the Nordic countries had quite an important role in the IOC from its beginning. Jørgensen mentions many discussions that took place between the Nordic members in the IOC and its founder, Pierre de Coubertin, that are of importance for international research on the subject. The French aristocrat's flexible attitude to the amateur question is illuminated, as well as his difficult role as intermediary, both in Nordic personal conflicts and in the super powers' political entanglements.

De Coubertin's antique metaphors are taken up in passing in Henrik Meinander's article, whose key word 'Word' refers to the public rhetoric and private every-day language of sport. By contrasting conceptual historical analysis with reconstructions of social history, Meinander shows how large the difference can often be between the rhetoric and practise of sports. This was the case not least at the beginning of the twentieth century, when a number of technological innovations rapidly changed the material structure of society, while public debate about the change was being carried on using historical concepts and ideas. Young sportsmen in the Nordic countries had very little to do with this elegant and arcane language; their slang was rich in sports terms, but by no means of the kind that referred to morals or hygiene.

In the same way as Henrik Meinander sheds light on the limits of public rhetoric, Matti Goksøyr questions how spontaneous the nationalist feeling at sporting events actually was in the inter-war years in Norway. His key word, 'People', opens up many perspectives. Goksøyr discusses Eric Hobsbawm's thesis that on the one hand nationalist feelings are ideal constructions of an elite and on the other hand express a genuine fellowship of the people. According to him this 'popular resonance' has been underestimated in Norwegian historical studies. Quisling nationalism led to scholars throwing out the baby with the bath water. The consequence was a reluctance to accept that the Norwegian national victory celebrations could be an expression of a deep collective feeling.

Erkki Vasara's key word, 'War', shifts the focus from feeling to action. His contribution focuses on the military during the inter-war years showing that the Finnish Home Guard, like the Estonian and German Corps, were strongly influenced by their experiences in the First World War. In contrast to the voluntary defence work in the other Nordic countries, whose small scale and almost peaceful appearance originated in the fact that they had avoided the horrors of the war, the Finnish Home Guards' priority was consciously a choice to prepare for a new 'inevitable' war with the Soviet Union. Similar priorities were established in the Baltic States, Poland and Germany where, as in Finland, with no outside prompting, sporting and military capabilities were given equal value.

The voluntary defence organizations in the Nordic countries were in symbiosis with the state. Johan Norberg's article on the internal relationship between the Nordic states and the expanding sports movements point to a comparable dependent relationship. His key word 'Organization' refers to the co-operation, which after much wavering following the Second World War, had become so enmeshed that it could be said that the state and the sports movement were one organization. Norberg considers this state of affairs, using as an analytical model the Nordic welfare state and clearly discerns a Nordic model of mutual support. The sports organizations have been allowed to retain their autonomy, but have in exchange for state funding, taken on a large measure of responsibility for public health.

In the Nordic nations, as elsewhere, competitive sport was for long seen as something essentially masculine and women could only by their own diligence, acquire time, space and publicity within this sphere. In her study around the key word 'Gender' Else Trangbæk investigates how much this emancipation process affected the general view of women. The example she takes is Danish women and sportswomen, who through their cautious yet tenacious breach of masculine sports conventions gave their femininity a new and more active character. As Else Trangbæk points out, competitive sports did not open up similar possibilities for men, because to a greater degree they built on already established male norms and traditions.

This volume is not a comprehensive historical presentation of sport in Nordic society. That is not its aim. The essential purpose of this volume is to point academics in new directions in this growing field of the social history of sport and to link interests to the Nordic world to the wider world. J.A. Mangan takes us into this wider world. He raises substantive points about the necessary subtlety of research approaches required in any consideration of continuity and change, the need for 'wallowing' rather than 'dipping' into the historical 'pond' and the necessity of ensuring an adequate consideration of the power of rhetoric as well as structure in any review of socialization through sport. These are all issues that have concerned the contributors to the Nordic world of this volume, but as Mangan demonstrates, they are issues that require greater attention in a global perspective.

10 THE NORDIC WORLD

NOTES

1. Erik Tawaststjerna, *Sibelius* (Helsinki, 1968), p.155.
2. Lars Olof Larsson, 'Den nordiska konstens betydelse', in *Frihetens källa. Nordens betydelse for Europa* (Stockholm, 1992), p.116.
3. Tawaststjerna, *Sibelius*, p.128.
4. For an excellent overview of Nordic history in English, see David Kirby, *The Baltic World 1772–1993* (London, 1990); and idem, *Europe's Northern Periphery in an Age of Change* (London, 1995).
5. Henrik Meinander, 'Den nordistiska kroppen', *Internationale idéstrømninger og nordisk kultur 1850–1914. Den 22. nordiske historikermøte: Oslo 13.–18. august 1994* (Oslo, 1997), pp.95–104.
6. Jan Lindroth, *Idrottens väg till folkrörelse. Studier i svensk idrottsrörelse fram till 1915* (Uppsala, 1974).
7. Matti Goksøyr, *Idrettsliv i borgerskapets by. En historisk undersøkelse av idrettens utvikling og organisering i Bergen på 1800-tallet* (Oslo, 1991), pp.310–14.
8. See for example Else Trangbæk *et al.*, *Dansk idrætsliv: den moderne idræts gennembrud 1860–1940* (bind 1: København, 1995); idem, *Dansk idrætsliv: velfærd og fritid 1940–96* (bin 2: København, 1995); Leif Yttergren, *Täflan är lifvet: idrottens organisering och sportifiering i Stockholm 1860–1898* (Stockholm, 1996); Erkki Vasara, *Valkoisen Suomen urheilevat soturit: suojeluskuntajärjestön urheilu- ja kasvatustoiminta vuosina 1918–1939* (Helsinki, 1997).

A Timeless Excitement: Swedish Agrarian Society and Sport in the Pre-Industrial Era

MATS HELLSPONG

Myth and Reality

The earliest references to agrarian sport in Sweden appear to be a mixture of myth and reality. A number of sources mention a peculiar and dangerous kind of 'wrestling' that was supposed to have its roots in early agrarian society. This was 'bältesspänning', where two men each equipped with a short-bladed knife were bound together with a belt. Each tried to cut his opponent while at the same time avoiding being cut.

During the first half of the eighteenth century 'bältesspänning' was reported by two authors from Småland, Petter Rudebeck and Samuel Krok[1] as still practised in Småland during the seventeenth century. Krok maintained that 'bältesspänning' was so usual at the parties in this province that the women used to take large sheets with them for wrapping up their injured menfolk. One author from the nineteenth century says that the people who practised 'bältesspänning' bound their knives so that only the tip was visible. They agreed upon how much should be bound.[2]

It is doubtful if 'bältesspänning' was a kind of sport. It was more like a ritual form of duel. And whether 'bältesspänning' is fact or fiction is debatable. Mortal duels were forbidden in Sweden by the seventeenth century. Perhaps 'bältesspänning' existed in the rural areas before and after this prohibition. Reliable sources are lacking. Indeed, Gunnar Olof Hylten-Cavallius, a pioneer of Swedish ethnology during the nineteenth century and an authority on the peasant culture of Småland, made a detailed study of the ancient Småland law reports to gather information about 'bältesspänning'.[3] Deaths in connection with these duels should have resulted in court actions. But he found no mention of 'bältesspänning' in the court proceedings.

Swedish traditional sports have their roots in prehistoric duels and games, but how the shoots from these roots have developed is impossible to say. We know from the world of the Icelandic sagas that games and competitions were a feature of the Viking Age and the early Middle Ages. We know little, however, about how the Viking heritage was kept alive during the Middle Ages.

In the Icelandic sagas there is mention of sports on special 'vall' (i.e. embankments) or flat grassland. A reference in 1794 to these games embankments, where the inhabitants met to compete in different sports, indicates they were still in use in Sweden during the seventeenth century.[4] When the modern sports movement arose in Sweden around the turn of the twentieth century, the old word 'vall' was used in different places when christening the new sports grounds.[5] Many Swedish sports grounds have still romantic-sounding names from the early Nordic Middle Age: 'Arosvallen', 'Slottskogsvallen', 'Tingvalla'. Modern sport has sought historic legitimacy by hinting at its descent from ancient sport!

The first source that gives almost exact dates for traditional sport in Sweden is *Historia de gentibus septentrionalibus* (The History of the Nordic People) by Olaus Magnus. Magnus was a Swedish priest in the period before King Gustav Vasa severed the ties of the Swedish church with Roman Catholicism. With his brother, Johannes Magnus, who was Sweden's last Catholic Archbishop, he went into exile during the 1520s and finally settled in Rome. There he wrote his Nordic history which was published in Rome in 1555.

Magnus refers frequently in his work to sport in Sweden at the beginning of the sixteenth century. It is sometimes difficult however to differentiate between what he himself had experienced and what belonged to a mythical Swedish history, or even to Greek or Roman mythology. He writes of lifting stones and tossing poles as mostly military exercises for soldiers. He mentions skating on both deer shanks (bones of deer greased with fat) and metal skates,[6] and provides information about speed competitions on skates.[7] The participants competed on a 'mirror-like lake' on deer shanks and the prizes were weapons, silver spoons and even horses. Magnus also describes horse races in which the loser's horse was the prize. The valuable prizes indicate that Magnus is writing about aristocratic sport. It seems that he was better acquainted with the sport of royalty and noblemen than that of the farmers and peasants. He does, however, mention the skiing skills of the Lapps. Regrettably there are very few direct connections between Magnus's invaluable information and what we know of traditional sport in Sweden during the eighteenth and nineteenth centuries. Written evidence of skating competitions is not available until the mid-nineteenth century.

We have very little information about traditional seventeenth-century sport in the countryside. From unconfirmed sources we are told that the old games embankments were still used for the larger sports competitions.[8] That the distinctive popular sports of Gotland existed in this century is clear from remarks by two different bishops on the island, recorded respectively in 1633 and in 1683.[9] An oral tradition of an annual wrestling competition in the parish of Hedesunda in Gästrikland dates back to the first half of the seventeenth century.[10] This competition, which took place every year on Midsummer's Eve, is well documented from the early to the late nineteenth century, when the authorities stopped it. As an annual event, a competition occurring on a specific day and known to the neighbouring parishes, it is unique in pre-industrial mainland Swedish agrarian society.

The Origins of Sport

To discover the origins of many indigenous sports is a hopeless task when considering simple and popular pastimes, like wrestling and stone lifting. With games such as ball games with elaborate rules it becomes possible, but it is both difficult and imprecise. By way of example, how old is the game 'pärk' on Gotland? Heiner Gillmeister has made a study of the philological history of various popular tennis-type games in Europe.[11] From a survey of certain words in 'pärk' and comparison between these and corresponding words in similar games in north western Europe (France, Belgium, Holland and Germany) he can show convincingly that 'pärk' came from north-west Europe, most likely from Friesland.

When exactly is harder to say. Gillmeister assumed that this had happened by the thirteenth century since trading contacts between Friesian and Flemish businessmen and Gotland were interrupted at the end of the thirteenth century.[12] Further, Gillmeister assumes that 'pärk' as well as the Friesian 'keatsen' and a similar ball game in Saterland in north-west Germany originated before 1415, when the 'modern' way of counting points in tennis, 15-30-40, was introduced. According to Gillmeister, 'pärk' could well have been changed at a later stage. Counting in multiples of ten is more logical and it is possible that the Friesian ball game could have been introduced to Gotland only in the late Middle Ages or even during the seventeenth century. We have no certain proof of the existence of 'pärk' in Gotland before the eighteenth century.

'Pärk' differs in many important ways from the Friesian 'keatsen' and the Flemish 'kaatsen'. The 'pärk' square, the square where the player serves and starts the game, is much smaller and the ball is much bigger. This means that the ball can be struck without gloves (as it hurts less) and that it can be kicked. Gillmeister sees this as a very old feature, as he is inclined to see a connection between tennis and football as territorial games? But the question remains as to how the rules on kicking in Gotland came into being if the game came from the Friesians who did not allow it. Of course, it should always be born in mind that games can change over the centuries. And it is precisely those popular games, played in small parishes and villages in the isolated countryside, which are likely to change according to local circumstances. Local conditions lead to locally made rules. The game of 'pärk' was definitely introduced from north-west Europe, most likely by Friesians. On this point we can agree with Gillmeister, as the terminology of the game leads us to that conclusion. But when this happened is an unsolved mystery. The counting, the size of the ball and the rules on kicking could well have changed over the centuries.

The island of Gotland has attracted historical researchers of sport for two reasons. On the one hand, a number of archaic games have survived there into the twentieth century, long after they disappeared from the Swedish mainland, if indeed they existed there at all. Today Gotland cherishes them as symbols of the island's individual culture and they still exist, though in more organized forms than in the past. There is still, however, an original form of local sport that has persisted unchanged in the countryside of Gotland for many centuries, the 'våg'. We do not know how old 'våg' is. Since in 1633 Bishop Hans Nielsen Strelow wrote that 'one parish [competed] against another', it follows that 'våg' existed in the early seventeenth century. It may be even older.

'Våg' is the most original of traditional Swedish sports. One 'våg' was a competition between two parishes or between two parts of the same parish or between two groups in the same parish, for example, free farmers against farm-hands or boys against girls. There were competitions in a number of different sports – usually three. The teams agreed on one sport, the 'sampsel' (play together) and each team also chose another, the 'frispel' (free game) which was kept secret until the day of the competition. Naturally each team chose as frispel a game it thought it could play better than its opponents and practised it in secret. Usually the teams won their own 'frispel' and the 'våg' was then decided by the 'sampsel'. Another characteristic of 'våg' was the written challenge to opponents. These challenges, 'våg-brev', were written in a stylized and flowery language. They stated the place and date for the 'våg' and how the post-våg party should be organized. Usually it was stated that the losing team would pay the greater part of the costs of the party.

The Gotland traditional sports were arranged in a way that had no equivalent on the Swedish mainland. They involved the whole local community. 'Våg' attracted a substantial number of local spectators. The fact that these sports were well integrated into local society, and were much more than recreation for farm-hands, ensured their survival on the island throughout the nineteenth century.

There are similarities between 'våg' and 'pärk' which encourage speculation about a connection between them. 'Pärk' is decided on the 'best of three' games and 'våg' is decided on 'best of three' different sports. The team that wins the two first rounds in 'pärk' or the first 'frispel' in 'våg' has won the whole match. This similarity may indicate that the 'pärk' players in

Gotland created the game of 'våg' by adding two other sports to inter-parish games of 'pärk'.

Another possibility is that the institution of 'våg' was introduced to Gotland at the same time as the 'pärk' game, by the same people, presumably Friesian immigrants. This seems less likely because we do not have any evidence of a competition like 'våg' in Northwest Europe. The common European features in 'våg' – the 'duels' between communities or groups and the importance of the party – do not, it must be said, appear stronger than those features that clearly separate Gotland from the rest of Europe – the written challenge, the combination of different sports and the secrecy over choice of sports.

It is possible that 'pärk' was introduced into Gotland from parts of Friesia, by immigrants or traders who may also have introduced the custom of playing 'pärk' between different trading-houses or between businessmen and farmers. The game may then have spread to the countryside. Neighbouring parishes initially played 'pärk' in the European way. Gradually, however, they included additional sports, for example, running and stone throwing. For this new, more extensive competition, 'våg', the principle 'best of three' was retained. Through judicious adaptation the sport became a Gotland custom. Just when this process of integration took place is difficult to say. It could have been in the Middle Ages that 'pärk' gradually became 'våg', which was certainly in existence then.

On the Swedish mainland it is difficult to find examples of early sports competitions or to date precisely the origins of the traditional sports. It is odd that we lack any reference to skiing competition before the second half of the nineteenth century. Numerous finds of skis exist from prehistoric time in the snow-bound areas of Sweden. The Lapps skill in skiing has been attested to by many authors. But there are no references to skiing competitions.

It is possible that in the pre-industrial agrarian society sports competitions were not planned but spontaneous. In some parts of the country, people used to row to Sunday church service in large rowing boats, 'kyrkbåtar' (church boats). Rowing home might easily have turned into a race home. These unofficial and spontaneous competitions might have their origin in a popular belief that the winner would be favoured by some higher power and informal competitions may have been considered as omens. During the seventeenth and eighteenth centuries many priests complained about the superstitious belief that the first home from the early morning service on Christmas Day would be the first to harvest in the coming year. This superstition led to keen horse and sleigh races on Christmas morning.

Competitions could also arise in agrarian society when it was a question of being first to gain access to something used in common and when the one who came first gained an advantage. In Lima in Dalarna during the eighteenth century there was common land on some local islands which was harvested after the church service on a certain day in the month of July. The first to get there after the church service could choose his fields.[13] Arrival was determined by a rowing race from the church.

Despite an apparent absence of organized competitions in mainland early agrarian society, trials of strength could, and did, arise spontaneously. The quickly improvised competitive game was always a possibility: arm wrestling on the inn table after cards and beers in the evening, a wrestling match in the stable yard, a stone-lifting contest at the side of the road on the way home, tests of strength and agility during a break in the harvesting. People in all societies have always liked to compete against friends, neighbours and fellow-villagers and the competitive instinct is easily aroused. For a brief moment sporting and physical achievement could bring the landless prestige and offer crofters and cottagers the chance to turn the social hierarchy upside down.

Idiosyncratic Features of Traditional Sports

In Gotland there was an overall champion 'våg' team and an overall winner in the individual games. At the Midsummer wrestling in Hedesunda during the nineteenth century, a 'king' was chosen during the night of Midsummer Eve, an honour he retained until the event the following year. Some renowned strong men could win many years in succession and were accordingly called the 'king' of two years, the 'king' of three years, and so on.[14] The expression was also common in the popular sports of Germany,[15] for example in riding games, but in contrast there was little ritual attached to the honour of being a Swedish 'king'. Generally, Swedish agrarian sports lacked traditional rituals probably because they were beyond the control of the towns and guilds.

In many rural sports winning was not important. In some ball games batting was the main aim. The game continued until it got dark or the players became tired and the result was not really important. Sometimes the rules stated that a draw was the equivalent of a win as in some skittle games where a maximum number of points was prescribed. Other games were more concerned with losing rather than winning, for example, those where someone had to burn (hit) somebody else in order to change places with him. The players could co-operate systematically to keep the 'burner' out of the group for long periods. Games even existed that ended in physical punishment for those who had made the most mistakes.

When sport took on a more organized form as, for example, the 'våg' game in Gotland or the wrestling in Hedesunda, who won mattered. But in everyday sport it was far less important and quickly forgotten. There were rarely rules about the length of the game or the size of the ground or indeed the location of the match. Roads and fields were typical venues. Games had rules for when the teams should change ends, but since there was rarely any scoring, not for victory or full-time.

Equipment was made by the participants themselves. The stone throwers, who tossed stones at a stick in the ground, chose their own stones from nature and worked on them to make them smooth and easy to toss. In the game 'slå trilla', in which two teams forced each other back and forth along a road by throwing a discus-like piece of wood back and forward and trying to stop it with long sticks, the disc and sticks were made by the participants. Sometimes local carpenters made equipment and in Gotland the balls for 'pärk' were made by local cobblers.

Ritual Features in Traditional Sports

In the main, Swedish traditional games were not greatly concerned with results. In many games it was irrelevant who won: scores were not counted and points rarely added up. Were they a form of ritual entertainment? Here is a well-known and often quoted passage from a narrative by Nils Loven, pseudonym Nicolovius, from Sweden's southernmost tip, Falsterbonäset in Skåne, from the beginning of the nineteenth century:

> On Shrove Monday the young people enjoyed some pleasant activities. In all villages there were races, 'wäddelöb', in which either two men competed against each other or a man against a dozen girls. The latter race was organised in such a way that a track was decided upon, usually one leading out about an eighth of a league from the village. The girls were placed at equal distances from each other. The girl who started the race, had a key in her hand which she passed on to the next girl, who passed it to the next and so on. When everything was arranged and the girls were in their places with their skirts tied up to their knees ready to run, a pistol shot signalled that the 'wäddelöb' had begun. Musicians, with many others, now followed the race on horseback playing a reel as the runners slowly started to run. ... The first girl and the man held hands for a short while, then let go of each other, and the man, who was now on his own quickly built up a big lead. If the girl let this deter her and slackened her pace, ... and if she did not consider it worth her while to continue to exert herself, the man's victory of course, was certain. But if she, though far behind, determinedly continued to run as fast as possible to pass the key on to the next girl, and if she in turn did not give up on seeing the man so

far ahead, the girls slowly started to catch up with the man, as each
new girl was fresh, and the man became exhausted, so that often the
girls won. Mostly, though, the man won, for there was always one
among the girls who lacked interest in the common endeavour, and
who partly by running in an affected way and partly by clumsily
handing over the key, left time for the man to get even further ahead.[16]

In the traditional sports in Sweden there were no competitions exclusively
for girls. On the other hand, the sexes, as in the passage above, sometimes
competed against each other, and then the men were given some kind of
handicap to make the outcome uncertain.

An interesting feature in the passage by Nicolovius, is the start where the
competitors hold hands while they slowly run the first part of the race. This
perhaps gives an impression more of a theatrical performance than of a
sport, especially when the actors are accompanied by musicians on
horseback. However, there may well have been a practical purpose to the
action. In Per Arvid Säve's description of foot races in Gotland in the mid-
nineteenth century[17] participants run across a field or along a road to snatch
a white handkerchief from a pole. The runners compete in twos and hold a
stick between them at the start. After three steps they let go of the stick and
the race begins. If one of them considers that the other has started too early,
he can ask for a new start. It is very possible, therefore, that such
arrangements may have had a practical function in traditional competitions.

Generally speaking, however, such ritual features were not frequent in
Swedish traditional sports, perhaps because these were rarely performed for
spectators.

The Appearance of Spectators

Traditional sports were usually performed without spectators, other than
neighbours or villagers from the parish. In reality the distinction between
competitors and spectators was not clear cut as passers-by could join in the
game if they had the time and inclination. The 'våg' game in Gotland was
an exception. Many interested parishioners gathered to watch for the
reputation of the parish was at stake. However, in Swedish agrarian society
sports were rarely used to assert a community's prestige in rivalry with its
neighbours. This is rather odd considering the strength of rivalry between
neighbouring parishes and its expression in many other ways, such as
collective fights and pejorative nicknames. In other European countries,
popular sports seem to have been used to express rivalry between
neighbouring villages: this is not the case in Sweden.

Traditional sports in other parts of Europe were often connected with the great feast days of the year. They were one way of celebrating religious festivals and were performed therefore before spectators. In Sweden sport was not part of the annual cycle of festivals with the exception of the Midsummer wrestling in Hedesunda, which did attract spectators.

Sweden and Europe

Swedish traditional sport was both similar and dissimilar to European sport in general. There was a strong wrestling and weightlifting tradition in Sweden but only wrestling became organized and competitive on the Swedish mainland during the early nineteenth century, in Hedesunda and in some other parishes in the neighbourhood. Stone-lifting occurred throughout Sweden whereas in the rest of Europe it was only popular in isolated regions such as Scotland, Iceland, the Basque country and the Swiss and Austrian Alps. It was less common in Germany and Holland.

In the case of winter sports the favoured position of the Nordic countries is evident. But skiing and skating did not become competitive until the modern sports movement. Country people never competed in skiing or skating. This reveals an absence of understanding of sophisticated competitive sport in Swedish rural culture. For the more complicated competitive forms of sports the Swedes took their models from abroad. But until the late nineteenth century for winter sports there was no external model to adopt and in northern Sweden there were almost no winter sports although this was the best region for skiing. Continental festivals, for example Lent celebrations, occurred only in southern Sweden and often included sport like the eighteenth- and nineteenth-century running and horse races in Skåne. Even in the southern, formerly Danish provinces, equestrian sports were limited.

In Swedish agrarian society, only spontaneous games for measuring strength or winning advantages such as the sleigh-ride from church on Christmas Day or church boat races were widespread. Running races had a long history, but were not common. They were strongest in Skåne. The Falsterbonäset race at the beginning of the nineteenth century was an offshoot from the German tradition of 'wettlaufen'. Races were popular amusements in many parts of Europe, not least among the shepherds of the Alps. However, races between women, mentioned in both Germany and England, were quite unknown in Sweden. Skittles, however, links Swedish and German popular tradition. Special grounds for skittle games were constructed in Germany at the end of the eighteenth century, and in Sweden at the beginning of the nineteenth century. In the Swedish countryside, 'country' skittles played in suitable open spaces, were more usual than games on purpose-built skittle grounds. 'Slå trilla' seems to have been confined to Sweden, Finland, Denmark and northern Germany.[18]

Interestingly, ball games such as football and hurling did not exist in rural Sweden. In this respect the Nordic countries resemble Germany. Ball games which involved bat and ball were more popular in the Nordic countries and Germany than, for example, in England. The northern French tennis game came by way of the Friesians to some areas of northern Europe including Gotland. It is surprising that the business contacts between the Hanseatic ports of Sweden and, for example, Holland and Flanders, did not lead to the dissemination of more sports such as the winter game 'kolven' from north-western Europe to Sweden.

Swedish rural sport in the eighteenth and nineteenth centuries reveals a relative lack of violence. In a European context this is somewhat exceptional. The violent western European games of the countryside towns and villages did not exist in Sweden. Nor, as we have seen, did violent rural games such as hurling and shinty. As Norbert Elias points out, it was that kind of popular game that most excited passion: 'forms of sport whose design most closely resembles that of a real battle between hostile groups have a particularly strong propensity for stirring up emotions'.[19] It is striking that the Swedish ball games and even 'slå trilla' were games where the participants did not have any physical contact. The absence of animal sports in almost all of Sweden contributes to the picture of sports in the Swedish agrarian society as relatively harmless and inoffensive. Nor has Swedish popular tradition anything to relate of confrontations between animals, such as cock-fighting, or between animals and men, such as bull running. The third form of animal sports, where people tormented and killed animals without putting their own safety in danger, is also unknown in most parts of Sweden. It did exist, however, in Skåne to a limited extent, mainly in the form of 'slå katten ur tunnan' (bang the cat out of the barrel). The even more brutal 'gåsridningen' (riding the goose) or 'dra huvudet av gåsen' (pull the head of the goose) common in northern Germany, occurred only in one known case in Sweden in Ystad in Skåne in 1699.

We can sense a Lutheran attitude towards tormenting animals as a popular amusement behind this state of affairs. When, during the mid-nineteenth century, an innkeeper in Malmä tried to revive 'slå katten ur tunnan' he was quickly stopped and his action criticized strongly as cruel. Perhaps we can see in this criticism, and in the total absence in Sweden north of Skåne of the games of animals torture, a forerunner of the attitude to violent sports, that marked the Swedish sports movement of the twentieth century? The pros and cons of professional boxing was discussed for decades in the Swedish parliament until finally it was forbidden in 1969.[20] Internationally this was a unique decision, but doubts about boxing had existed in the Swedish sports movement since the end of the nineteenth century. During the 1920s professional boxing was forbidden in many cities, including Stockholm, and the 'Svenska Boxningsfürbundet' (the Swedish Boxing League) did not become a member of the Swedish National Sports League until 1939. Is there a connection between the absence of cruel animal sports in Swedish agrarian society during the eighteenth and nineteenth centuries and the Swedish programme of legislation at the end of the twentieth century against corporal punishment for children?

Disappearing and Changing Traditional Sports

Traditional sports may seem timeless but do change, of course. One of the most characteristic features of these sports were differences in rules from community to community. Each village practised its sports in its own way. Written rules for traditional sports did not appear until about 1900, when folklorists, educationalists and sports experts began to write them down. But by then most of the sports were already history. In Gotland, however, 'pärk', stone-throwing ('varpa') pole tossing and other games still existed and the written recording of rules led to their standardisation.

Mainly during the second half of the nineteenth century further competitive elements were added to traditional sports. Wrestling, which had concluded with throwing the opponent to the ground, now began to include wrestling in a recumbent position. In stone-lifting the traditional round stone was difficult to grasp and in the nineteenth century to improve performance, stones with handles began to be introduced and lifting competitions began. If the participant managed to lift a big flat stone, a smaller stone was added to it and so on.

In 1886 Captain Viktor Balck, 'the father of Swedish Sport', published the first volume of his handbook on sports, *Illustrerad idrottsbok* (Illustrated Book of Sports) and for the first time modern sports were presented to the Swedes in a systematic and thorough way. In 1880 Balck had led a group of gymnasts on a tour of England, Belgium and Denmark, and had come into close contact with English sport. But the *Illustrerad idrottsbok* not only covered English and other modern international sports, it also included some traditional domestic sports, among others 'pärk', rounders, 'söt och sur' and 'tre slag och ränna', all of them different kinds of ball games. Balck, who was a deeply patriotic man, would gladly have seen old Swedish competitive activities take their place beside modern sports. His hope was never realized. None of the traditional sports and games survived in the twentieth century, except 'varpa', a throwing game in Gotland, that now has its own league in the Swedish National Sports League.

In the 1880s when Balck advocated traditional sports in *Illustrerad idrottsbok*, he tried to modernize, regulate and standardize them in order to adapt them to the modern sports world. The game 'slå trilla' can serve as an example. It was one of the most common competitive rural games in the nineteenth century. Two two-man teams faced each other on a road. One player threw a round piece of wood towards the opposite team who were supposed to stop this 'trillan' with their sticks. It was then thrown back from the point where it had landed. In this way the two teams forced each other up and down the 'sports field', usually a highway. Balck tried to modernize this game in his handbook.[21] He laid down how big the 'trilla' and the sticks should be. He specified a maximum length for the field. Balck wanted to introduce goals, although traditionally there were neither goals nor scores. He also suggested time limits for the matches. The team which won most games within the time limit won the match. In contrast in the traditional game the result was never clear and of little interest. Balck also recommended that the teams should change sides to counteract advantages from sun, wind or any geographical features. All this was well meant, but despite Balck's good intentions, 'slå trilla' has completely disappeared in the twentieth century. Indeed, it is remarkable how few traditional competitive games have survived as modern sports. It is also astonishing that no form of baseball has caught on in modern Sweden, considering the earlier widespread popularity of traditional games which involved hitting a ball. In fact, traditional sports had died out in many parts of the country by the time modern sports were introduced during the last decades of the nineteenth century. The exception is, as usual, Gotland, where the institutionalization of 'våg' and the place of sport in the local community ensured its survival. But even here it was in danger when modern sports were introduced.

The local folklore movement, which grew in importance at the end of the nineteenth century, however, saved the popular sports of Gotland. Various clubs in the only city in Gotland, Visby, became passionate defenders of traditional island sports and thus, ironically, town dwellers came to play an important role in preserving rural custom. The sports of Gotland became a kind of regional icon, a symbol of the island's individuality. In 1912 a special club was created for Gotland sports and in 1925 this club, for the first time, arranged the 'Stångaspel'. It is still today the climax of the annual traditional sports events in Gotland and an ever growing popular festival.

There is a remarkable continuity in Swedish traditional sports until the second half of the nineteenth century. Their form and function does not appear to have changed much in the previous centuries. A thirteen-year-old farmer's boy, Lars Andersson, from Nyckleby farm in Västergötland, wrote in his diary on Sunday, 6 May 1860 that he played skittles with three other boys on a drying-ground near the farm. On Thursday evening of the same week he played 'trilla' on the highway with the same boys. On Friday evening of 25 May he again played 'trilla' with six other boys and later in the evening the boys played ball in a field.[22] Some decades later the picture was to be completely different. Skittles, 'slå trilla' and rounders were abandoned by then and replaced by completely new sports such as football and bandy, which had no roots in Swedish popular culture.

Richard Holt has criticized the tendency of some historians of sport to make too rigid a distinction between 'traditional' and 'modern' sports. He asserts that this separation is based on a romantic view of rural society before industrialization as a 'Garden of Eden' with sports of a completely different character from modern ones. He suggests that in fact change occurred slowly in different ways in different places: 'As we shall see, the early nineteenth century was less unambiguously "traditional" and the late nineteenth century less 'modern' than appearance might suggest.'[23] While adequate evidence for this assertion is still required, he may be partially correct as regards Britain, where *some* modern sports evolved out of earlier domestic sports but nevertheless did change quite substantially and dramatically in the last quarter of the century! However, with regard to Sweden, he is quite wrong. The break in the continuity was clear cut. In a European, and indeed a British context, his ideas need modification.[24] In Sweden sports certainly did not evolve in the way he opines they did in Britain.[25] In Sweden, at the end of the nineteenth century a number of new sports appeared which had no predecessors in traditional culture. Sport became newly cosmopolitan and unambiguously modern.

NOTES

 1. Petter Rudebeck, *Småländska Antiquiteter.* The Royal Library manuscript collection, Stockholm, ch.32. Samuel Kork, 'Urshults Pastorats inbyggares seder', in N. Werner, *Småländska Hembygdsböcker* (1922), p.19.
 2. A.E. Holmberg, *Eorden under hednatiden* (1852), p.252.
 3. Gunnar Olof Hylten-Cavallius, *Wärend och wirdarne' Ett försök i Svensk Ethnologi 1–2* (Stockholm 1863–68).
 4. Johan Fischerström, *Tal hallet vid Praesisii nedlaggande uti Kongl. Vetenskaps Academien den 20 september 1794* (Stockholm, 1794).
 5. Henrik Sandblad, *Olympia och Valhalla. Idehistoriska aspekter av den moderna idrottsrörelsens framväxt* (Stockholm, 1985).
 6. Olaus Magnus, *Historia om de nordiska folken* (Stockholm, 1976), ch.15:14.
 7. Ibid., ch.1:25.
 8. See note 4.
 9. For mention of sports in Gotland see Hans Nielsen Strelow in his work *Cronica Guthilandorum* (1633) and Haquin Spegel in his work *Rudera Gothlandica* (1683).
10. Mats Hellspong, 'Brottning som folklig lekl', *Rig* IV (1991).
11. Heiner Gillmeister, *Kulturgeschichte des Tennis* (Munich, 1990).
12. Ibid. p.54.
13. Carl von Linne, Dalaresa, *Iter dalekarlicum, jämte Utlandsresan, Iter ad exterosm och*

Bergslagsresan, Iter ad fodinas (Stockholm, 1953), p.105.

14. Mats Hellspong, 'Brottning som folklig lek', *Rig* IV (1991), p.118.
15. Leopold Kretzenbacher, *Ringreiten, Rolandspiel und Kufenstechen. Sportlicher Reiterbrauchtum von heute als Erbe aus abendländischer Kulturgeschichte* (Klagenfurt, 1966), p.180.
16. Nicolovius, *Folklivet I Skytts härad I Skåne I början av 1800-talet* (Stockholm, 1957), p.134.
17. Per Arvid Säve, *Gotlandska lekar*, Herbert Gustavson (Uppsala, 1948).
18. See Mats Hellspong, 'Slå trilla. En lek på gränson mellan folklig och modern idrott', *Rig* I (1990). In Germany the game has been called among others Trudelspiel or Verdriewen.
19. Norbert Elias, 'Introduction', in N. Elias and E. Dunning, *Quest for Excitement: Sport and leisure in the civilizing process* (Oxford, 1986), p.49
20. Mats Hellspong, *Boxningssporten i Sverige En studie i idrottens kulturmiljö* (Stockholm, 1982).
21. See Mats Hellspong, 'Slå trilla. En lek på gränson mellan folklig och modern idrott', *Rig* I (1990).
22. Britt Liljewall, *Blondevardag och samhällstbrändring. Studier kring västsvenska bondedagböcker från 1800-talet* (Gothenburg, 1995) p.139–40
23. Richard Holt, *Sport and the British: A Modern History* (Oxford, 1989), passim.
24. J.A.Mangan and Stephen Bailey will shortly reflect on the possibility of a more subtle evolutionary model of both British and European sport in a research paper currently in preparation.
25. For an interesting contradiction of the Holt thesis and its inadequecy on a fully explanatory model see Roger Hutchinson, *Empire Games: The British Invention of Twentieth-Century Sport* (Edinburgh, 1996), ch.1.

Politics and Gymnastics in a Frontier Area post-1848

JØRN HANSEN

Gymnastics have been a symbolic part of the struggle for national identity between Danes and Germans. This struggle was nowhere more violently expressed than in the late nineteenth century in the town of Flensborg, which today lies within the German province of Schleswig-Holstein[1] immediately south of the Danish–German border. The late nineteenth century political manoeuvrings and disagreements are well documented. Regrettably, the role of sport in the creation of the respective national movements in the border area is not. This essay repairs this omission.

The War of 1848

On 23 March 1848 the March Revolution reached Schleswig-Holstein. In the struggle for a democratic constitution, the citizens of Schleswig-Holstein established a provisional government in Kiel. The provisional government was supported by an army unit of about 3,000 men confronting a Danish force of 11,000 recruited in North Schleswig. The numerically outnumbered army unit, meanwhile, was joined by a corps made up of a number of voluntary revolutionary 'Turner' (gymnasts) and 'Burschenschaft' (student club) students from the University of Kiel and the College in Tønder. The slogan that was to symbolize the unity of Schleswig and Holstein with Germany was 'Jungs – holt fast!' (Youth – hold firm). Carrying the banner of the German unification movement, the students marched side-by-side under the Schleswig-Holstein blue, white and red flag, with German mercenaries and Prussian officers. The army was composed in all of about 6,000 men.[2]

On 26 March the corps with the army moved northwards. The student section of the corps consisted of 126 men and was led by a law student. The 80 strong Turnen section was led by a bookbinder. Within the corps there were two young men from Flensborg, Johann Freidrich Esmarch and Daniel Sauermann. Esmarch, who was 25 years old, had studied at Kiel and was then working as an army surgeon; Sauermann was 26 years old and worked as a saddler in his father's workshop in Flensborg. Both later became the founders of the Turnen movement in Flensborg. On 30 March the corps marched to Åbenrå to the joy of the pro-German part of the population. The very next day it was in retreat towards Flensborg. In Flensborg it prepared itself for a decisive battle against the Danes, who had moved up to Bov, north of the town. On 9 April the Danish forces moved to Nystad. There a three-hour-long battle was fought. The superior Danish force was too powerful for the Schleswig-Holsteiners; they pulled back and the Danes took Flensborg, this time to the joy of the pro-Danish part of the population.[3]

The losses were modest: on the Danish side there were 15 dead and 77 wounded, on the Schleswig-Holstein side 36 dead and 121 wounded, and some 1,000 prisoners were taken, about one-sixth of the defeated army.[4] For Turnen corps and student sections the loss was relatively large. Seven were killed in the Nystad battle and three died later, while 16 were badly wounded. Among the prisoners taken was Esmarch, while Sauermann, who knew the area well, managed to escape. Esmarch and a number of other students were held captive for nine weeks on the Danish ship *Dronning Maria*.[5]

Immediately after the Danish troops took Flensborg, the Danish King visited the town, where he proposed a toast to the newly-appointed Councillor of State, a former professor at Kiel, Christian Flor, who acted as the adviser to the Danish army.[6] In 1844, in his efforts to make the Schleswig people 'more Danish', Flor had been the inspiration behind setting up the first Danish folk high school in the village of Rødding in North Schleswig. The Danish army continued its onslaught through South Schleswig and two days later reached Slien. But on 12 April the German Federal Diet acknowledged the provisional government in Schleswig-Holstein and Prussia now sent a 30,000-man force against the Danes, who were defeated and had to retreat to Jutland and the islands. Russia put pressure on Prussia and a complete Danish defeat was avoided. In September 1848 in Frankfurt, the German National Assembly agreed to a cease-fire.[7]

The cease-fire was broken many times, but on 2 July 1850, the Danes managed to get a separate peace agreement with Prussia, after which the Schleswig-Holstein army had to look after itself. On 25 July, at the battle of Isted, the Danish army inflicted a final defeat on the Schleswig-Holsteiners. The provisional government was disbanded and Schleswig-Holstein remained under Danish rule until 1864. Russia and England were guarantors of this arrangement. As a consequence of the Turner involvement in the 'folk army's' revolt, the Danish state proscribed the Turnen Movement in Flensborg and its surroundings in 1852.

Influential Danish politicians, without deference to the political realities, wished to bind the German Holstein Duchy to Schleswig as part of the Danish state. Consequently in 1864, army units from Prussia and Austria advanced into Schleswig and with their superior forces quickly crushed the Danish defences. The battle at Oeversee and the fighting over the earthworks at Dybbøl were given the same great symbolic value by the pro-Germans as the Battle of Nystad in 1848. In 1873, by the side of the highway from Flensborg to Nystad and Bov, on the 25th anniversary of the Battle of Nystad, the 'Flensburger Turnschaft' (Flensborg Gymnastics Society) erected a memorial to the fallen members of the Turnen corps.[8]

Schleswig-Holstein remained part of the German Reich until 1920. Following Germany's defeat at the end of the First World War, a referendum in 1920 led to the division of Schleswig, so that North Schleswig became part of Denmark, and was called South Jutland, and South Schleswig became part of Germany and was called Schleswig. The border was drawn south of Tønder but north of Flensborg, where it has remained.

German and Danish Vormärz in Kiel

After the war of 1848–59 the Danish government purged the leading civil servants in Schleswig. In the first six months of 1851, 243 were dismissed. The new civil servants came mainly from the north and the requirement of two years' study at the University of Kiel, that had until then been obligatory for civil servants in Schleswig-Holstein, was waived. The University of Kiel was in disgrace, and ten of its professors were dismissed. It was their partisan politics that had contributed to the active participation of the students and gymnasts in the revolt against the Danish state.[9]

However, the University of Kiel was not only the source of an emerging German nationalism; some of the important Danish nationalist movements derived from the university. Paradoxically, in a number of instances both national movements shared a reliance on exercise and on the 'Burschenschaftsbewegung' (the student club movement) influenced by the German (father of) 'Turnvater', Friedrich Ludwig Jahn.

Compulsory physical education in the form of gymnastic exercises was first introduced in the grammar schools and primary schools in Schleswig-Holstein in 1838 by the Danish King Frederik VI.[10] It was based on training programmes at Dessau, Schnepfental and Berlin. As Duke of Schleswig-Holstein, the Danish King had the right to do this. However, it did not happen entirely fortuitously. The King was an enthusiast. Indeed, the author of the first school manual on the new gymnastics *Gymnastik für die Jugend* (Gymnastics for Young People) published in 1793, Johann Christof Friedrich GutsMuths (1759–1839), had dedicated it to 'His Royal Highness Frederik, Crown Prince of Denmark, Defender of Human Rights'.[11] The Crown Prince and Frederik VI were, of course, the same person. These gymnastics courses were located where benefit could be had from militarily trained youth and where there were facilities and space for buildings. However, the buildings did not materialize until 1848. Nevertheless the schools introduced obligatory gymnastic exercises without them.

The implementation of a scheme of national gymnastics revealed a hiatus between GutsMuths and Jahn. For GutsMuths liberal education was the inspiration; for Jahn national-revolutionary training was the motive. Friedrich Ludwig Jahn (1778–1852) had a decisive influence on German nationalism. In 1806, he experienced the ignominious German defeat by the French at Jena and thereafter his ambition was the restoration of German nationalism. His book *Deutsches Volkstum* (German Nationhood), published in 1808, was central to these endeavours and was published in several editions during the nineteenth century.

The purpose of the book was to bolster the spirit of the people and use this spirit as the foundation for a strong German state. 'Volkstum' was a combination of 'national characteristics' and the feeling of national solidarity that gave the state life and renewal producing unity with freedom. Physical exercise and games were a central part of this national renewal. They ensured fitness for defence. According to Jahn they were to be called by the old Germanic word 'Turnen' (gymnastics). In 1811 the first Turnen group trained in Hasenheide in Berlin. At the Battle of Leipzig in 1813 many Turner took part, and after the War of Independence the Turnen Movement expanded rapidly. In 1816 the first club was established in Hamburg and in 1818, five years after the victory over Napoleon, there were 12,000 Turner.[12] Jahn now introduced a 'Volkstümlichen' (nationalistic) slogan into the Turnen movement: Frisch–Fromm–Fröhlich–Frei! (fresh–pious–happy–free). It was this slogan with the four Fs that adorned the Turnen banners.

In his struggle for German unity and independence, Jahn was also the father of the German 'Burschenschaft' movement, a strongly nationalistic student organization known especially for its Wartburg festivals. In October 1817 these German student societies celebrated the 300th anniversary of the Reformation and the fourth anniversary of the victory at Leipzig. At the end of the festival a book burning was arranged of 'lampoons of the fatherland' – anti-nationalist books. Among the participants was a law student from Flensborg, Christian Paulsen, who was a student at the University of Gättingen at the time.[13] Christian Paulsen later became a professor at Kiel and a good friend of Christian Flor.

The movement advocated a 'popular' army and, in principle, freedom, equality and solidarity, but in reality it was often autocratic, militaristic and chauvinistic. In 1819 one of the 'Burschenschaft' Turner murdered August von Kotzebue, a conservative author who was in the pay of the Russians. This action led to a ban on the Turners and Jahn was arrested. (The ban lasted until 1842, but in fact Turnen activities were resuscitated from the 1830s onwards.) Jahn was released in 1825 but was thereafter under continuous political surveillance. In 1840 he was rehabilitated and in 1848 he was elected to the German National Assembly in Frankfurt. He also received honorary doctorates from the universities of Jena and Kiel.

The Wartburg festivals played an important part in the birth of nationalism at the University of Kiel. Previously there had been no strong German-oriented student movement. German professors saw this as an effect of 'Danicism'. Students at the university were not Danish nationalists, but many seemed satisfied with the status quo. As late as 1815, for example, Kiel students celebrated the coronation of Frederik VI,[15] regardless of the fact that Denmark was allied with Napoleon and the Germans had won the War of Independence against him. But change was on the way and it was promoted by a number of younger professors. An important figure in this transition was the professor of history, F.C. Dahlmann. At the 1815 university festival to celebrate the Battle of Waterloo, he gave the principal speech, in which he talked about Germanism in both duchies – that is, both Schleswig and Holstein. Dahlmann, however, was not himself a political revolutionary in the mould of Kiel professors such as Nikolaus Falck and Carl Theodor Welcker, who published *Kieler Blätter* (Kiel Letters) and formed the debating and literary society 'Die Kieler Harmonie', which became the fount of national-liberal thought. In the same year as his Waterloo speech Dahlmann became secretary for the landed nobility in Schleswig-Holstein and immediately took a more reserved attitude to democratic ways of thinking. Nevertheless, as far as German nationalism goes, 1815 was seen as the beginning of the Schleswig-Holstein movement, and from then on the Kiel students celebrated on the anniversary of Waterloo at the gateway to Kiel. In 1817 these students took part in the festival at Wartburg, where the slogan 'Holsatia sei's Panier!' (Holstein forever) was changed to 'Germania sei's Panier!' (Germany forever).[16]

The University of Kiel was not exclusively pro-German. Ironically, the German 'Burschenschaftsbewegung' produced the first Danish nationalist in Schleswig-Holstein. In 1817 Christian Paulsen took part in the festival at Wartburg. In 1825 he was appointed Professor of Law at the University of Kiel. Colleagues and friends tried to persuade him to support the Schleswig-Holstein cause but, in contrast to their 'Germanism', he increasingly expressed views on the 'Danishness' of Schleswig as demonstrated by the inhabitants' 'national characteristics', a term he took straight from German Romanticism and from 'Turnvater' Jahn. Paulsen's most important publication in support of 'Danishness' was highly significant. It was written in German, was published in 1832 and was called *Ueber Volksthümlichkeit und Staatsrecht des Herzogthums Schleswig; nebst Blicken auf den ganzen*

Dänischen Staat (Survey of the National Characteristics and Constitutional Law of the Duchy of Schleswig; as well as an Overview of the whole Danish State). In this polemic against Uwe Jens Lornsen, the former Counsellor, and Professor Falck, Paulsen denied that Schleswig and Holstein had the same relationship with the Reich. There were the different and important 'folk qualities' in Schleswig, where half the population were Danish speakers, although German was both the legal and administrative language and the language of the upper classes. This polarization contributed to the repression of Danish 'national characteristics'.[17]

The 1848 revolution forced Paulsen to give up his professorship at Kiel, but before that with his friend and colleague, Christian Flor, he had contributed to the establishment of the Danish movement in the Duchy of Schleswig. In 1826 Christian Flor had taken up the lectureship in Danish language and literature at the University of Kiel. From the mid-1830s onwards he was closely connected with N.F.S. Grundtvig (1783–1872), who was the best known apologist for popular Danish nationalism. Flor's connection with Grundtvig led to close contact with representatives of the Danish movement among the townspeople and farmers in Schleswig. From then on Flor was the one who put Christian Paulsen's ideas in writing, and by the end of the 1840s he had made Danish nationalism popular throughout North Schleswig, later to become Danish South Jutland. Flor, for example, was behind the creation of Danish newspapers, of which *Dannevirke* is the best known; and supported Peter Hiort Lorenzen, who in the Assembly of the Estates of the Realm in Schleswig spoke Danish, contrary to custom. In addition, Flor wrote speeches for the 'pure Schleswiger', the people's spokesman Laurids Pedersen Skau, whose 'trademark' farmer's coat bore a strong resemblance to the old German Turner uniform. At the height of his success Laurids Pederskin Skau addressed over 6,000 people at the festival of Skamlingsbanken, in May 1843, an event which was to acquire great symbolic significance.[18]

As an important, perhaps the most important, means of disseminating Danish nationalism, Christian Flor established the first folk high school in North Schleswig. Due to the nationalist revival among the farmers, it was inevitable that it would be located in Schleswig and the choice fell on Rødding to the north, where Danishness was stronger than, south of Flensborg.[19]

The high school in Rødding opened on 7 November 1844, and from the start physical exercise was an important element of popular national revival. King Christin VIII donated gymnastics apparatus to the school and during the summer there was swimming in the river nearby. As early as 1818, in a small book called *Om Skoleopdragelse* (About School Education) Flor had argued in favour of the beneficial effects of a school having a large open space 'with all kinds of gymnastic apparatus, that could be entrusted to the farm boys to be used as they wanted'. In his view if the place were also situated by a lake, where there was swimming for 'the sake of a constantly clean body', it was the very best arrangement possible.[20]

The Prussian defeat of the Danes in 1864 made it impossible to keep the folk high school in Rødding as it lay south of the Kongeaa border and in 1865 the high school moved north of the border to Askov. At the inauguration at Askov on 3 November 1865 he expressed the wish 'that the School now in Askov, as in Rødding, should bring luck to the cause of the struggle for Danishness'. Flor's last contribution to the high schools in Denmark was the collection of funds for a gymnasium for the Askov school – a collection that was not a complete success and Flor felt obliged to be the biggest contributor.[21] The gymnasium was opened in the autumn of 1872, and over many decades produced a number of instructors, who contributed to the diffusion of popular gymnastics – first German-oriented Danish gymnastics based on GutsMuths, Nachtegal and Jahn, then Ling's Swedish gymnastics. South of the Kongeaa border 'Danish' gymnastics were as yet unknown, as after 1864 the Turnen Movement held all the cards in its hands.

'Jungs holt fast' (Youth – hold firm)

After the defeats at Bov and Nystad in 1848, there was discussion among the pro-Germans as to whether the poor physique of the soldiers had contributed to defeat. They romanticized the Turner students' contribution at Nystad and concluded that their fitness had been a major factor. As a consequence, a Turnen campaign was launched in Schleswig with the slogan 'schlappe Jungmannschaft braucht Turnervereine' (weak teams need Turnen clubs). It led to the formation of 'Männerturnvereins von 1849' (the 1849 Men's Turnen Club) in Flensborg. Behind this innovation were the two former fighters at Nystad, the doctor, Johan Friederich Esmarch, and the saddler, Daniel Sauermann.[22]

Nevertheless, until 1864 the Turnen movement in Schleswig soldiered on in poor conditions. The Danish state kept a close eye on its political activities and, as mentioned earlier, Turnen clubs were banned from 1852 to 1856. When the ban was lifted in 1856 Esmarch and Sauermann reorganized the Turnen club in Flensborg under the name 'Flensburger Turnerschaft' (Flensborg's Turnen Society). Daniel Sauermann now became something of a nationalist hero. In 1863 he participated in the third German Gymnastics Festival in Leipzig, where 20,000 gymnasts celebrated the 50th anniversary of the victory over Napoleon, and was acclaimed as Schleswig-Holstein's freedom fighter in the war of 1848–50.[23] From 1864 the Turnen movement in Schleswig grew rapidly.

In 1866, following the Prussian victory over Austria, Schleswig acquired the status of a Prussian province. Denmark and the pro-Danish Schleswigers hoped that the Great Powers would give Schleswig back to Denmark. However, after the defeat of Napoleon III at Sedan in 1870, there was no real foundation for this hope and the pro-Danish Schleswigers had to adapt to the way things were, carrying on a lengthy and emotional struggle against the pro-German Schleswigers. The victory at Sedan, like the victory at Leipzig in 1813, was a symbolic moment for the Turnen movement, and the fifth anniversary of the Battle of Sedan was seen as a suitable occasion for the movement in Flensborg to inaugurate a club banner with the four 'Fs'. In the same year, the club went on its annual march to Oeversee to a special Turnen event. At the Battle of Oeversee in February 1864, the Prussian and Austrian forces had inflicted on the Danes a decisive defeat. Sport and politics were one.[24]

The Turnen movement spread, with the active support of the club in Flensborg, to three of the bigger North Schleswig cities, Tønder, Aabenraa and Haderslev. In these cities clubs were formed, which merged with 'Deutscher Turnerschaft' (the German Turnen Association).[25] Turner now played an important part in efforts to 'Germanize' North Schleswig.

Between 1864 and the mid-1880s, German influence in the Flensborg area both spread and stabilized. Danish feeling, which in 1864 had been strong in this area, decreased when the city was modernized and German was introduced as the compulsory school language. North Schleswig, where in 1880 a Danish language club had been formed and in 1888 a Danish constituency organized, now became the focus of Danish–German antagonism. From the end of the 1880s the government in Berlin with Bismarck at its head wished to Germanize this area; in 1888 German was introduced as the school language and all sermons were in German.[26] With the aim of supporting Germanization both culturally and politically, the 'Deutscher Verein für das nördliche Schleswig' (the German Club for North Schleswig) was formed in 1890. It had 59 local divisions by 1909 and acted as a pressure group on governmental bodies. It was dominated by German officials and was connected with the radical right wing 'Altyske Forbund' (the All-German Society). In 1897, when E.M. Köller became Prefect in Schleswig-Holstein, the German Club supported the heavy-handed treatment of pro-Danes and the expulsion of undesirables, without German nationality. One ground for expulsion was the organization of mass excursions to Denmark.[27] The Club bought Knivsbjerg at Genner, not far from Aabenraa to use for popular festivals in support of the German state.

Knivsbjerg, after Skamlingsbanken the highest place in the province, quickly became built up with pavilions, Turnen and sports grounds and youth hostels. In 1896 the first Turnen festival was held there. Students from Kiel, school children from Haderslev and Turners from Flensborg and the clubs in North Schleswig participated. The festival became an annual event, in which the 'Flensborgs Turnerforeninger' (Flensborg's Turnen Club) took part 'in Turnertreue und mit Turnerdank an den sportlichen Wettkämpfen und den politischen Kundgebungen' (with Turnen loyalty and with Turnen gratitude in sporting competitions and political manifestations).[28]

In 1896 the first stone of the Knivsbjerg tower was laid and in 1901, on the anniversary of the German victory in 1870, a so-called 'Vaterlands-Monument' (a monument to the fatherland) was inaugurated. The whole facility was shaped like an ancient place of worship, with 12 rock columns forming a circle around a pedestal of granite. On the base of the pedestal was the slogan of the Turnen movement from the 'Vormärz' era: 'Jungs holt fast'. On the four sides of the pedestal there were sacrificial altars and on the pedestal itself there was a seven metre high copper statue of Bismarck with the national sword and crown. Beneath Bismarck was written 'Up ewig ungedelt' (forever together), expressing the eternal link between Schleswig and Holstein and their association with the German state.[29]

After the First World War, pro-Germans were convinced that the coming election in Schleswig would probably reveal a Danish majority in North Schleswig and they feared for the safety of the monument under Danish rule. They decided, therefore, to remove the statue, and a few years later moved it to Aschberg at Hytten Bjerge (Hüttener Berge) south-east of Schleswig, where they established a meeting-place with a youth hostel and sports facilities. However, after the new border was drawn, Knivsbjerg was retained as a meeting-place for the German minority. It acquired great symbolic meaning for the Nazified German minority north of the border, especially in the period between 1933 and 1945. On 16 August 1945 the granite pedestal and buildings were destroyed in an explosion caused, it appears, by Danish saboteurs, keen to destroy a Germanic shrine after the Nazi defeat. This action was later condemned by Hans Hedtoft, the Danish Prime Minister[30] and in 1949 the Danish state paid for the partial re-establishment of Knivsbjerg, which became again a well-frequented location for the German minority's cultural activities. The excellent sports facilities were considered especially important to the continuation of the activities of the minority.[31] The Flensborg Turnen club has retained its strong links with Knivsbjerg. In 1990 'Turn und Sportsbund' (Turnen and Sports Club) Flensborg sent a team of young handball players to the Knivsbjerg festival and at the festival Dr H.A. Rossen gave those who had been members of the TSB for more than 50 years the Knivsbjerg-prize that he himself had founded – a heavily symbolic gesture.[32]

'South Jutland will Win'

The defeat of 1864 had a great impact on the formation of Danish national feeling. Danish cultural and intellectual life prior to the defeat, of course, had been influenced by German culture. After 1864, both culturally and economically, Denmark was influenced by Great Britain. The consequence of the marksmanship movement and the growth of an indigenous physical culture, in the form of Nordic gymnastics and British ball games, had the same source[33] – ever-increasing anti-German feeling in Denmark. In high school circles, for example, Ling Swedish gymnastics became dominant,[34] and after 1861 the Danish public authorities supported the creation of 'De danske Skytteforeninger' (Danish Marksmanship Clubs) following the creation of National Rifleshooting Associations, which acted partly as a kind of Home Guard and partly to prepare young Danish men for national defence.

Those in the marksmanship movement who also organised gymnastics, were described as 'platoon commanders' as in the marksmanship corps and in time platoon commander training was formalized. In 1889 'Delingsførerforeningen af 1899' (1899 Club of Platoon Commanders) was formed after a course at N.H. Rasmussen's club in Copenhagen. At a general meeting at Askov High School in 1896 the club decided, after consultation with, among others, the High School teacher Poul la Cour, to change the name to 'Skyttesagens Gymnastiklaererforening' (The Club for Gymnastics Teachers for Training the Population in Marksmanship). In the following year the club's first newspaper *Ungdom og Idræt* (Youth and Sport) was published. It exists to this day under the name of *Dansk Ungdom og Idræt* (Danish Youth and Sport) and is published by the large popular Danish sports organization 'Danske Gymnastik- og Idrætsforeninger' (the Danish Gymnastics and Sports Club).[35] Under the heading 'Vor Graensekamp' (For the Border Struggle), a lecture that Poul la Cour gave at a meeting in Højstrup Skov in Zealand, was printed in *Ungdom og Idræt* in 1898.

The public lecture opened with patriotic community singing: 'Slumrer sødt i Slesvigs Jord' (Slumber Sweetly in Schleswig's Earth) – the song that had echoed in la Cour's head during a walking tour of Dybbøl. In his speech, la Cour said: 'it was impressive to walk down there between the graves. They are around you, at the fence, in the field and in the garden. Many different thoughts and memories well up, when one walks there. Here was a small country's army with muzzle-loading weapons that stood bravely against a bigger country's army with breech loading weapons.'[36] Such odds, he added, were unfair to a small population, who nevertheless fought heroically. In the later struggle for South Jutland, la Cour believed in the importance of the high school, the intellectual life of Denmark and education to the struggle for South Jutland. In his speech he informed his audience: 'The Germans understand that the high school is dangerous. When last winter, as was the custom, I should have given a talk in Bredebo, between Ribe and Tønder, it was forbidden on the grounds that anyone, who was connected with a Danish high school, was not allowed to speak.'[37] In 1897 E.M. Köller became Prefect for Schleswig-Holstein, and supported Germanization in North Schleswig. The ban on talks by la Cour was part of this effort. La Cour finished his speech to the Schleswigers with the exclamation: 'We love you, Schleswigers, with all our soul. Look at the crowd that has gathered together, without talk of "Højre" (right wing) or "Venstre" (left wing) ... And so I would like to end with a cheer for everything that is Danish.'[38]

The following year *Ungdom og Idræt* included a discussion about 'the goal for "Skyttesagen"'. The discussion was initiated by A. Nordahl-Pedersen from the folk high school in Djursland. He raised the issue of 'the people's fight to be a people'. Laurids Nielsen, a pacifist, then entered the discussion and asserted that should there be war many marksmen would hang up their rifles.[39] There was a strong reaction to his opinion from some of the active marksmen. One, who signed himself simply as '303', informed Nielsen: 'You cannot talk about "love for our folk poems and the history of our fatherland" and at the same time give up everything without a fight. You cannot cherish love for history without opening your eyes to – and understanding – the fact that the previous generation, who failed to raise their men and youth against a foreign assault, is finished with.'[40]

Others, who also felt provoked by Nielsen, referred, as did '303', to the history and poetry of the fatherland. However, in the long run it was not the discussion for or against pacifism or militarism that was important for the marksmanship movement – it was South Jutland. This was made clear in the newspaper in 1898 by the Schleswiger, H. Sørensen, from Kvissel High School.[41] Sørensen was convinced that South Jutland could not be retaken immediately with weapons in patriots' hands, but instead they should create in Denmark an 'energetic and, in addition, provenly nationalistic young people' who could be persuaded to win over the Schleswigers to their views. In this way

the Schleswigers who live between us and the Germans, cannot do anything else but turn to the North, when a comparison is made between Danish and German young people, and this they will do. Young German people train themselves mainly for the sole purpose of becoming soldiers – of the kind that their Kaiser wants: submissive defectives. Danish young people train themselves to be good citizens, who can both fit into society and defend their homes. For people with sane judgement – and that the Schleswigers have – the choice is not difficult. They are influenced by all that is sane and good in Denmark. The 'Skyttesagen' has helped to bring the Schleswigers back to us in mind and heart …This situation is better both for us and for them than, for example, the situation in 1870 when we won with weapons in hand.[42]

The reference to 1870 was to the Franco-Prussian War, which had raised Danish hopes that a victorious France would return Schleswig to Denmark. Prussia won, of course, and the German Empire became a reality. However, Danish nationalism acquired an ever stronger anti-German bias. North of the border especially, the Danish folk high schools contributed to the formation of a nationalist frame of mind.

In 1898 there was an unsigned article in *Ungdom og Idræt* about the status of Schleswig-Holstein over the preceding 50 years. According to the article, 1848 was a year of freedom, rich in memories, when a firm allegiance of the people to the throne was established and 'the word Danish became an honorary title common to all', from worker to royalty:

> In face of the danger to the fatherland, individual interests were set aside. Young men, who were busy working to shape a future for themselves, came together voluntarily to fight for the fatherland. The student forsook his books, the carpenter his workshop, the farmer his plough to defend home and hearth side by side.[43]

Danish Sport in North Schleswig

After 1880 it became common for young pro-Danish North Schleswigers (Schleswigers, as they mostly were called) to attend a folk high school in Denmark. After a period at the school they went back to their homes to advance the cause of Danish patriotism. Little by little it also became usual for a number of idealistic young people from north of the border to spend time working on the pro-Danish farms south of the border. In these ways, Swedish gymnastics, as a national symbol, first spread to the areas that were situated south of Kongeå, not far from Askov. H.P. Hanssen has recounted how in the 1880s, when he was a pupil at Askov, on la Cour's initiative pupils and staff introduced Swedish gymnastics into Denmark. They were assisted by a group of Swedish students, who stayed in Askov and visited North Schleswig, where they were housed by villagers in København.[44] In 1892 the pro-Danish North Schleswigers built their first village hall in the province of Skrave, north of Rødding. Shortly afterwards 'Skrave-Skodborg selskabelig Forening' (the Skrave-Skodborg Social Club) introduced

Swedish gymnastics. Østerlindet and other villages followed. By 1907 there were more than 30 halls. The Danish-Swedish gymnastics movement now gained ground in North Schleswig.[45] In time, other sports were introduced. During and after Köller's Germanization effort the work of the visiting proselytizers was hampered because as Danish citizens they could be expelled by the German government. Pro-Danish north Schleswigers, of course, could not be expelled but were harassed in other ways. Meetings of a national or political purpose were not allowed and as a result the famous and lawful Schleswiger 'coffee-meetings' became popular.

In 1899, under the heading 'Hvor der Kaempes' (Where They Fought), H. Sørensen published in *Ungdom og Idræt* excerpts from a number of letters he had received from Schleswigers, harassed by the police south of the border. One village hall was permitted to open only some seven months after it was ready. When the first meeting was held and Reverend Poulsen of Bov wanted to profess his faith, it was forbidden – permission from the government was required to hold church services. The public authorities also stepped in to forbid a women's social. The society that had built the hall was considered a political club and at political meetings, according to German legislation, women were not allowed.[46] Other letters referred cheerfully to 'the subversive coffees' and bitterly to harsh expulsions. There were reports of gymnastics sessions under the strict supervision of the police. The police could not stop the gymnastics movement, however, and in 1903 the forerunner of 'Søderjydsk Idrætsforening' (Schleswiger Sports Club), 'Nordslesvigs Fælles Idrætsforening' (North Schleswig's Common Sports Club), was founded. It embraced all Danish sports in the border area.

'Nordslesvigs Faelles Idraetsforening'

The club was founded on 15 November 1903 at a meeting at which representatives from seven clubs participated: Fjelstrup, Nustrup, Vojens, Rødding, Skrave, Øster Lindet and Haderslev. One of the veterans of the national struggle in North Schleswig, J.H. Schmidt, was chosen as president. He recognized the importance sport had for young people. Schmidt had earlier been a teacher in Snogbæk for 11 years but had left when the authorities forced him to participate in German festivities. He settled down in Haderslev and became the business manager for the 'Foreningen af 6. Oktober' (The Club of 6 October). This had been started with capital of 500,00 DKK by Danish Members of Parliament in order to safeguard Danish land. In this position, and as director of the 'Nordslesvigs Kreditforening' (North Schleswig's Credit Club), he became the force behind the fight for land. Land deals of more than 30 million DKK passed through his hands.[47] Ownership of land was later estimated to have been the central element in maintaining the Danish character of North Schleswig: it was the pro-Danes who held onto the land, while the pro-Germans were more concerned with education and official power.[48] The deputy president of the club, Mads Gram, from København, later president for many years, was also an enthusiastic supporter of both gymnastics and ball games.

The first important task for Nordslesvigs Faelles Idraetsforening was to train instructors. Ingeborg Appel of Askov travelled to gymnastics festivals in North Schleswig acting as director and judge, as well as selecting young Schleswiger 'platoon commanders' for courses in Askov. 'Skytteforeningen i Danmark' (The Danish Marksmanship Club) gave free lessons at these courses, while food and lodging was paid with grants from the 'Sønderjydsk Centralforening' (Schleswig Central Club).[49] Gymnastics did not, however, achieve the same dominant position in Nordslesvigs Fælles Idrætsforening as it had in the equivalent clubs in Denmark. The club did not include shooting for obvious reasons but ball games were included, first football for the men and then basketball for the women. In time, since the authorities were less interested in ball games, these became more important than gymnastics for several reasons. Ball games were not considered as military education, while gymnastics were. Furthermore, there was no age limit at the time for ball games, so that when the authorities started to limit gymnastics for the very young, they played football.[50]

In 1905 Nordslesvigs Fælles Idrætsforening held its first anniversary in Sønderborg. There was gymnastics, with teams from Skrave and Nybøl, as well as football and basketball. In 1906 parliamentary elections made a meeting difficult to arrange and the next meeting, took place in September, 1907. There was football, basketball and gymnastics. In the afternoon, the participants entered the sports-ground to the sound of music. During the procession others joined in and the procession grew larger and larger on its way through the village and the triumphal arch of the festival field. After the sports there were songs and speeches. These were supposed to be politically neutral, but the symbolic meanings in the songs 'Se, det lyser for vort Øje' (See How it Shines for our Eyes) and 'Løft dit Hoved' (Raise your Head) could not be misunderstood by the initiated.[51]

Kirstine Boesen, the Gymnastics Issue and the Football Club

In 1906 the local county chairman in North Schleswig prohibited the pro-Danes from giving gymnastic lessons to children and adolescents. Other county chairmen in North Schleswig even went so far as to forbid gymnastics lessons completely in the village halls. These decisions by the Prussian authorities were challenged in law. It was ruled that the ban was valid only for young people over compulsory school age. Nevertheless, the police continued to arrest those who taught gymnastics to those under 18. Gymnastic lessons in South Jutland were now held behind locked doors with the curtains drawn. Teachers who were caught were fined between 100 and 300 DEM. Any teacher from north of the border was expelled.

A grotesque form of persecution aimed at the proscription of high school gymnastics occurred in Skærbæk. Kirstine Boesen was the daughter of the landlord of the Danish village hall in Skærbæk. After a course in Askov folk high school, she returned to her village in 1906 to teach gymnastics illegally. The police soon made their appearance, forced their way into the village hall and told the children to go home. When they refused the police unsheathed their swords and chased them out. This was far from being the end of the matter. In the spring of 1907 Miss Boesen was fined 100 DEM. She refused to pay. When the police came to arrest her, a local pro-Dane, Andreas Svendsen, paid the fine. Then in the winter of 1908–9 Miss Boesen started gymnastic classes again, this time in the villages of Bredebro and Hvidding. For some time all went well, but finally a policeman managed to catch her in the act. In *Ungdom og Idræt* in 1910 under the heading 'Landsfarlig Gymnastik' (Nationally Dangerous Gymnastics) there was a report that Miss Kirstine Boesen from Skærbæk had been fined 200 DEM. Should Miss Boesen decline to pay the fine, the court in Tønder decided, she would serve 20 days in prison. She again refused to pay. On 9 August 1910 she was arrested and put in Skærbæk prison. This arrest roused so much opposition that she was quickly moved to Tonder prison. Kirstine's father sent a complaint to Berlin. Five days later she was released. The matter had been given so much painful publicity, both in the country itself and abroad, that the government in Berlin overruled the local authority's action. *Ungdom og Idræt* announced her release and home coming and the Boesen case was also extensively reported in the daily papers.[52] Prussian authoritarianism for once had been defeated.

Ball games were not proscribed by the German authorities. Still, on occasion, they faced the same problems as gymnastics. In 1911 Nordslesvigs Fælles Idrætsforening received an invitation to join the 'Norddeutsche Fussball-Verbund' (the North Germany Football Association), the only official football association in north Germany. In the invitation, the association's neutral political character was stressed. However, the pro-Danish Club did not accept the invitation and the association, decided to disqualify it and informed the 'Dansk Boldspil Union' (the Danish Ball Game Union). Danish clubs were banned from playing against the North Schleswigers and a forthcoming match in Alborg was cancelled by the Danes.[53] Bureaucracy took priority over nationalism.

The Goal Achieved

It was due to German foreign policy that North Schleswig was returned to Denmark. In 1914 all pro-Danish club activities were forbidden and young pro-Dane Schleswigers had to fight for Germany. If they failed to answer their call up, they lost the right to their parental farm and land. Many were killed in the Great War, among them a number of young 'platoon commanders' from Nordslesvisk Faelles Idraetsforening. In 1918, hope of freedom was reawakened among the pro-Danes. During the war, the pro-Danish newspapers in North Schleswig had been forbidden to mention 'the North Schleswig question'. In October, 1918 censorship was abandoned. In *Ungdom og Idræt*, in November 1918, Eigil Jørgensen, who considered himself a man of the people, anticipated coming events: 'The Schleswig question is topical again ... suddenly we have our own voice again and can speak and write of what is of such vital importance to us.'[54] The workers' and soldiers' rebellion in Germany now caused the collapse of the German Empire. For a short time the Schleswiger villagers became part of a socialist republic, with positive consequences for North Schleswig, because: 'it meant ... that the members of the Opposition ... in Berlin, with whom H.P. Hanssen had had a good relationship for many years ... now came to power in Germany ...'[55] The speech that Hanssen made in the Berlin Parliament about North Schleswig's reunion with Denmark was noticeable for its moderation and as *Ungdom og Idræt* commented, 'Here lies the explanation for why we can now, more or less, talk and write as we wish. Our claim was recognized everywhere as just.'[56]

The revolution in Germany made Danish reunion with North Schleswig possible, but where should the border be drawn? Hanssen was a realist, but that was far from true of all. From the gymnastics headquarters on Wodroffsvej in Copenhagen, N.H. Rasmussen issued the following statement: 'Danish patriotism will increases in the south in the future: gymnastics will be Danish with ... Danish speeches and songs. Gymnastics should be included in everything as time passes to carry the Danish flag down to Dannevirke. Just see to it!'[57] On 30 January 1919 Nordslesvigs Fælles Idrætsforening held its first post-war board meeting. In February, with other club representatives at a general assembly, it discussed *inter alia* linking Fællesforeningen with a Danish umbrella organization after reunion. There were two possibilities, either to join 'Dansk Idræts-Forbund' (The Danish Sports Club) or 'De Danske Skytte og Gymnastikforeninger' (the Danish Marksmanship and Gymnastics Club), earlier called 'Danske Skytteforeninger' (Danish Marksmanship Club). Marksmanship and gymnastics clubs were closely connected with the high school gymnastics movement and the choice was not difficult. Consequently at the delegates' meeting in Nr. Hostrup in March 1920, it was unanimously agreed that Nordslesvigs Faelles Idraetsforening would join De Danske Skytte og Gymnastikforeninger. The agreement was formalized in the following letter by the new President, Johannes Juhl from Branderup:

> Hereby I request that 'De Danske Skytteog Gymnastikforeninger' takes 'Nordslesvigs Fælles Idrætsforening' into its association. We have been cut off from the marksmanship clubs since the disastrous year of 1864 ... At all times 'De Danske Skytteog Gymnastikforeninger' has supported us with advice and action and we are convinced that it is only within this association's framework that we feel at home and will find a continuing development of common benefit to country and people.[58]

The summer of 1920 saw reunion festivities throughout North Schleswig. King Christian X participated in many of them. *Ungdom og Idræt* contained lengthy descriptions of most of them. However those in Tønder and Højer, both with German majorities, were tensely anticipated. In Tønder, nevertheless, the pro-German Mayor made the welcoming speech in Danish. A local minister was recorded by *Ungdom og Idræt*: 'It was difficult to recognize Tønder. Its style was Danish. I could not avoid noticing either that whereas earlier there were very few signs written in Danish, now there were many ... "Does Tønder look like this?" one could hear people say. Individuals also said: "Flensborg would also have liked to look like this"!'[59]

In Højer the Mayor's welcoming speech for the king was in German. *Ungdom og Idræt* reported that: 'The King replied in Danish ... while the Germans, that is to say the pro-Germans, gathered in the market place by one of the well-known Turkish oaks that the Germans had been busy planting in South Jutland to symbolize the "separation" from Germany in 1848 and "the homecoming" in 1864, the ... King received them down by the so-called King's stone, south of the village.'[60]

The high-point of the festivities was the celebration at the Dybbøl earthworks on 11 July 1920 where, according to a report in *Ungdom og Idræt*, up to 100,000 people gathered. The event was a carefully planned folk festival to symbolize Danish unity but before it was over, there were a number of serious confrontations. H.P. Hanssen was accused of an opportunist border policy, that according to many, had resulted in the pro-Danes in Flensborg and South Schleswig being left in the lurch. One of the most severe critics of H.P. Hanssen was the editor Andreas Grau, of Flensborg. However, both were allowed to speak at the Dybbol event.[61] First, the King and then H.P. Hanssen spoke. He stressed that it was due to the victory of the Allied and Associated Powers that North Schleswig had gained its freedom.

H.P. Hanssen was followed by Andreas Grau, who spoke directly to the population south of the border and stressed that the border was clearly drawn between Danes and Danes. The last speaker was the Prime Minister, Neergaard, who addressed these famous words to the pro-Danes south of the new border: 'You will not be forgotten. It will be a question of honour for each government to support you and to its utmost capacity maintain the language and national character that you have so bravely forfeited.'[62]

'Sydslesvigs danske Ungdomsforeninger'

From the mid-1880s onwards the situation for the pro-Danish South Schleswigers changed considerably. The pro-Danish inhabitants had now become a clear minority.[63] By the turn of the century this minority was better organised than earlier. The old clubs like the townsmen's clubs and language clubs, constituency clubs and school clubs all gained ground. The organization of sports, however, took time. Not until November, 1903 was the 'Flensborg Gymnastikforening' (Flensborg Gymnastics Club) formed. Holger Fink, who had gone to Flensborg to teach business, took the initiative.[64] The club was given permission to use the hall in the townsmen's club for exercises and performances and attracted a group of young men and women. They chose to buy their gymnastics apparatus in Copenhagen, as the Danish apparatus was more suitable for Ling gymnastics than the German Turnen apparatus. A tax of more than 800 DEM was placed on the apparatus, so that the club began in debt. The wealthy wholesaler, Lorenz Poulsen, gave them an interest free loan. The gymnastics went well for many winters.[65] The club soon paid back the loan. When I.P. Müller had his book *Mit System* (My Method) translated into German and other languages, the Flensborg Gymnastikforening managed to persuade him to start his foreign publicity tour in Flensborg. The authorities, however, did not want to allow a pro-Danish club to organize a popular lecture on Müller's method. Luckily, many members of the Flensborg Gymnastikforening often went to the sun bathing institute 'Luft, Licht und Sonnenbad Helios' (Air, Light and Sun Bathing Helios). It agreed to act with Flensborg Gymnastikforening as co-organizer of the lecture in return for a share of the profits. 'Collesseum', the largest hall in Flensborg, was completely filled for the lecture and the entrance fee of 1 DEM provided ample funds for Flensborg Gymnastikforening to rid itself of its irritating debt.[66]

In 1907, in Frøslev, north of Flensborg, an enterprising gymnastics splinter group from the local pro-Danish choral society, 'Frøslev Gymnastikforening', started up under the leadership of the blacksmith, Johan Meyer, who had had a 'platoon commander's' training at Ryslinge.[67] In 1912 a Danish club for young people was established in Flensborg and members from Frøslev also took part in the club's activities. The club took the name of 'Ungdomsforeningen for Flensborg og omegn' (Club for Young People in Flensborg and Surroundings).[68]

Flensborg and Frøslev were the only places in South Schleswig where 'Danish sport' existed before the First World War. At the outbreak of war in 1914 all Danish club activities were forbidden everywhere in the region. With the defeat of Germany Danish activities in Flensborg and surroundings were reintroduced. Johan Meyer from Frøsleve related how, with the club from Flensborg, he visited the Søndereborg club in the summer of 1919, after an invitation from their principal, Andreas Grau. A joint march to the Dybbøl earthworks was planned. The pro-Germans however, organized a counter march and met them with the 'Schleswig-Holstein' song. The pro-Danes sang 'Vift stolt pa kodans bolger' (The Proud Waves of the Baltic). At Dybbøl roughly 300 pro-Danes were met by nearly 1,500 pro-Germans who disturbed the Danish meeting, according to Meyer, by howling the German song. The pro-Danes withdrew, singing the national patriotic Danish song of 1848, 'Den gang jeg drog af sted' (The Time I Left That Place). In Sønderborg the German navy could not guarantee the safety of the pro-Danes and they returned to the steamer in some disarray. When the steamer left the quay it was to the sound of their singing of the Danish national anthem 'Det er et yndigt land' (It is a Lovely Country).[69]

The popular vote in 1920 led to the border being drawn between Flensborg and Frøslev. Frøslev became Danish while Flensborg remained German. The pro-Danish Flensborg club decided to continue meeting once a week. The first meeting was reported by Jacob Kronika, who between 1919 and 1925 published a German paper for the Danish minority called *Neue Flensburger Zeitung* (New Flensborg Paper). Many pro-Germans knew, therefore, that the club usually met on Wednesdays and at the beginning of one meeting a large group of people gathered outside the door and started to sing 'Schleswig-Holstein Meerumschlungen' (Schleswig-Holstein Surrounded by Water). Inside the club the pro-Danish answered with 'I Danmark er jeg født, der har jeg hjemme …' (In Denmark I was born, there I have my home …) The situation did not develop any further and remained a contest in patriotic songs! Matters became worse, however, a little later when the pro-Danish in Flensborg decided to organize a ball game. A ball was found and a public field, 'Exe' at Frisergade, was chosen as a playing field. Young people of both sexes played in the ball game. They spoke in Danish. This was noticed. An ever-increasing crowd gathered. Every now and then antagonistic shouts were heard. On the way home the pro-Danes were closely followed by the pro-Germans and a 'battle' resulted. There was plenty of ammunition in the form of turf, bits of wood and shoes, and there were willing combatants. The following day the newspapers contained details of 'Slaget I Mathildegade' (the Battle at Mathildegade).[70] Tension between pro-Danes and pro-Germans clearly remained.

It was in 1920 also that the pro-Danish Flensborg club, for the first time, was given support from the Danish government; Prime Minister Neergard put 500 DKK at the disposal of the young people for their activities. In 1923 the club got its own meeting place 'Hjemmet' (Home). At the opening of Hjemmet, the president suggested to the pro-Danish 'Flensborg Ungdomsforening' (Flensborg's Club for Young People) that it gather all the existing clubs for young people from Flensborg and surroundings into a joint club. On 28 September 1923 the 'De mellemslesvigske ungdomsforeninger' (The Mid-Schleswig Club for Young People) was started. In 1924, when the Danish club for young people from the town of Slesvig was included, there was a further change of name to 'De sydslesvigske ungdomsforeninger' (The South Schleswig Club for Young People). In 1947 the name was changed yet again to 'Sydslesvigs danske Ungdomsforeninger' (the South Schleswig Danish Club for Young People).[71] 'Sydslesvigs danske Ungdomsforeninger' still exists. Sport still defines Danishness.

Conclusion

On 10 February 1920 the North Schleswigers voted to return to Denmark. In *Morgenposten Fyens Stiftstidende* of 10 February 1995 it was noted that 75 years had passed since a reunification, that was both a fine precedent for the settling of a territorial dispute and a possible precedent for peaceful co-existence in Europe. This was the opinion shared by the rest of the Danish press and also by the majority of Danish politicians. However, recent European history has shown repeatedly that apparently peaceful co-existence can change overnight into violent confrontation: events sadly have given the lie too often to the optimism of press and politicians. Perhaps Schleswig's history may offer a too little known precedent for the resolution of conflict as a consequence of the spirit of nationalism. It certainly also offers clear evidence that sport is too often political – a war without weapons.

NOTES

1. *Schleswig-Holstein* is the German word for the province (land). In Danish it is called *Slesbig-Holsten*. Since 1920 the Danish–German border has been drawn through the middle of Slesvig. *North-Slesvig* is the German word for the part of Slesvig which became Danish, while the Danish word is *Sønderjylland*. The Danish word for the part of Slesvig that became German is *South-Slesvig*, while the German word is just *Slesvig*.

2. Lorenz Rerup, *Slesvig og Holsten efter 1830* (Copenhagen, 1982), p.124 and Uwe Heldt, '125 Jahre Turn-und Sportbund Flensburg. Ein Beitrag zur Entwicklung von Turnen und Sport in Flensburg', *Kleine Reihe der Gesellschaft für Flensburg Stadtgeschichte*, 21, 1 (1991), 41.
3. Compare Rerup, op. cit. and Heldt, op. cit.
4. Rerup, p.124.
5. Heldt, p.45.
6. Jens Peter Ægidius, *Christian Flor. Paedagogen, politikeren, folkeoplyseren* (Odense Universitetsforlag, 1994), p.271.
7. Rerup, p.128.
8. Heldt, p.157.
9. Rerup, p.132; Heldt, p.31.
10. Heldt, p.20.
11. Jørn Hansen, 'Gymnastik og sport – det borgerlige samfund og industrisamfundet?', *Idrætshistorisk Årbog* (1989), 14.
12. See also Dieter Düding, 'Friedrich Ludwig Jahn und die Anfänge der deutschen Nationalbewegung', in Horst Ueberhorst, *Geschichte der Leibesübungen*, Part 3/1 (Berlin, 1980); Egmont Zechlin, *Die deutsche Einheitsbewegung* (Frankfurt/M-Berlin 1967), pp.48–59; Inge Adriansen, *Fædrelandet, folkeminderne og modersmålet* (Publications from Museumrådet for Sønderjyllands Amt Sønderborg 1990), p.29 and Heldt, p.17.
13. Johann Runge, *Sønderjyden Christian Paulsen. Et slesvigsk levnedsløb* (Flensborg, 1981), pp.46–7.
14. Zechlin, pp.48–9; Adriansen, pp.29–31 and Heldt, pp.17–19.
15. Peter Brandt, *Studentische Lebensreform und Nationalismus. Vor- und Frühgeschichte der Allgemeinen deutschen Burschenschaft* (1771–1819/23), unpublished, p.372.
16. Compare ibid., p.373; Ægidius, p.58 and Heldt, p.32.
17. See Rung; Rerup, pp. 45–8 and Adriansen, pp.46–57.
18. Ægidius, pp. 189–91 and Sørent Mørch, *Den sidste Danmarkshistorie. 57 fortaellinger af fædrelandets histori* (Copenhagen, 1996), pp.106–7.
19. Ægidius, op. cit. and Gunhild Nissen, ' Udfordringer til Højskolen. Danske folkehøjskoler 1844 til 1994', *Foreningen for Folkehøjskolers Forlag 1994*, ch.1.
20. Christian Flor, *Om Skoleopdragelse, Indbydelsesskrift til den offentlige Examen I Borgerdydskolen Sptbr. 1818*, and Ægidius, pp.33, 234.
21. Ægidius, pp.299–302.
22. Heldt, pp.48–53.
23. Ibid., p.54.
24. Ibid., p.167 and Rerup, pp.191–2.
25. Heldt, p.165.
26. See also Hans Schultz Hansen, *Danskheden i Sydslesvig 1840–1918 som folkelig og national bevaegelse* and Gottlieb Japsen (pub.), *Dansk og tysk i Sønderjylland* (Copenhagen, 1979).
27. Japsen, pp.34–6.
28. Heldt, p.165.
29. Adriansen, p.178; Heldt, pp.164–5.
30. Rerup, p.421; Adriansen, p.178.
31. Adriansen, p.178.
32. Heldt, pp.165–6.
33. Jørn Hansen, 'Sport' og 'dansk idræt', in *Idrætshistorisk Årbog 1990*; Jørn Hansen, 'I form for 100 år siden. Gymnastiklærer J. Lauritsen og Odense, Gymnastikforening', in Odensebogen (1996).
34. The introduction of Ling-gymnastics into Denmark is described in detail by Ove Korsgaard, *Kampen om kroppen. Dansk idræts historie gennem 200 år* (Copenhagen, 1982) and by Else Trangbæk, *Mellem leg og disciplin. Gymnastikken i Danmark i 1800–tallet* (DUO Aabybro 1987).
35. *Ungdom og Idræt*, 1 February 1897, and John Engelbrecht, *Vil du taende, må du braende. Fra delingsfører til gymnastik-instruktør. Den danske delingsfører gennem 100 år 1889–1989* (GIL 1989).

36. *Ungdom og Idræt*, 14 (1898), pp.407–8.
37. Ibid. p.410.
38. Ibid. pp.412–13.
39. See *Ungdom og Idræt*, 26 (1898).
40. *Ungdom og Idræt*, 29 (1898), p.606.
41. *Ungdom og Idræt*, 26 (1898), p.628.
42. Ibid. p.631.
43. *Ungdom og Idræt*, 23 (1898), p.566.
44. Adler Lund, *Sønderjydsk Indraetsforening. Et Bidrag til Skildring af Dansk Ungdomsliv i Sønderjylland* (Haderslev, 1932), p.11.
45. *Ungdom og Idræt*, 8 (1907).
46. *Ungdom og Idræt*, 18 and 29 (1899), pp.476–7.
47. Adler Lund, pp.19–20.
48. See also Japsen and Schultz Hansen.
49. Adler Lund, p.22.
50. Ibid. p.24.
51. Ibid. p.25.
52. *Ungdom og Idræt*, 34 (1910); Adler Lund, pp.37–41 and Chr. Pedersen (ed.), *Dansk Idraet i Graenselandet* (Haderslev, 1957).
53. Adler Lund, p.27.
54. *Ungdom og Idræt*, 46 (1918), p.377.
55. *Ungdom og Idræt*, 49 (1918), p.394.
56. Ibid. pp.394–5.
57. *Ungdom og Idræt*, 50 (1919), p.423.
58. Letters from Johannes Juhl to *De Danske Skytte- Gymnastik- og Idrætsforeninger*, Adler Lund, p.106.
59. *Ungdom og Idræt*, 30 (1920).
60. Ibid.
61. Rerup, pp.322–4.
62. *Ungdom og Idræt*, 30 (1920) and Rerup, p.347.
63. Schultz Hansen, pp.358–9.
64. Ibid. p.335.
65. Holger Fink: 'Minder fra Flensborg', in *Dansk Ungdom Sydslesvig 1923–1948*, Sydslesvigske Danske Ungdomsforenings Jubilaeumsskrift edited by Franz Winginder and Sig. Kristensen, p. 27.
66. Ibid. p.28.
67. Schultz Hansen, p.337.
68. *Dansk Ungdom i Sydslesvig*, p.64.
69. Johan Meyer, 'Oplevelser sammen med unge danske flensborger', *Dansk Ungdom i Sydslesvig*, pp.30–1.
70. Jacob Kronika, 'Danmark kommer lnaermere' in, *Dansk Ungdom i Sydslesvig*, pp.39–40.
71. *Dansk Ungdom i Syudslesvig*, pp.62–5.

The Power of Public Pronouncement: The Rhetoric of Nordic Sport in the Early Twentieth Century

HENRIK MEINANDER

On the morning of 29 May 1894 the steamer *von Döbeln* entered the harbour of Helsinki, the capital of the Grand Duchy of Finland. Among those on the deck were a crowd of interested members of the Stockholm (Sweden) 'Gymnastikförening' (gymnastics society), who had travelled over the Baltic to participate in Finland's second general gymnastics festival. They received a warm reception at 'Södra kajen' (the southern harbour). After a student choir had sung Finland's national anthem 'Vårt land', there followed in succession welcoming speeches and cheers. The group's figureheads, Major Viktor Balck and his friend Frithiof Holmgren, Professor of Physiology at the University of Uppsala, got the most cheers because they were widely known in the Finnish sports and gymnastics worlds. Balck was famous as a dynamic sports leader, while Holmgren was renowned for his stirring speeches, in which he often dwelt on the common history of the two countries and so awoke a silent longing among the Finns, who wished that the Grand Duchy could free itself from the Russian empire and be again joined to Sweden. For many centuries Finland had been an integral part of the Swedish empire and not until 1809 did it become part of the Russian empire, after a short war of conquest.

The gymnastics competition went according to plan, and the last item on the programme, on 3 June, was a combined competition in athletics, won by a student, Hjalmar Fellman. All this was good and worthy, but at least by the big farewell party that same evening most of the participants must have realized that the marches and performances were neither the only nor necessarily the most important purpose of the event. As the evening wore on, the speeches increasingly and openly alluded to Finland's Swedish past and the Finns' cultural resistance to absorption by Russia. The only thing that curbed the tone of the speeches was the risk that police spies had infiltrated the audience.

Not surprisingly, it was Holmgren's speech that was received with most rapture and enthusiasm. His exuberant speech to the Finns at an equivalent competition in Stockholm (Sweden) in 1891 was still fresh in their minds and when the professor, after a few well-chosen words about spring, youth and the struggle for life, looked to the future he saw the illusion of Finland's independence: 'Life is a continuous struggle and perhaps the person struggling is happier than the one who has reached his goal and rests on his laurels. Keep on with the struggle. It keeps the blood flowing and the spirits high. Do not let go, Finnish gymnasts, but hold on and never loose your hope.'[1]

Frithiof Holmgren's speech that pleasant early summer evening in Helsinki raises two questions. Firstly, the contrast between the political message of the speech and the other arrangements at the festival, with its traditional performances and competitions, is a reminder that there is often tension between the rhetoric and practice of sport. In the Nordic countries this was most apparent around the turn of the century. Informal sport during the 1880s and the 1890s became more formal, and at the start of the twentieth century a rapid social and structural transformation took place in the sphere of leisure time. At the same time the discussion about the political, cultural and medical purpose of sports was expressed in visions, which only exceptionally reflected the present. They were mostly associated with visions of the past or the future. Why was this?

Secondly, Holmgren's tactful incitement of the Finnish gymnasts is a good example of how social ideas, expressions and views gained ground in the Nordic countries before the First World War. The Lutheran educational tradition in the Nordic countries led to the rate of literacy among the population being clearly higher than in Central and Southern Europe; but despite this, it could be difficult for new ideas to gain ground. The reasons for this are obvious; sparse population, difficult physical conditions and great distances to the urban centres in Central Europe. During this time, meanwhile, many significant improvements in contact were made, thanks especially to a number of technical innovations. The region became less peripheral and the Nordic countries from 1910 onwards *de facto* in many ways now had a visible position in the sports culture of Europe. How is this change viewed by the Nordic academic community?

Competition is Life

A little after the gymnastic festival in Helsinki, or, more precisely, at the beginning of August 1895, over 6,500 educationists met in Stockholm for the seventh Nordic Schools' Congress. Among the many speakers was Viktor Balck, whose topic 'Sports and physical exercises in connection with upbringing' was charged with arguments for more games and sports in school. Balck had been campaigning for this for almost two decades and was now considered the spokesman for the whole Nordic sports movement.

For this reason his arguments had rhetorical importance.

Balck pointed out, as so often before, that games and sports were more mentally stimulating than gymnastics, because to a greater extent than gymnastics they developed self-discipline, courage, energy and an appetite for fair play. And naturally the Anglophile Major reminded his audience that the backbone of the British empire was its healthy sport: 'From it derives the personal courage and the liking of energetic, sometimes audacious actions, that has contributed to make the British soldiers, seamen, colonialists and explorers what they are today.'[2]

Henrik Sandblad has pointed out that Balck, in addition to obtaining inspiration from the British empire, borrowed much of his thinking from Frithiof Holmgren, who wrote enthusiastic social-Darwinian articles and speeches about the dynamics of sports in the 1870s and 1880s. Balck's contribution in 1895 consisted of mostly the same arguments that Holmgren had used in the preface to *Illustrerad Idrottsbok* (The Illustrated Sports Book), published in Stockholm between 1886 and 1888. Balck's thesis that 'Sports without competitions is dead. Competition is life' was a highly simplified reproduction of Holmgren's animated view of sports, according to which competition increases man's vitality and with it enlivens and develops his nature.[3]

This 'gospel' according to Holmgren also inspired others in the Nordic countries, especially in Denmark where his preface was reproduced in 1890 in a book on sports edited by the Victor Hansen, a leading exponent of Danish sport. The excuse given by Hansen, for his apparent plagiarism, was that Holmgren's views had universal applicability: 'There has arisen all over the country [Denmark] a vital urge for the youth to become what youth foremost should be – young, healthy and buoyant.'[4] A similar enthusiasm for Holmgren's view was also found in Finland. There were two reasons: his supportive references to a common past and the conviction that Holmgren had discovered something crucial in competitive sports.[5]

Was this really the case? Holmgren's two main themes – Vikings as role models and Darwinism as reality – in fact were not part of the language of school and park playing fields. The nostalgic allusions to a forgotten Viking mentality had it roots in the political Scandinavianism of the 1850s. Holmgren had himself experienced the political enthusiasm of the fifties but used the Viking analogies sparingly. This was rarely the case with his enthusiastic followers. In consequence, references to the Nordic peoples' dormant prowess became increasingly removed from the context of everyday life and were mainly used as historical ornaments in public discourse, and by 1910 the Viking 'craze' was over.

Yet it is important to remember that all languages have idiomatic expressions and sayings that forge associations with the past. They can be examples of true continuity in the use of the language, but often they are products of a conscious revival or an invented tradition. An apt and clear example of this is the old Nordic expression 'idrott' (sport) and its Finnish equivalent 'urheilu' and their use from the end of the nineteenth century onwards. Both terms were reintroduced by ideologically receptive educationalists and physicians who wanted to make the point that modern competitive sports could be understood as a continuation of the pre-industrial games and competitions of northern Europe.[6]

The introduction was successful and led to the wide use of the ancient terms. They inevitably lost many of their historical connotations, but by no means all. They still prompted memories of the Viking period and Nordic glory. Another category of Viking romanticism and the *Kalevala*-inspired constructions[7] that had had time to enter common usage in sports language were old Nordic and Finnish names for the sports clubs and places. Here also the original meanings and associations died out partially but not completely.

Thus language is neither linear nor an exclusive reflection of the socio-economical context. But its acceptance depends on the ability to refer to a reality, or more specifically, on an ability to create a meaningful illusion from it. In most cases the rhetoric joined the new and the unknown to the old and familiar. It seems that Viking romanticism and old Finnish language 'ornaments' met the need of spectators, more precisely the parents and teachers, for a positive rationale for the young's peculiar and strong interest in the new competitive games and sports of the modern age.

Positive comparisons between the new and the old were a way of criticizing society. The rhetoric of Viking romanticism produced paradoxically visual pictures that contained a vision of a different future. Reinhard Koselleck's thesis is, true enough, that similar visionary terms are made with the help of new concepts,[8] but the question is whether subconsciously reborn expressions are not also neologisms. Similar comparisons with pre-industrial games and competitions were made, as is known, even by the father of the Olympic movement, Pierre de Coubertin, who was noticeably good at camouflaging novelties in togas and tunics.[9]

A parallel can be found in Freudian rhetoric. It is obvious that the ability to interpret and propagate novelties by using antique myths was and is still one of the secrets of Sigmund Freud's great popularity in the western world. Freud's classical education and literary ambitions made it possible for him to write his scientific observations about the psyche in a language that was both understandable and attractive to the bourgeois reader. The psychoanalytic predilections of his biographers have enticed them to neglect this aspect of his work; their proximity has led to blind spots. This is true, for example, of the renowned historian of ideas, Peter Gay, despite the fact that long before his impressive works on Freud, he wrote *Style in History*, a brilliant analysis of the mutual attachment between form and context in all written culture.[10] Gay points out the peculiarities in the diffusion of the Freudian vision, but fails to consider the conceptual receptivity of his wide circle of readers.[11] He could usefully have learnt from Freud's readable style.

Consideration of Freud's attractive language leads directly to a consideration of one of the cornerstones of Holmgren's rhetoric, the Darwinian vocabulary. As in the case of psychoanalytical jargon it contains numerous neologisms. Holmgren and his contemporaries in the 1890s may have lived happily without knowing that they might have an Oedipal complex, but could any of them have avoided using expressions such as 'the survival of the fittest', 'evolution' or 'the natural choice'?[12]

Liberal Control

The popular use of Darwinian concepts was frequently visionary in the promotional texts on sport at the turn of the century. Some embraced the simplistic belief that fighting hardened the human race, but often in conjunction with the belief that sport developed the social conscience of the young. In the Danish educationist Oscar Hansen's influential book *Opdragælselære*, published in 1898, for example, organized games were recommended because they stimulated a willingness to compete with a discipline that inculcated both initiative and obedience. The 'survival of the fittest' to Hansen seemed like a struggle for a more humane existence, while evolution seemed to him a clear opportunity to move society in a positive direction.[13]

Opdragælselære reproduced almost word for word the moralistic propaganda disseminated by British educationists during the 1860s and 1870s that had been spread in a simplified form by newsletters and foreign visitors. Sometimes reiteration led to citations of citations. The prize for this was clearly won by the Norwegian journal *Den høiere skole*, when in 1899 it published a translation of the Austrian review of the French book *La supériorité des Anglo-Saxons*. The review concluded predictably with high praise for the character-building education and consequent successful imperialism of the British.[14]

Hansen did not refer specifically to Darwin, but to the sociological interpretations of Herbert Spencer, whose moral teaching has often been treated in a pejorative sense as the crudest social Darwinism. However, the Nordic supporters of Spencer did not view him as being an apostle of self-absorbed egoism. They interpreted individualism as a naive common-sense form of altruism, as Hansen did, as it allowed for feeling for others, especially relatives and friends.[15] Moreover, Spencer's interpretation of Darwinism was mainly used by them as intellectual ammunition in the ideological war with the Establishment and its inflexible conception of culture.[16]

Oscar Hansen's call for more playgrounds and sports facilities for the public was based on the Spencerian axiom that all rational education and social planning should be based on physical needs. The axiom contrasted strongly with the conservative college and university circles' neo-humanism and embraced the ideal of a more open and egalitarian society. The playground was seen as a source of social mobility, a place for breaking down class barriers. Hansen belonged to 'Venstre', the liberal group in Denmark's cultural and political life, which saw in Spencer a convincing spokesman for a society where all individuals were treated as equals in the struggle to ensure 'survival of the fittest'.[17]

Hansen's textbook was meant for students training to be elementary school teachers who, on reading it, would understand that the elementary school by itself could not ensure social equality. Wider reforms were needed, and sport was seen increasingly as a concrete example of positive action that was already beginning to take place at the grass-roots level. The British and German playground movements, which had spread widely during the 1880s, inspired a group of liberals in 1891 to found a society in Copenhagen to demand municipal playgrounds[18] and within ten years similar initiatives had been taken in Kristiania (from 1925 Oslo), Stockholm, Helsinki and many other Nordic cities.

It was not only educationists who found a political message in Spencer's attitude to the body. Public-minded physicians who took a full part in the debate and planning of the new society were equally keen on reform. To their way of thinking the Spencerian arguments were justified both from a physiological and a psychological point of view. The physiological reasons were based on the results of research into the over-exertion and bacteriological dangers to which schoolchildren were exposed, while the psychological reasons reflected the arguments of the educationists. Modern society needed citizens who had been shaped by games into individuals, to quote the Norwegian doctor, Thomas Mohn, with 'quick wits, self-confidence, self-reliance, consideration, endurance ... in other words discipline'.[19]

It is neither accidental nor insignificant that the liberals' focus of attention was the human physique. The Nordic vision of a new society, 'self-sufficient' and independent of any central European guardian, saw the body and its liberation as an important cultural metaphor. Similar analogies were drawn in central Europe, but a Nordic variation on the theme of political, social and physical emancipation could be clearly recognized.[20]

The arguments of educationists and physicians demanding the emancipation of the body did not, however, have total liberation in mind. They distinguished themselves from the conservative sports enthusiasts, in that they did not see the 'survival of the fittest' as a question of national assertion or readiness for war but more as a process of democratization. But in the background there was a clear attempt to steer and control the process, to see that the natural tendency of the young to play did not run wild but was kept within limits.

The differences between the conservative and liberal views of sport were clearest during the decade before the First World War, when the question of schoolchildren belonging to national sports organizations arose. In Denmark, Sweden and Norway these organizations were led by military or commercial people. In general, these organizers supported a more conservative view of society than educationalists and physicians, and were convinced that the voluntary central organizations should be responsible for sport for schoolchildren; only they had the organizational networks to ensure the effective recruitment of members.

The liberals thought, however, that the existing organizations lacked the educational and medical expertise that was needed to steer young people in the right direction. They thought that the view that organizations could manage without this kind of guardianship was based on ignorance and arrogance. The dispute was defused in the Nordic countries during the 1920s when the parties agreed compromises. None of these agreements, however, solved the basic question of which overall public body would really direct and monitor the young in their different activities.[21] The discussion continued, therefore, well into the 1950s and died down only when the invasion of American youth culture made the whole issue seem anachronistic.

The recently published study by Henrik Berggren of the rhetoric used in the Swedish youth movement between 1900 and 1939 sheds new light on this conflict of views. At the beginning of this century many central ideas on how society was changing concentrated on the concept of 'youth'. The control of the coming generation meant control of the future. Berggren distinguishes between two general views on youth. The one was that the young with their idealism and abundant energy were a great source of renewal in society; the other stressed their fragility and argued that society should protect these 'budding plants'. The prevailing view was still the belief that the youth of the new century represented a strange, and in the positive sense, uncivilized element in western culture.[22]

Berggren's analysis was a part of a political debate in Sweden, but his analysis is also relevant to the debate on the expansion of sporting activities throughout the Nordic countries. Liberals and conservatives argued about the organization of activities, but they were agreed that they had to attempt to maintain a balance between release of energy and protection of vulnerability. A further dividing-line, of course, was between the differing debaters and the performing young. The former used their energy to define, govern and criticize the young, while the young in their turn, expressed themselves through action.

Niels Kayser Nielsen, referring to this situation, has reminded us that the Nordic sports movement at the turn of the century had many of the symptoms of a youth revolt.[23] The notion that young people of the new century were a strange element was thus not an illusion. It was based on rapid changes in technology and the infrastructure of society. The point was that these changes were understood very differently by the different age groups at the time. Diversity of view between old and young was the product of interpretation, not fragmentation.

The older generation considered change from an historical perspective. Motor cars and the electrified towns were compared with the horses and candle light of former times; the increasingly rational rhythm of work and the cult of leisure time contrasted with the previous decades' social life, over which there had still hovered something of the rigid formalism and sleepy tempo of the pre-industrial society. The children of the 1880s had already a more existentialist attitude towards the transition; they grew up with the substantial reforms in society and their first formative sensations were essentially connected with technical breakthroughs and extensive social change. The result was a permanent feeling of destruction and construction, that was put into words and action.

This feverish feeling was not the experience of the adolescents of the 1910s, who belonged to a generation that did not reflect as much on history and technical novelty. Their attitude can be seen in the sports papers and slang of schoolboys in the 1910s. The rapid advance of the sports movement had from the end of the 1890s led to the setting up of competitive-minded central organizations and an increasing number of modern sports facilities. Between 1900 and 1910 substantial space was cleared for large sports grounds in all the Nordic capitals. When these organizational frameworks and architectural infrastructures were established, the expansion went ahead swiftly and without lengthy ideological debate. This instrumentalism was reflected in the language of sports, which lost much its emotional charge and became increasingly one-dimensional in its emphasis on statistics and results.

A Moral Purpose

The differences between the generations can be clearly demonstrated. The older generation's view on the young's sport is strikingly depicted by the

Swedish headmaster Carl Svedelius.[24] During the 1910s he distinguished himself as a resourceful and influential spokesman for sport for schoolchildren. Svedelius strongly recommended all forms of sport and always supported his recommendations with pedagogical and physiological arguments. His arguments regarding health were the basis of his exhortations on the matter. Healthy children were more amenable to spiritual stimulation and this led to sport as a crucial part of upbringing in two ways. On the one hand it increased the pupils' academic ability; and on the other it improved their mental health – to use a more fashionable period term – their character.[25]

Svedelius's apologia for more sports was imbued with a sense of responsibility and rationality. Many of the things he said were modern and topical, reflecting the belief that pupils' self-discipline and personality developed best when allowed enough freedom. But behind his arguments for more space and time for this liberation there was still a conventional belief that interference was necessary and in a good cause. This argument had played a central role in the public debate from the 1880s to the 1910s. Svedelius was surely greeted with approving nods and comments when in August 1915 he gave a talk to Swedish teachers, in which he stressed the exceptional importance of pupils in secondary schools being in good physical condition: 'School has ... the positive aim of trying to lay a solid foundation for the greatest possible degree of health, strength and zest for life not least for those who at some time will be civil servants and become more or less influential bearers of national development.'[26]

Svedelius's careful use of expressions such as 'solid foundation', 'civil service' and 'national development' shows how strongly he was influenced by a traditional utilitarian way of thinking. There was no talk of a total emancipation of the youth; his purpose was, on the contrary, to strengthen the moral framework of society through a development of the pupils' self-discipline. Svedelius relied mostly on the twin concepts of self-discipline and self-help, that since the 1880s had been keywords in Anglo-Saxon-inspired reformatory pedagogics. In short his purpose was the same, namely 'that pupils were to be educated to self-discipline, at the same time as their sense of responsibility was stimulated'.[27]

The same views can be found in a widely acclaimed speech by the Norwegian arctic explorer Fridtjof Nansen at a meeting of eductionalists in Kristiania (Norway) in 1900. Nansen was born in 1861, the same year as Svedelius, and like him advocated an upbringing that developed pupils' self-reliance. His criticism of the secondary schools' inflexible curriculum was in itself neither unique nor new, but the speech found support because it was given by a scientist who had skied across Greenland and made numerous scientific surveys of the Arctic Ocean. Nansen was the most popular person in the Nordic countries at the turn of the century and was seen generally as the personification of the modern man. There was personal experience behind his words: 'it is naturally good to bring up one's children to become good and well-behaved, but it isn't enough; it is equally important to produce individual, strong-willed people'.[28]

Nansen preached a belief in the value of skiing, but his attitude to the modern sports movement was not wholly supportive. On the contrary, he pointed out in his speech that a large part of competitive-oriented sport had relapse into a 'corrupt' hunt for records and fame. This did not fit his image of sport as a form of moral upbringing; 'sport was supposed to educate and strengthen the body and soul and take us out into nature'.[29] On this point Nansen was more extreme than Svedelius, but common to both of them was the conviction that sport should not be allowed to become an end in itself. It was governed by the natural need for physical activities and longing to get back to nature, but it had to be kept within reasonable bounds while fulfilling its educational role.

Nansen's worship of nature reflected the typical contemporary middle-class reaction against the alleged unhealthiness and demoralizing effect on young people of the expansion of city-life. This reaction was critical of 'civilization', in that it questioned the benefits of technical innovations for mankind, and it resulted in Nansen writing a book on the theme of nature versus culture. The book was published in 1916 with the title *Frilufts-liv* (Outdoor Life). It contained many stirring descriptions of the author's skiing expeditions through snow-covered forests and mountain scenery. Nansen summarized his reactionary thoughts in an epilogue, where he deprecated the 'advances' of civilization: 'But now then! One can see the funnels of trains through the stillness, the train going back and forth, the black smoke bellowing out from the tunnel openings up into the blue sky – and the so-called culture moves higher and higher up with its big hotels.'[30]

In a study of Nansen's public life, Bodil Stenseth states that during the 1890s the press portrayed him as an ideal model for Norwegian youth.[31] The two-pronged message in his criticism of 'civilization' also coincided with the emerging ideology of the youth movement, in whose rhetoric there was a constant dialectic between traditional torpor and contemporary awakening. Nansen criticized modern society but still contributed to it through his scientific achievements. A similar dualism can also be found behind the slogans of the youth movement, that often made it appear inimical to culture. It was pointed out that the young held the promise of a new mankind, but at the same time their power of renewal could be described as an echo from a purer past. History and the future joined forces in an attack on the present.[32]

The Futurists in Sport

Nansen and his generation veered towards an idealization of the nation and the more 'natural' life of the past. The younger generation, born mainly during the 1880s, of ideologically-conscious writers and leaders viewed the past more as a polite preamble to dismissive demands for a faster pace into the future. Henrik Berggren has pointed out that their stress on action and novelty curiously could well be interpreted as a camouflaged attempt to carry through older and more traditional educational aims. But he also admitted that to say this might be to underestimate the genuine avant-garde nature of the youth rhetoric in the 1910s.[33]

One of the most active, in word and deed, sports ideologists in the Nordic countries during the 1910s was the Finnish journalist Artur Eklund (1880–1927), who both in his writings and in actions demonstrated a strong desire to welcome the future. He had some success as a sportsman and pointed out on several occasions that only those who had experienced the thrill of the race could understand what sport really is. The assertion was aimed at the older generation, who like Svedelius and Nansen thought that the value of sport stood or fell because of its usefulness to society. Eklund had read his Nietzsche and Bergson, both of whom questioned the significance of rational goals, and therefore stressed that it was impossible and highly unsatisfactory to talk about the instrumental purposes of sport.[34]

In a essay written in 1914 Eklund dealt with the strong criticism of competition fever by the famous German author Max Nordau. According to Eklund, Nordau's attack was based on a total lack of knowledge about the new experiences of young people on sports grounds. Nordau had not understood that 'sport is a way of expressing a person's self-assertion, a boisterous, joyful sense of life'.[35] In other contexts he pointed again and again to the weaknesses in the utilitarian arguments. If one practised sports for one's health then it was a question of medical gymnastics and if one practised them with a moral purpose then one was more a teacher than a sportsman.[36] Eklund's references and style reveal that he had been influenced by Bergson's compatriot Georges Sorel, who, starting from the Bergson theory of the primacy of intuitive over analytical knowledge, had formulated a strategy for political action. Sorel understood that one could create a revolutionary feeling by evoking a collective spirit of increasing and continuous haste.[37] In his case the goal was social revolution and socialism, but many others saw his strategy as a formula for wider action. Without doubt Eklund belonged to them, and with his pure futuristic ideas, was convinced that the feeling of freedom obtained its power from the fact that one impatiently awaited the future.

Around 1910 Eklund began to work wholeheartedly for the nationalistic consolidation of the Swedish-speaking inhabitants of Finland. A few years later he helped build up an underground resistance movement that played an important part in the nation's fight for independence in 1917–1918; and he was probably more successful than any Scandinavian in presenting sport as an expression of the need to be absorbed by strong movements and feelings.[38] Eklund's essays were also futuristic in the sense that he showed little understanding of a nostalgic longing to return to nature. On the contrary, there was an obvious delight in his pronouncement that culture continuously advanced; 'life becomes more complicated and multifarious, the machines take over more and more the work of humans'.[39]

Eklund admitted that there was some truth in the accusations that modern top-level sport was losing its element of play and becoming work-oriented. But at the same time he pointed out that this singularity of purpose was the secret behind the vitality of American society, as it was driven by 'intensive willpower, straight-backed resolution, absorption in the task of the moment, and the doubtless unreserved use of the last drop of strength and energy'.[40] Taylorism[41] did not therefore appear to Eklund as a heartless mechanization of life. Instead rationalization was a means of introducing principles of sport into work, as it meant 'the highest possible ability by means of the most appropriate technique and careful practice'.[42] Eklund's words mirrored a worship of speed as a symbol of vitality that was typical of modern thinkers in the 1910s as an expression of the maximization of all forms of human sensation. The increasing speed, movement and rhythm of sport were direct offshoots of the intuitive desire of the young to continually increase the level of sensation.[43]

It is too easy to describe the sports debate of the 1910s as solely a clash between the generations. Many of Eklund's contemporaries were just as concerned as the older debaters lest this worship of speed in one way or another lead to a cultural catastrophe. They were of the view that western civilization had been afflicted by a structural degeneration that could not be cured by physically and mentally charged sensations. These views were shared in Finland, for example, by Eklund's critics within the so-called Swedish cultural camp, who rejected his demands for a linguistic polarization in Finland as irrational and short-sighted.

The distrust shown by these Swedish-speaking academics of Eklund's activist recipe, however, did not apply to sport but to language and society. But according to Eklund everything was connected. In his view their cultural pessimism was an expression of an over-sensitive mentality and an aesthetic snobbishness that could be put right by sport. This was a hasty conclusion that resulted in Eklund's failing to distinguish between the older form of nostalgia and the new cultural pessimism, concerned not with technology as such but with the irrational preoccupation with the future for which he himself was spokesman.[44]

In an inspiring analysis of this degeneration scenario Stephen Kern has compared the cultural pessimists' ambivalent attitude to the future with contemporary reactions to the sinking of the *Titanic* in 1912. On the one hand people were fascinated by the ocean liner's technical finesse and luxurious comfort; on the other they pointed out that pride in the worship of speed and human inventiveness had led to a catastrophe. This dismay decreased of course when the likelihood of wrecks and other disasters diminished at the same rate as new techniques were introduced. But at the back of their minds there was still an evil foreboding that modern civilization was like the crew of the *Titanic*: proud, comfortable, arrogant and disdainful of icebergs suddenly appearing in the misty oceans of the future.[45]

The First World War was undeniably just such an iceberg. The reaction was clearly strongest among the central European intellectuals, whose worship of machines quickly evaporated when they were confronted with the modern technology of war.[46] Denmark, Norway and Sweden managed to stay outside this Armageddon, while Finland was drawn into this continental 'man mincing-machine' during the last year of the war. Eklund's reaction to the war was almost like that of the travellers on the top deck of the *Titanic*; first curiosity, then increasing anxiety and finally uncontrolled panic. The end result was disillusion as to the future and a greater understanding of the cultural pessimists' view of European civilization. He wrote congratulatory book reviews of Oswald Spengler's culturally pessimistic best-sellers and like him called for ways to be free of the yoke of democracy and communal culture. Sport was still Eklund's password, but the reason for this was no longer what it had been.[47]

Not all the enthusiasts for the future gave up so easily. Especially not those who, like the Danish author and later Nobel laureate Johannes V. Jensen (1873–1950), held to the view that dedication to sport reflected a democratic instinct, because it promoted equality of opportunity. Jensen's worship of speed and machines had been preceded by a culturally pessimistic view of society.[48] Jensen's ideological development, therefore, provides an interesting comparison with Eklund's, which, of course, went in precisely the opposite direction – from optimism to pessimism. Jensen and Eklund stood on opposite sides of an historical watershed. Jensen had suffered the 'Weltschmerz' and decadence of the 1890s as a young student in Copenhagen (Denmark); Eklund grew to maturity during the dramatic constitutional crisis that flared up between the Russian government and Finnish nationalists between 1899 and 1905. By 1900 Jensen had already got over his anxiety about the modern world and during the next three decades wrote numerous novels in praise of life, while Eklund was pulled more and more into political activities and seems to have been susceptible to the feeling of depression that spread all over Europe after the First World War.[49]

Other factors led to their increasingly divergent views. Eklund's optimism was boosted by Finland's Declaration of Independence in December 1917, but two months later the Russian Revolution spread to the former Grand Duchy. The civil war ended with the victory of the White Government troops, and Eklund became one of those journalists who expressed themselves in fulsome terms because of this. Nevertheless it is apparent that the war blunted the edge of his belief in the future. Jensen was spared similar shocks: Denmark was neutral in the war and he continued to write as productively and positively as earlier.

The Social History of the Word

There is a further issue to be considered – the written word in its social context. It is possible to compare the rhetoric of Frithiof Holmgren and Viktor Balck and to see how they combined the myths of Viking romanticism with Darwinian concepts. It is, however, more difficult to determine what real meaning their ideological constructions had for the Nordic sports movement. Holmgren was often quoted at, and Balck frequently invited to great sports festivals, but how far did their rhetoric stimulate or reflect a collective way of thinking?

Jan Lindroth's thesis on the development of the Swedish sports movement reveals that Balck had a great influence on its organization. My own thesis contains an analysis of his pedagogical thinking. But neither of us has considered sufficiently the extent of the impact of words on the development.[50] One difficulty of connecting rhetoric with practice lies in there being an obvious danger associated with any reconstruction of the history of ideas. Laurence Veysey believes correctly that there is a real risk sometimes in making too much of the rationality and cohesion of past ideas. A too precise interpretation of confused and hazily-formulated thoughts leads to the improvement of certain parts of them and the distortion of the original message.[51]

Too much, in turn, can be made of Veysey's fears. It is very apparent that some actors on the historical scene have thought carefully about the logic of their ideas and their implications for society. Carl Svedelius's position on sport was based on a thoroughly thought-out pedagogical point of view; his commitment to the beneficial effects of sport in schools was a consequence of this. It was not by chance that Artur Eklund's essays attracted attention all over the Nordic countries; they reflected and expressed a belief in the future, typical of the time, and were truly representative.[52]

The slang of Nordic schoolboys lends itself well to the analysis of language with sporting and physical connotations at the turn of the century. One of the classics studies of urban slang of the Nordic countries is the collection of words by Ruben Berg in 1900.[53] Berg's list was the foundation for Wilhelm Uhrström's similar collection in 1910, from which we can see that the slang used in Stockholm (Sweden) around the turn of the century was varied, particularly in two regards. Firstly, there were numerous expressions to describe a friend's or opponent's social position and the many pejorative expressions for secondary school pupils – one used especially for the pupils in lower status secondary schools was 'rallbuse' or 'rallare' (navvy).[54] Secondly, there were many expressions for describing physical movement and ball-games. References to running included expressions like 'skubba' (dash away), 'skala' (peal off), 'skota' (hasten away), 'lägga i väg' (take to one's heels) and 'luffa' (amble/wander), while football and rounders needed a whole collection of technical terms with which to describe every detail of the play. 'Bolla, bolla' (to dribble) is easy to understand, but what of expressions like 'knorva' or 'sulle'? 'Sulle' meant the area where the ball-player waited for a suitable moment to make a dash for the goal. 'Knorva' is especially interesting because it, like a number of other slang-words, had two very different connotations. On the one hand the player was 'knorvad' if he was hit by the ball; on the other he would 'knorva' himself by failing an examination. Another expression was 'en halva', which meant both catching a ball that has bounced once on the ground and also the second sip from a glass of vodka.[55]

These double meanings clearly indicate the social milieu of the school, street and boys. Sport was not considered moral or healthy, but part of school or workplace or leisure and references to it included a number of slang-words that linked it with the social context; the body, the word and the surroundings created, in other words, a meshed chain of meaning.

No equivalent slang dictionary of the early twentieth century can be found in the other Nordic countries, but there is in Helsinki Heikki Paunonen's extensive studies of the connection between the Finnish- and Swedish-speakers' slang before the Second World War. Helsinki was still a bilingual city circa 1910 and this was reflected in its slang, which was a combination of the two languages. In many cases this slang was seen as the lingua franca and this was especially the case of sports terms, where the key expressions were identical in the Finnish and Swedish variants of the slang. Paunonen does not dwell especially on the sports vocabulary, but mostly on the amazing range of expressions for women as sex objects, but he points out that sports expressions, as in Stockholm, were often also used in other contexts.[56]

The existence of a bilingual slang in Helsinki was also made quite clear at the end of the 1980s when this author interviewed Swedish-speaking

Helsinkians who had been active sportsmen during the 1920s and 1930s. Despite the fact that the inter-war years were marked by a more bitter language feud than the early years of the century, it was almost impossible to have these sports veterans remember matches or competitions, where the language war would have been more important than the sporting occasion itself. This could have been taken as an expression of mental reconciliation if the veterans had not, when speaking about the society as a whole, pointed out the language tension at the time.[57]

The explanation for this remarkable inconsistency became clear on a closer analysis of the interviews. Most of the sports veterans used a lot of bilingual slang expressions when they reminisced over their sporting past. To them sport was still closely connected with Helsinki slang, almost equally strongly as at the time when they protested to the umpire and swore at their opponents in the intertwined language. The common slang indirectly contributed towards creating an atmosphere of reconciliation. There was also another reconciliatory factor, namely the rules, time and space of the game, that created a kind of microcosm where play took pride of place. The more intense the sportsman's involvement in his play the less intensive was the language issue.

Gender and Sport

Another interesting category of contrasting sports rhetoric at the turn of and the early years of the century involved women and an intensifying competitiveness. Although the social emancipation of women had gone far further in the Nordic countries than in central Europe, sport was still strongly male-dominated. Women certainly participated in sport and the press wrote admiringly of female rowers, skiers and swimmers, but no official roles were available to the 'fair sex' in the developing sports organizations.

Not only men found it difficult to accept the idea that women should practise competitive sports. Equally strong opposition came from leaders of the Finska Kvinnors Gymnastikförbund (The Gymnastics Association for Finnish Women), that was founded in 1896 as a protest against the administrative exclusivity of men's networks. The association's main spokeswoman against women's competitions was Elli Björkstén. In the inter-war years she received international recognition for her approach to women's gymnastics that laid stress on grace, health and beauty.[58]

According to Elli Björkstén male competitive sports were obsessed with a myopic hunt for records, in itself questionable both on physiological and psychological grounds. In a speech in 1911 she largely reproduced the plethora of criticism directed at modern sports all over Europe and the

United States from the mid-nineteenth century onwards; the body developed unharmoniously, fame corrupted the spirit and over all competitive events there hung an ominous circus atmosphere. She also pointed out that competitive sport was especially harmful to women, as it destroyed or distorted their natural feeling for rhythm and balance.[59]

One of Elli Björkstén's domestic opponents was Anni Collan. In the early part of the century she became the most vociferous advocate in the Nordic countries for women's sport. In 1910, with some like-minded colleagues, she founded the journal *Kisakenttä* (Athletic Field). Its initial aim was to advance modern developments in female gymnastics, sports and games. Gradually the journal adopted a more conservative standpoint, but during its first five years of publication a lot of space was devoted to Collan's arguments.[60]

Central to these arguments was the belief that neither male nor female competitive sports had found their ultimate form. This belief was widespread in Nordic pedagogic circles and especially among those female teachers who, like Anni Collan, believed that women's involvement in the expanding sports movement could be their moral and social redemption. In the autumn of 1911 the gymnastics teacher Sigrid Fontell, for example, wrote that female sport was not only as valid as male sport, but that it also offered outstanding opportunities for trying out new forms of activity.[61]

Interestingly enough, the belief in these possibilities could result in the same unfettered worship of the future that existed among those who most categorically defended free competition and the pursuit of records in sport. Despite many irreconcilable ideas about competitive sports, Anni Collan and Artur Eklund were agreed that the chief question was how both to free and maximize the exploitation of society's main source of energy – the young. In the futuristic view of the universe of Eklund and others, the answer was a total immersion in the new culture of machines. For Collan and her supporters full emancipation depended, in addition, on how quickly the young could realize that their inherent energy would be freed by interaction with nature.

As is known, the cult of nature was to take on many visible forms of expression in Europe. The scout movement spread amazingly quickly in the wake of British cultural imperialism, and in central Europe the German 'Wandervögel' movement became a mass phenomenon. In Germany alone there were over 600 free hostels for young ramblers in 1913.[62] In the spring of 1911, only one year after Baden-Powell started his first scout group in Great Britain, young Finnish scouts, complete with British uniforms, could be seen in Helsinki.[63]

When the Wandervögel movement attracted attention in the Nordic countries, Anni Collan, one of the founders incidentally of the Finnish scout movement, published in *Kisakenttä* long quotations from the ramblers' cult book *Jugend* by Carl Wagner: 'The forest with its captivating scents, noises, running water, the hills with their breezes and wide views, the sea with its energy and poems are a home for young people. It is there one must go to find strength and life!'[64] What was new in this worship of nature was not only the attempted seduction of the young but the strong appeal to the contemporary women's movement, which supported the relationship between vitality and nature.[65]

The most important pioneer in this regard was the Swede Ellen Key, whose writings were obligatory reading for the liberal educationists and pioneering feminists of the Nordic countries and German-speaking world. The main message of her work *Missbrukad kvinnokraft* (Misdirected Energy of Women [1896]) and *Barnets århundrade* (The Century of the Child [1901]) was that the improvements in the standing of women and men in society should not diminish their natural joy and curiosity in life and their own personalities. In short, men and women should be equal when it comes to natural fulfilment.

Key's ideas became important in Finnish feminist circles particularly with regard to the reform of suffrage in 1906, when Finnish women were given the right to vote – the first in Europe. Her ideas were also well received by women gymnasts and sports enthusiasts like Anni Collan, who saw their efforts as attempts to advertise female capabilities in society. As a clear hint to her own society, Anni Collan reported, following a visit to the United States in the spring of 1914, that the Americans, in contrast to the Europeans, had clearly realized that sports stimulated and advanced female gender roles.[66]

The report contrasted pointedly with the impressions of her compatriot, Lauri Pihkala, during a similar visit the year before. Pihkala belonged to the younger generation of Finnish sports journalists, who were influenced by Artur Eklund, and welcomed the expansion of competitive sports. He went to the United States to learn as much as possible about the training methods of the American top sportsmen. Anni Collan considered play and sports grounds to be ideal places for an equal dialogue and interplay between the sexes.[67] Pihkala, on the other hand, following his stay at the University of Pennsylvania, became convinced that the sports' revolution of an earlier time had forced girls' and boys' interest in sports into two very separate directions. The physical activity could be the same, but the psychological response was very different: 'A boy will train, when it is pointed out that the result [the chance of winning] will then improve. A girl, on the other hand, when it can be shown that the training will improve her [performance] skills.'[68] In short, men train to compete; women train to perform!

The Benefits of the Periphery

Collan and Pihkala clearly differed over women and competition, but as to other matters, they returned with very similar impressions from the American 'fairyland'. These included not only their admiration for the rationality and enthusiasm that seemed to characterize the whole sports culture of the United States, but the certainty that they had seen their country's future. This belief was a common one. The vision that America was Europe's tomorrow was widely prevalent in the 'old world' and its roots went back at least to the French Revolution. The young Finns' reports showed an almost total belief in the American dream.

The Nordic nations seemed to embrace the view more wholeheartedly than other European nations. One reason for this was apparently that during the preceding decades the Nordic countries had experienced faster social and cultural change than the rest of Europe. Central and western Europe were in the lead until the Second World War, but thanks to the effective reception of new technology the Nordic countries from the 1880s slowly but surely started to close the gap.[69] The Nordic peoples' more open attitude towards the United States was founded on a feeling of solidarity. The Nordic countries and North America, from a cultural point of view, were both European 'border' countries that developed quicker than the centre of their civilization; this fact transformed the collective values and priorities of both communities faster than in central and western Europe.

An early witness of the Nordic peoples' positive attitude towards the new technology was the Spanish consul in Helsinki, Angel Ganivet, who in 1898 published his observations in book form, *Cartas finlandesas*. Ganivet had a keen eye for small, but telling details in everyday life. He was surprised especially by the presence of women in the public and social life of the city and the straightforward absorption of new technology. The telephone was used as freely as a 'kitchen utensil'. Consultation by telephone was commonplace, ensuring the speedy transmission of information. Other forms of communication were equally advanced. The railways functioned almost as well as in Germany, the steam-engine effectively connected the great inland lake districts and everywhere one could see bicyclists: 'The bicycle has caused total madness, and women have taken to it as a tool of emancipation. I cannot go for a walk without bumping into a young woman bicyclist.'[70] According to Ganivet the Finns had the same mechanical attitude to culture as had the North Americans. A technical novelty was accepted without a murmur if it was believed to be useful and everywhere the lazy supporters of efficiency made themselves felt. And when this state of mind was joined to the natural toughness and unbearable constant calmness of the Finns, the whole society seemed to work like a machine.[71]

Ganivet's observations and conclusions are revealing up to a point, but it is clear that he had little insight into the complex reasons for the arguments that at the time characterized discussion in the Nordic countries about change, technology and the nature and role of youth in modern society. If he had, he could have pinpointed those traditions, perceptions and attitudes that separated the Nordic and American people. In particular, Nordic evolution was, to a far greater degree, influenced by central European intellectual trends and patterns. Despite an infatuation with the United States and a worship of machines the Nordic people were bound by the European custom to discuss and plan the future with the help of myths and messages from the past.

NOTES

1. Mauritz Wænerberg, *Drag ur Helsingfors Gymnastikklubbs lif. Tecknade af Movitz* (Helsingfors, 1901), p.114.
2. Viktor Balck, 'Om idrott och kroppsövningar i uppfostrans tjänst', *Sjunde nordiska skolmötet i Stockholm den 6., 7. och 8. augusti 1895* (Stockholm, 1896), p.207.
3. Viktor Balck, 'Om idrott', p.211; Frithiof Holmgren, 'Företal', *Illustrerad Idrottsbok, Del 1* (Stockholm, 1886), pp.i–v; Henrik Sandblad, *Olympia och Valhalla: Idéhistoriska aspekter av den moderna idrottsrörelsens framväxt* (Stockholm, 1985), pp.159–72, 321–59.
4. Victor Hansen, *Illustreret Idrætsbog: Udarbejdet paa Grundlag af Victor Balcks illustrerad Idrottsbok. I del* (København, 1890), p.7.
5. Henrik Meinander, *Lik martallen, som rågfältet: Hundra år finlandssvensk gymnastik* (Helsingfors, 1996), pp.23–4.
6. Leena Laine, *Vapaaehtoisten järjestöjen kehitys ruumiin-kulttuurin alueella Suomessa v. 1856–1917* (Lappeenranta, 1984), pp.293–302; Henrik Meinander, *Towards a Bourgeois Manhood: Boys' Physical Education in Nordic Secondary Schools 1880–1940* (Helsinki, 1994), pp.71–2.
7. Sandblad, *Olympia och Valhalla*, pp.100–2.
8. Henrik Berggren and Lars Trädgårdh, 'Historikerna och språket: teoretiska ambitioner och praktiska begränsningar. En taktisk programförklaring', *Historisk Tidskrift* (1989), 369–73. See even their main source in this question: Peter Schöttler, 'Historians and Discourse Analysis', *History Workshop 27* (Spring 1989), 48–53.
9. Richard D. Mandell, *The First Modern Olympics* (Berkeley, 1976), pp.49–73.
10. Peter Gay, *Style in History* (London, 1975).
11. Peter Gay, *Freud* (Viborg, 1996), pp.472–80.
12. See for example Ulf Danielsson, 'Darwinismens inträngande i Sverige', *Lychnos 1963–1964* (Stockholm, 1964), pp.198–99.
13. Oscar Hansen, *Opdragelselære* (København, 1898), pp.268–9. For a closer analysis of Hansens pedagogic point of view, see also Vagn Skovgaard-Pedersen, *Dannelse og demokrati: Fra latin- til almenskole. Lov om højere almenskole 24 April 1903* (København, 1976), pp.156–60.
14. Leon Kellner, 'Engelsk ungdom', *Den høiere skole* (Kristiania, 1899), pp.131–4. For a further look of this reception, see Henrik Meinander, *Towards a Bourgeois Manhood*, pp.181–6.
15. Ulf Danielsson, 'Darwinismens inträngande', pp.325–6.
16. Henrik Meinander, 'Mellan nyhumanism och nordism. Aspekter på det nordiska läroverkets systematisering 1800–1950', *Historisk Tidskrift för Finland* (1993), pp.206–11.

17. C.N. Starcke, 'Herbert Spencer. 27. April 1820 – 8. Decbr. 1903', *Det ny Aarhundrede 1903–1904*, (København, 1904), pp.436–44.
18. Tim Knudsen, *Storbyen støbes: København mellem kaos och byplan* (København, 1988), p.153.
19. Th. Mohn, 'Gymnastikens stilling i skolerne', *Den norske lægeforenings smaaskrifter* (Kristiania, 1906), p.14.
20. Henrik Meinander, 'Den nordistiska kroppen', *Internationale idéstømninger og nordisk kultur 1850–1914: Den 22. nordiske historikermøte: Oslo 13.–18. august 1994* (Oslo, 1997), pp.95–104.
21. Henrik Meinander, *Towards a Bourgeois Manhood*, pp.190–7.
22. Henrik Berggren, *Seklets ungdom: Retorik, politik och modernitet 1900–1939* (Stockholm, 1995), pp.44–50.
23. Niels Kayser Nielsen, 'Et overset kapitel – om sporten og gårdmandslinjen i dansk idrætshistorie', *Den engelske sports gennembrud i Norden* (København, 1990), pp.178–91.
24. Carl Svedelius (1861–1951) played a visible role in the educational debate in the Nordic countries in the 1910s and 1920s. For further analysis of his life and letter see both Henrik Meinander, 'Karaktärsdaning framförallt. En skiss av Carl Svedelius, pedagog och idrottsideolog av nordiska mått', *Svenska idrotthistoriska föreningens årsskrift 1991* (Stockholm, 1991), pp.85–102; and Sverker Sörlin, 'Filolog i sportkostym – rektor Carl Svedelius', in Ronny Ambjörnsson and Sverker Sörlin (eds.), *Obemärkta. Det dagliga livets idéer* (Stockholm, 1995), pp.89–110.
25. Meinander, 'Karaktärsdaning framförallt!', pp.88–95.
26. Carl Svedelius, 'Fysisk fostran. Föredrag hållet i Hankö den 13 aug. 1915', *Verdandi* (1917), 42.
27. Carl Svedelius, 'Värdet av olika slag av skoldisciplin', offprint from the journal *Verdandi* (1912), 8–9.
28. Fridtjof Nansen, 'Idealitet og karakter', *Nansen røst: Artiklar og tal af Fridtjof Nansen. II 1897–1915* (Oslo, 1915), p.271.
29. Ibid., p.275.
30. Fridtjof Nansen, *Frilufts-liv: Blade av dagboken* (Kristiania, 1916), p.57.
31. Bodil Stenseth, *En norske elite: Nasjonsbyggerne på Lysaker 1890–1940* (Oslo, 1993), pp.119–20.
32. Henrik Berggren, *Seklets ungdom*, pp.68–71.
33. Ibid., pp.60–1.
34. Henrik Meinander, 'Idrottsmannens bevekelsegrunder. Artur Eklund och 1910-talets idrottsrörelse', *Historisk Tidskrift för Finland* (1991), 4–29.
35. *Finskt Idrottsblad* (1914), 163.
36. Artur Eklund, *Idrottens filosofi* (Helsinki, 1917), 31–2.
37. Stephen Kern, *The Culture of Time and Space 1880–1918* (Cambridge: Massachusetts, 1994), pp.103–4.
38. Henrik Meinander, 'Artur Eklund, idrottsjournalist i första världskrigets skugga', *Pressklipp, fil och forsk. Brages årsskrift 1990* (Helsinki, 1991), pp.57–71.
39. Eklund, *Idrottens filosofi*, p.15.
40. *Finskt Idrottsblad* (1916), 54.
41. A scientific management movement of the early twentieth century. It is widely associated with the name of its leading advocate, the American engineer F.W. Taylor, whose main work, *Principles of Scientific Management* (1911), was soon available in all Nordic languages.
42. Ibid., p.56.
43. Artur Eklund, *Idrottens filosofi*, pp.117–29; Kern, *The Culture of Time and Space*, pp.110–24.
44. Henrik Meinander, 'Idrottsmannens bevekelsegrunder', pp.9–18.
45. Stephen Kern, *The Culture of Time and Space*, pp.107–8.
46. High Cecil and Peter H. Liddle (eds.) *Facing Armageddon: The First World War Experienced* (London, 1996), pp.709–816.
47. See for example Artur Eklund, 'Spengler och den tyska nationalismen', *Nya Argus* (1924), 181–4; Meinander, 'Idrottsmannens bevekelsegrunder', 28–9.

48. Niels Kayser Nielsen, 'Idrott, rörelse, tid och rum omkring 1990. Johs. V. Jensen och
    möjligheten för en civil, demokratisk kroppskultur', *Finlands Idrottshistoriska förenings
    årsbok 1995* (Joensuu, 1995), pp.182–6.
49. Ibid., pp.182–3.
50. Jan Lindroth, *Idrottens väg till folkrörelse. Studie i svensk idrottsrörelse till 1915*
    (Stockholm, 1974); Meinander, *Towards a Bourgeois Manhood*.
51. Laurence Veysey, 'Intellectual History and the New Social History', in John Higham and
    Paul K. Conkin (eds.), *New Directions in American Intellectual History* (Baltimore, 1979),
    pp.21–3.
52. Henrik Meinander, 'Artur Eklund, idrottsjournalist i första världskrigets skugga', p.60.
53. Ruben G. Berg, *Skolpojks- och studentslang. En ordsamling. Bidrag till kännedom om de
    svenska landsmålen och svenskt folkliv* XVIII.8 (Stockholm, 1900).
54. Wilhelm Uhrström, *Stockholmska: Slang, vulgarismer och skämtord* (Stockholm, 1911).
55. Ibid.
56. Heikki Paunonen, 'Från Sörkka till kulturspråk: Iakttagelser om Helsingforsslangen som
    språklig och sociokulturell företeelse', *Historisk Tidskrift för Finland* (1989), 585–622;
    Idem, *Suomen kieli Helsingissä: Huomioita Helsingin puhekielen historiallisesta ja
    nykyvariaatosta* (Helsinki, 1995), pp.2–27.
57. Henrik Meinander, 'Bilingual Sportsmen: Swedish-Speaking Sports culture in Inter-war
    Helsinki', *International Journal of the History of Sport*, 10 (1993), 418–26.
58. Henrik Meinander, *Lik martallen, som rågfältet*, pp.41–67.
59. *Kisakenttä* (1911), 6–9.
60. Henrik Meinander, *Lik martallen, som rågfältet*, p.40.
61. *Kisakenttä* (1911), 57.
62. *Tidskriften F.F.F.* (1923), 79–80.
63. *Finskt Idrottsblad* (1911), 41–4.
64. *Kisakenttä* (1911), 72.
65. Henrik Berggren, *Seklets ungdom*, p.210.
66. Anni Collan, *Kertomus opintomatkasta Pohjois-Ameriikan Yhdysvaltoihin vuonna 1914:
    Voimistelullisia matkakertomuksia II* (Porvoo, 1916).
67. Ibid., pp.22–23, 94–96, 303; *Kisakenttä* (1915), 226–7.
68. Lauri Pihkala to R.F. von Willebrand 15.5.1913, *SLSA 378, Helsingin yliopiston kirjasto*;
    Kisakenttä (1913), 133.
69. Marjatta Hietala, *Services and Urbanization at the Turn of the Century: The Diffusion of
    Innovations* (Helsinki, 1987), *passim*.
70. Angel Ganivet, *Suomalaiskirjeet*, Translated into Finnish by Kaarle Hirvonen (Porvoo,
    1964), p.90.
71. Ibid., pp.91–3.

From Balck to Nurmi: The Olympic Movement and the Nordic Nations[1]

PER JØRGENSEN

Athens and Amsterdam

In the period from the first Games in 1896 (Athens) until the ninth Games in 1928 (Amsterdam), Pierre de Coubertin's concept evolved from what John MacAloon aptly called a 'fin-de-siècle curiosity'[2] into a world-wide cultural occasion. It was by no means a frictionless process.

Until 1908 (London) the Olympic Games struggled for survival. From 1912 (Stockholm) and until 1924 (Paris) the Games grew both in extent and credibility, especially with the introduction of the Winter Games in 1924. After 1928 the Games were distinctive and well-established international occasions.[3] The mass media now followed them closely and Olympic stars like Johnny Weismuller (United States) and Sonja Heine (Norway) were also international stars. The greatest star, however, was the Finnish runner, Paavo Nurmi (1897–1973), who won his ninth gold medal in 1928. Then, immediately before the Olympic Games in 1932 (Los Angeles), he was declared a professional. By 1928 the Olympic Games had become a venue where discussions on amateurism, professionalism, politics, gender and giantism were regularly on the agenda.[4] These themes were also topical in relation to the Olympic movement in the Nordic countries.

In international sport the period 1894–1928 may be described as one of struggle between centralism and decentralism. Coubertin and the International Olympic Committee (IOC) initially tried to take complete control of both the form and the content of the events of the Olympic Games. However, in fact, it was the international associations that took control of the rules and regulations of specific sports, and the influence of the IOC was correspondingly limited. It developed into an organization, in the words of David B. Kanin, which merely selected and monitored the cities where the Olympic Games were to be held, and was mainly occupied with its own philosophy and privileges.[5] With these roles, the IOC gradually developed organizationally from a 'family concern' into a modern, although not completely streamlined, organization.[6] A similar situation in which central sports federations lost ground to sports associations characterized the Nordic countries.

The Swede, General Viktor Balck (1844–1928), and the Finn, Paavo Nurmi, symbolize, at one and the same time, both the origins of the Olympic Games and its evolutionary realities. Balck represented the upper class, which organized the Olympic Games and constructed the Olympic idea around key concepts such as Olympism, amateurism, nationalism and internationalism. Nurmi, represented the working and middle classes – the main sources of the participants. He also represented the minority among the participants who achieved status as world celebrities. By the 1920s these stars were increasingly the living symbols of the Olympic Games. They were also increasingly important elements in the commercial activity which international sport was also on the way to becoming – with professionalism and sham amateurism as inevitable consequences. Finally, on account of their international visibility, the stars helped to propagate the nationalism that characterized the Olympic movement from its first moments. When Nurmi won, Finland won!

The Launch of the Modern Olympic Games

On 23 June 1894 Coubertin formed the first International Olympic Committee (IOC) in Paris. The first Chairman was the Greek, Demetrius Bikelas, and the first Olympic Games were held in Athens in 1896. Coubertin then took over the Chairmanship himself and retained it until 1925, when he was replaced by the Belgian, Count Henri de Baillet-Latour.[7]

Victor Balck had a prominent position in the first IOC. He was a member of the Paris committee of 1894,[8] belonged to the inner circle, was one of Coubertin's supporters for many years and co-operated closely with Coubertin – especially in connection with the early Olympic Games.[9] He remained on the committee until 1921. At that time, his compatriot, Sigfred S. Edström, the organizer of the Olympic Games in Stockholm in 1912, had just joined the IOC, where he was to be a dominant figure over the next 31 years, admired especially by Coubertin himself.[10] Sweden is clearly the Nordic country that was most active and influential at the top levels of the IOC during the period from 1894 to 1928 (see Table 1, p.73). It was the only Nordic country to have two members of the IOC for most of this period. The other countries never had more than one.[11]

Even though Balck was an enthusiastic advocate of the Olympic idea, he did not have immediate success in obtaining the backing of his native country, and only one sportsman from Sweden participated in 1896. Coubertin did not have the support of his native country either, and the French team that lined up in 1896 was rather thin, and included a couple of tourists who happened to be in Athens.[12] Nor was international support overwhelming in the early years. Coubertin put great pressure on the IOC members to set up national Olympic committees. This was achieved at first in only a few countries and the Nordic countries were not among them. Balck wrote to Coubertin that the Crown Prince was interested and that a lot of work was being done on the matter. Yet the only thing that Balck could promise was that 'Everything possible will be done'.[13] However, this was not enough. Sweden did not possess a national Olympic committee until 1913 – the last of the Nordic countries to have one (see Table 1).

In 1894 Balck could look back on a long and impressive career in the sports world, as leader, instructor, debater and writer. For a long time he had had a central position in both school sports and association sports. He belonged to the Swedish upper class, had good connections with the power centres in society including the royal family and understood how to use his connections.[14] His sports activities in Sweden were based on Swedish (Ling) gymnastics. Efforts to change these gymnastics, for example by introducing apparatus, made him enemies among the more orthodox Ling supporters. These circles did not become any more sympathetic when he demonstrated an increasing interest in sport over the years. However, for a long time he regarded gymnastics as more important than sport and he considered it one of his achievements that he had made Ling Gymnastics known abroad, though his enemies did not agree with this. They claimed that it was not Balck who made the Ling system known internationally but the other way around.[15] The same circles, heavily involved in Ling gymnastics, had little time for the Olympic idea. In 1897 this impatience was expressed in a rejection in principle of the Olympic Games as an idea, and in 1912 in a rejection in practice (disassociation) when Sweden was the Olympic Games host nation.[16] In Denmark, too, there were gymnastics opponents of both the Olympic Games and modern sport.[17]

In the Nordic countries, especially Denmark and Sweden, gymnastics and to an extent the rifle-club movement have been given a special position in the history of sport as something particularly Nordic and gymnastics was regarded by its supporters as nobler and purer than sport. Gymnastic supporters claimed that gymnastics in contrast to sport served greater causes: patriotism and nationalism.[18] The relationship between gymnastics and the rifle-club movement on the one hand and sport on the other, however, was not just a Nordic concern at the turn of the century. In the rest of Europe, too, riflemen and gymnasts considered their activities to be more worthwhile than sports activities. For instance, when Coubertin tried to involve the French rifle-club movement in the Olympic movement in 1895, he was told that it was astounding that he could imagine that shooting could consider being 'a mere branch incorporated and fitted into a whole series of sports'.[19] Even before the Congress in 1894, which led to the formation of the IOC, the president of the Belgian Gymnastics Association categorically refused to participate. His Association, he wrote to Coubertin, 'had always believed, and still believed, that gymnastics and sports are two contrary things and has always fought against the latter'.[20] Gymnastics was a process; sport a product. The introduction to the Belgian Gymnastics Association's own statutes also confirms that being a gymnast was something special. It stated 'De Belgische turners zijn broeders.'[21]

The IOC, Upper-Class Club

The leaders of the Olympic movement, the IOC, generally came from the very highest class in society. In our day, a self-elected assembly of mainly elderly men, chiefly from the upper class, naturally does not seem to be particularly representative, let alone democratic. But around the turn of the century, the leadership of a number of organizations, both in the world of sport and outside it, consisted of men from the upper middle class and upper class. In the Nordic countries, most of the top leadership in the sports movement was recruited for many years chiefly from the military and from business. And even though election to leading positions in the Nordic sports movement was democratic in principle, the general rule was that the sitting leadership had their own candidates elected.[22]

However, the composition of the IOC differed significantly from that of the early Nordic sports leadership in one respect – in regard to the participation of the very top class in society, the nobility. In Sweden there were very few representatives of the nobility in the early sports leadership and in Denmark none.[23] In the IOC, on the other hand, there were many aristocrats, and this was also the case, relatively speaking, in the Nordic Olympic Committees (NOC) (see Table 1). The clergy, however, were conspicuous by their almost total absence, both in the IOC and in the Nordic sports leadership.[24] Both the nobility and the clergy have played major roles as social reformers in the Nordic countries, in such fields as culture, education and physical education. Their absence from the sports establishment in the Nordic countries, was due to the fact that this establishment was part of a modern class breakthrough. The Nordic countries were 'led into' the twentieth century by the middle class, which at the turn of the century was the leading class, politically, culturally and socially.[25]

The Olympic movement, of course, came to be regarded as a major international force, for example by Coubertin himself as early as 1896.[26] But this was not obvious to all at the time. As late as 1911, one educationalist, in an open letter to Coubertin, maintained that the Olympic Games' 'influence on all that concerns education in the family, the schools and in the army really amounts to nothing at all'.[27] This belief that the Olympic movement was irrelevant to modern life apparently did not survive for long. John Hoberman points out that the modern relevance of the Olympic Games has provoked vigorous discussion.[28]

TABLE 1

THE NORDIC MEMBERS OF THE INTERNATIONAL OLYMPIC COMMITTEE (IOC), THEIR OCCUPATIONS AND THE YEARS FOR THE ESTABLISHMENT OF THE NORDIC NATIONAL OLYMPIC COMMITTEES (NOC), 1894–1928[29]

Denmark (NOC, 1905)		
1.	Colonel Niels V.S. Holbeck	1899–1906
2.	Captain Torben Grut	1906–12
3.	Colonel Fritz Hansen	1913–22
4.	Head of Department, Ivar Nyholm	1922–31
Finland (NOC, 1907)		
1.	Baron Rienhold von Willebrand	1908–20
2.	Consul Ernst Krogius	1920–48
Norway (NOC, 1900)		
1.	Captain, Count Heinrik Angell	1905–7
2.	Thomas Heftye	1907–8
3.	Colonel Johan T. Sverre	1908–27
4.	Master of the Royal Hunt, Sir Thomas N. Fearley	1927–50
Sweden (NOC, 1913)		
1.	General Viktor G. Balck	1894–1921
2.	Count Clarence von Rosen	1900–48
3.	Director, J. Sigfred Edström	1920–52
(Executive Board 1921–52, Vice President 1937–42 and IOC President 1942–52)		

With five officers, five businessmen or civil servants and three members of the nobility (one of whom was also a serving officer), the Nordic representatives in the IOC in the period 1894 to 1928 differ little from the other IOC members as regards their social class recruitment. This is hardly surprising since the assembly was self-elective. Self-election was criticized by the Nordic countries on several occasions in the period. Two examples will suffice.

The first example comes from the early years of the IOC. Prior to 1899 Balck looked after Danish interests in the IOC. For example, for the IOC meeting in Le Havre 1897 Balck received meticulous, written instructions about the Danish wishes.[30] Even when Denmark had its own IOC member Colonel Niels Holbeck in 1899, Balck was still asked to help. Thus when problems arose about Danish participation before the Olympic Games in Paris in 1900, it was Balck to whom the Danes went for advice and assistance and not the newly appointed Danish IOC member.[31]

In 1906, when Holbeck wished to resign, Denmark nominated, on Holbeck's very strong recommendation, the extremely well-qualified Captain Fritz Hansen for the position.[32] Hansen was an efficient, well-informed, although extremely self-willed chairman of the Danish Sports Federation. He was also Chairman of the Danish Olympic Committee. However, the IOC chose a man completely unknown in Danish sports circles, Captain Torben Grut. Eugen Stahl Schmidt, who had founded the Danish Sports Federation in 1896, protested about the appointment policy of the IOC in a private letter to Coubertin. What Schmidt did not know was that it was Coubertin himself who had found Grut. He had simply asked the military attaché at the French Embassy in Copenhagen to find suitable candidates.[33] Several candidates were suggested, but the choice fell on Grut. It naturally caused surprise that a locally supported candidate, who in addition was chairman of the National Olympic Committee, was rejected in favour of an unknown person. But one reason could be that perhaps Balck had a finger in the pie, and another that the IOC did not necessarily regard the NOCs as partners. The IOC regarded its own members as being ambassadors from the IOC to the respective countries. In the Nordic countries, in contrast, the National Olympic Committees, who were subject to national sports organizations, were regarded as national spokesmen to the IOC. And this is also how they functioned in practice.

Schmidt suggested in his letter to Coubertin that IOC members should be appointed by their national committees. Coubertin edited the letter to ensure its anonymity and published it in *The International Olympic Bulletin* in order to make the point that the IOC was above private and political interests and was completely independent.[34] Later, Coubertin clung to this view tenaciously.[35] However, Hansen was subsequently selected to the IOC when Grut resigned in 1912.

The second example is drawn from the 1920s in the form of a joint Nordic action at the 1925 IOC meeting in Prague. The Nordic countries proposed that the IOC members should be appointed nationally. The IOC policy of self-election remained a thorn in the Nordic flesh. It was decided, therefore, at a meeting of De Nordiske Rigs-Idrætsforbunds Fælleskomite (the Nordic States Sports Federations Joint Committee) to authorize the Swedish NOC to propose that the composition of the IOC 'be based on proposals from the National Olympic Committees'.[36] The letter was sent in May 1925, but when no answer had been received by October 1926, a reminder was sent. This prompted a response but it was dismissive. The IOC selected its representatives itself, as Coubertin had already made quite clear, maintained the new president, Baillet-Latour.[37] In 20 years nothing had changed!

Socialization and Amateurism

What interest could Balck, a middle-aged Swede, deeply involved in and highly placed in the Swedish sports system, have in the revival of the Olympic Games? Allen Guttmann, among others, has put forward the view that Coubertin's motives for creating the modern Olympic Games were a mixture of nationalism, internationalism and idealism.[38] It was a question of upbringing – *noblesse oblige*. Balck and Coubertin resembled each other closely.

Coubertin was greatly interested in education. The same is true of Balck. But while, throughout his life, Coubertin had a philosophical belief in the potential of sport, this was not wholly true of Balck. While Coubertin published thousands of pages on this theme, the ideological perspectives of sport were generally given a low priority by turn-of-the-century Swedish sports leaders, as Jan Lindroth has pointed out. This applied, for example, to a marked degree to Sigfred Edström (later President of the IOC) but in part also to Balck. It is true that Balck had a fully developed view of sport. He endorsed a widespread belief in the benefits of sport, such as 'mental well-being', 'character formation', 'moral improvement', 'patriotism', 'internation-alism' and 'democracy'. However, he expressed his view of sport only in unpublished material such as lectures and talked about 'the power of example' as the best means of propaganda. Practice before theory.[39] Like other Swedish sports leaders he concentrated on creating an organizational framework for the practice of sport. It was not necessary in his view to argue the case for sport.

These Swedish sports leaders differed little from their peers in the other Nordic countries in this. It was only in Denmark that sports leaders were forced to assert the benefits of sport. This was because the public authorities in Denmark were not interested to the same extent as in Finland, Norway and Sweden in supporting the sports movement,[40] in part because Denmark had a strong rifle club and gymnastics movement.[41]

The beginning of modern sport in the Nordic countries can be traced back to the 1830s in the case of Denmark and Sweden, and somewhat later in the case of Norway. It was thus pre-industrial, as industrialization came to the Nordic countries at the end of the nineteenth century. This pre-industrial sport was based on a 'sportification' (modernization) of activities that already existed locally, so it was not a question of importing sports activities from abroad in the first phase of 'sportification'.[42] The Nordic activities were riding (with the exception of Norway), sailing and rowing. But of course international 'modernization' of these activities had already occurred.[43] Balck and many other Nordic sports leaders were fascinated by English sport and culture. But they were more pre-occupied with the organization of, and education through sport than in profound philosophical discussions about the precise nature of the attributes of sport. Yet arguably it was sports' rules and regulations, that made it such an effective instrument of socialization.

Ideology can be explicit. By way of example, ideology can be seen plainly in the way sports organizations organize sport. In Denmark middle class[44] values as regards hygiene, time-keeping, clothing and behaviour were transferred through sport to the working class. Within sport, these values were mainly transferred via amateurism and rules and regulations.[45] The result was a socialization that occurred mainly on the sub-conscious level. The middle class ordered the world as the best of all worlds, namely their own, should be ordered. The ideology of sport, reflected in the establishment and structure of the middle-class sports organizations as well as their rules and regulations, did not therefore differ in principle from the ordering of a number of other public and semi-public institutions of the time. The purpose was hegemonic control within a democratic framework.[46]

The rules on amateurism of the period in the Nordic countries differed somewhat from country to country. However, there was shared interest in the introduction of 'ethical rules' into, or in connection with, these rules. This was most clearly reflected in the joint-Nordic amateurism rules, on which there was agreement in principle in 1905. Here the word professional was nowhere to be found.[47] These amateur rules, which incidentally were similar to Danish rules dating from 1897, distinguished between 'amateur' and 'non-amateur', the latter term being only partly comparable with 'professional'. A person was a non-amateur if he infringed 'ethical rules' or 'financial rules'. The financial rules excluded the professional participant, a person who received money or payment in kind, for performance. The ethical rules excluded the participant, for example, who had a disreputable reputation, had debts, behaved badly, insulted a referee or leader, criticized his sports organization publicly or was unsuitably dressed. If these infringements occurred, the participant could lose his amateur status.[48]

Interest in the ethics of sport remained strong throughout the period. Thus, at a congress in 1925 the Nordic countries jointly decided to attempt to raise international ethical standards at the IOC meeting in Prague the same year: 'The Congress decided to support every effort aimed at elevating a disciplinary and chivalrous spirit in the sportsman.'[49] Countless numbers of Nordic sports men and women were excluded from sports over the years for infringing ethical rules about behaviour on and off 'the sports field'. The infringement of ethical rules was the reason for some 98 per cent of all exclusions in Denmark in the period 1896–1918. Real professionalism was extremely rare.[50] The new joint Nordic rules were adopted in Denmark and Norway, but never in Sweden. The problem for the Swedes was not the content of the 'ethical' rules, but the 'financial' rules under which, for example, Swedish swimming instructors no longer would have been amateurs. Skiers in Sweden skied for money prizes, and the rowers did not consider workers to be amateurs. The attitude of the Swedish rowers was not shared by other Swedes (or Scandinavians) and this led to a break between the rowers and the other sports.[51]

The Olympic Movement did not formulate and introduce rules on amateurism until 1925, and these did not involve 'ethics'. But exclusions could be made on ethical grounds. One of the more curious examples is the exclusion by the United States of triple-jump athlete Dan Ahearn from the Olympic Games in 1920. He had refused to sleep in a bed that was too short. It was only when his team companions threatened a boycott that he was restored to favour.[52]

Amateurism and the Olympic Games

Coubertin himself had a relaxed attitude to amateurism. He regarded the amateurism question as a little ridiculous but agreed to amateurism rules for tactical reasons.[53] The English thought they were important: 'To me, sport was a religion with its church, dogmas, service ... but above all a religious feeling, and it seemed to me as childish to make all this depend on whether an athlete had received a five franc coin as automatically to consider the parish verger an unbeliever because he received a salary for looking after the church.'[54] But Coubertin gave in. He was a pragmatist and often behaved tactically when required.[55] This has led many historians to laud him as a great strategist, while others such as Hoberman regard it as yet another example of the fact that 'the Olympic movement has never possessed an ethic'.[56]

Amateurism was gradually introduced into the Olympic movement to such an extent that it was finally perceived as one of the most important characteristics of the movement. At both the Olympic Games in Athens in 1896 and in Paris in 1900 professional fencers competed and in St Louis in 1904 professional cyclists participated. After that, the net tightened and by the 1912 Stockholm Olympic Games the principle of amateurism was fully instituted.[57] As early as 1900, however, there were efforts to ensure that only amateurs participated. For instance the Danish swimmer Peder Lykkeberg had to submit a written declaration to Coubertin that he was a Danish citizen and that he was not a professional. A covering letter from Holbeck, the Danish IOC member, confirmed this.[58] Nevertheless, as mentioned above, it was not until 1925 at the IOC meeting in Prague that the first 'Olympic' definition of amateurism was adopted.[59] This did not solve the problem.

On the one hand, the new definition was simple, as it placed on record that: 'An amateur is one who devotes himself to sport for sport's sake without deriving from it, directly or indirectly, the means of existence. A professional is one who derives the means of existence entirely or partly from sport.'[60] On the other hand, it was clear to most people that the definition encapsulated class distinction. The rich are those who have money and money was necessary in a number of sports as early as 1925, if there was to be any hope at all of achieving international standards. Instead of serving an ethical purpose, the regulations on amateurism, in the words of Andrew Strenk, encouraged many participants to do precisely what they were not supposed to do. It was simply impossible for many athletes to 'comply' with the regulations without lies, trickery and hypocrisy.[61] This was particularly true for athletes from countries where there was no support available from a well-developed sports system. Those from the Nordic countries were better placed than most to exist within the framework of amateurism. The Nordic sports system, based on publicly supported voluntary associations and organizations, to a great extent could afford facilities, trainers and travel expenses. However, this by no means prevented Nordic athletes from colliding with the amateurism regulations.

The most famous Nordic sportsman to experience difficulties with the Olympic amateurism regulations before they were removed from the Olympic charter in 1974 was the Finnish runner Paavo Nurmi. He appeared on the Olympic scene in 1920 and won three gold medals. In 1924 he won a further four, while in 1928 he won 'only' two gold and three silver medals. It was not simply the fact that Nurmi won nine gold and three silver medals and set 22 official world records in distances from 1,500m to 20km that made him so popular. And it was definitely not his way with the media, because it was virtually impossible to have him speak a word. What was widely admired was the way in which he ran and won. Apparently, he did not run against his competitors but against his stopwatch. In the 1920s he was a symbol of perfection. Some people called his perfection mechanical, others joyless, but everyone was fascinated.[62] His victories were based on his assiduous training, which was unprecedented at the time, and at an athletics meeting in 1924 this enabled him to set world records in the 1,500m and 5,000m races with only a one hour interval in between. At the Olympic Games later in the year he also won the same two distances, likewise with an hour's interval between them.

Nurmi intended to finish his Olympic career by winning the marathon at the Olympic Games in Los Angeles in 1932. Shortly before that he had run the distance in a time that remained the unofficial world record until after the Second World War. But immediately prior to the Games Nurmi was declared a professional. For a long time, he had had, in the words of one race organizer, 'the lowest heart beat and the highest asking price of any athlete in the world'.[63] What caused Nurmi's downfall were a number of races in Germany in 1931, after which he was accused of having received excessively large amounts to cover expenses.[64]

It was a clear case according to the rules. Nurmi could be a training addict, could go all over the world, be away from family and friends for long periods, delight thousands and fill the coffers of the race organizer, but he was not allowed to be able to live from it. A committee consisting of Edström, another Swede called Bo Ekelund, Avery Brundage and the German, Karl Ritter von Halt, disqualified Nurmi. Naturally the Finnish reaction was vehement. The whole Finnish team threatened to return home from the United States, and Asea Electric, the Swedish company where Edström was director, was boycotted in Finland.[65] Nevertheless, the Finnish team stayed and participated in Los Angeles, but the fact that two Swedes had been involved in the condemnation of a Finn confirmed in Finland, a former Swedish colony, many prejudices about the Swedish chauvinistic and imperial mentality. At the IOC meeting in Prague in 1925, it had been recommended that the international associations decide their own amateurism rules instead of conforming to common rules. This was in accordance with developments in the Nordic countries at the time and it could have saved the Olympic movement much debate later on. But the proposal was rejected and was not adopted until fifty years later.[66]

Two complex issues in the amateur-professional debate were the refunding of expenses and loss of earnings. Both issues arose early in the Olympic movement and as early as 1905 the IOC agreed that amateurs could have expenses refunded. However, this by no means solved the problem, particularly because the various international associations had different definitions of what constituted 'expenses'.[67] The problem of loss of earnings was never solved. When it was raised in Prague in 1925, it was decided to forbid compensation for loss of earnings completely. One of those most strongly opposed was Sweden's Sigfred Edström, the later chairman of the IOC, who gravely warned that it would 'open wide the flood gates'.[68] The Nordic countries disagreed on the question. Sweden and Finland were against compensation for loss of earnings, Denmark and Norway were in favour, and had already allowed for this in their rules. However, Denmark virtually granted general compensation, while Norway only allowed compensation in special circumstances. In order not to destroy Nordic co-operation, Sweden and Finland decided for the time being to respect Denmark's and Norway's decision to pay for loss of earnings, but only in 'extremely limited cases'.[69] The hope was that tan IOC decision in Prague on loss of earnings would be followed by all the Nordic countries.[70] As mentioned above, the IOC ruled against the idea.

As early as 1927, however, the IOC decision was reversed. FIFA had voted to allow loss of earnings compensation in soccer. FIFA considered it contradictory that if one player's employer paid wages when the player was away from his job playing soccer, while another soccer player's employer did not, then the first player was an amateur while the other was a professional, if he had his loss made up. With the prospect of either having 'professional' soccer players at the Olympic Games in Amsterdam in 1928, or cancelling the soccer tournament, the IOC decided to give temporary permission for loss of earnings compensation. In protest English soccer representatives stayed away from the Olympic Games and after the Games the IOC annulled its decision. It was not until after the Olympic Games in Helsinki in 1952 that the IOC once again supported loss of earnings compensation.[71]

Olympism and the Nordic Countries

Apart from the standard rules of sport, which are necessary to ensure fair competition, over the years the Olympic movement has added a number of rituals and symbols – the motto, the entry march, the oath, the torch and the rings – all to suggest that order exists in a chaotic world. Uniquely, the Olympic movement also has a philosophy called Olympism to promote – among other things, international understanding and peace through sport. The philosophy was constructed mostly by Coubertin. However, apart from a small elite, few were aware of it in the Nordic countries until well into the twentieth century. In Denmark, for example, Coubertin as a person and Olympism as an ideology were virtually ignored in the largest and most sports-orientated Danish newspaper, *Dagbladet Politiken,* until immediately before the Olympic Games in Berlin in 1936.

Between 1894 and 1935 Coubertin's name occurred only twice – both times only briefly, and he was not quoted.[72] That the Olympic Games were based on a specific ideology was never mentioned. Then in 1936 Coubertin and his creation of the modern Olympic Games were given coverage in *Politiken* in connection with the Berlin Games. In addition, for the first time, the modern Olympic Games were linked with ancient Greece. Nevertheless, down the years various Olympic Games involving Danish participation had been given long and expansive coverage, but the Olympic ideologist, Coubertin, and the Olympic ideology, Olympism, were never referred to.

This is not the same as saying that there was no 'Olympism' in the daily sports columns. Concepts like amateurism, decent behaviour and fair-play required of Olympic participants, can be found in several sports reports of the time. They appear continually as general requirements but never as explicit 'Olympic' concepts.[73] Of course, many basic concepts in Olympism are shared European ideals typical of the social groups who were particularly conspicuous as sports innovators at the time – men from the middle class, as were those who wrote about sport.[74] Beyond the Nordic countries, too, many years passed before Coubertin as ideologist and Olympism as an ideology were known.[75] Both Coubertin and Olympism drowned completely in the World Exhibitions of 1900 and 1904,[76] and many were surprised that the Games survived until 1912 at all. Years were to pass before the Games were seen in a chronological context and not as isolated world championships.[77]

Years of international anonymity in no way diminish Coubertin's large-scale and lifelong contribution to the Olympics and Olympism. No one can take from Coubertin the fact that he more than anyone created the modern Olympic Games with 'a unity and integrity of rule, purpose and form'.[78] This made the Games modern, in keeping with the times, and thus they survived and differed from their predecessors – not only the original ancient Greek games, but the so-called pseudo-Olympic games of which there had been over a score between 1612 and 1893[79] including, in a Nordic context, the Swedish 'Olympic Games' of 1834 and 1836 in Ramlöse near Helsingborg.[80]

It must not be forgotten that Coubertin was a man of his time and that this influenced the form and content of 'his' Olympic Games. It has been emphasized, and with reason, that Coubertin 'was in many important aspects a transitional figure, a man in passage between his era and our own'[81] and, as R.G. Osterhoudt points out, the Olympic Games, as a sporting occasion, form a bridge between the optimistic nineteenth century when they were devised and the more pessimistic twentieth century when they were to take place.[82] Coubertin matured in *la belle époque* with its belief in human progress. He shared this experience with many reformers in Europe and the Nordic countries.[83] In Coubertin's construction of Olympism, the huge influence of the English school and sports system and their concept of 'fair play' must not be underestimated.[84] In passing, it should be noted perhaps that while English sport was not imported wholesale into the Nordic countries since the early modern Nordic sports were based on earlier indigenous activities, there can be no doubt that English sport exercised a great influence over the Nordic countries.[85]

From England came industrialism, liberalism and sport in the course of the nineteenth century, and English culture was generally positively perceived by the middle class in the Nordic countries. In the case of Denmark, the attraction of England was also nationalistic. To be pro-English was to be anti-German, as Jørn Hansen describes elsewhere in this volume.[86] In the world of sport too there was a positive attitude towards the English.[87]

The Nordic Countries, Nationalism and Gender

Nationalism affected the Olympic Games at an early stage – in fact before the first Games of 1896 were even held. The Germans declared that they had not been invited to the Congress in Paris in 1894 and that Coubertin had insulted them. Germans were invited to Athens, but in a private capacity.[88] Germany was not officially invited, because certain French delegates threatened to stay away in protest on account of the Franco-German War of 1870.[89] These sorts of disagreement have continued ever since, and examples are legion. During the Olympic Games in 1896 Coubertin protested that he was being pushed to one side, with the result that a furious Greek newspaper accused him of being 'a thief seeking to rob Greece of her inheritance'.[90] After the outbreak of the First World War in 1914, Sir Theodore Cook, the English member of the IOC, resigned because the German members had not been excluded, and after both world wars the losing countries were kept out by the winning countries.[91]

Balck claimed, as did Coubertin, that a nation's sports life expressed its vitality. More than this, he was of the opinion that sport ensured national survival: 'we do not allow ourselves to be defeated by our neighbours in the west or east'.[92] Of course, it was contrary to the Olympic ideal of internationalism to see sport through such narrow national spectacles. Paavo Nurmi also 'used' sport in the service of nationalism but with a difference. Whereas Nurmi helped to put the new Finnish state on the world map, Balck helped to create a militarily and mentally strong Sweden.

The Olympic movement tried to distance itself from overt chauvinism as for example in its fight against unofficial point tables ranking national performances in the Games. But it was impossible to put a stop to these informal lists.[93] Good international results were important for a country. Sport leaders and the mass media were all agreed on this. Of course, as can be seen from Table 2, the Nordic countries were not equally successful in achieving Olympic glory.

During the 1920s Finland made a breakthrough in the Olympic Games. Long-distance and intermediate-distance runners like Paavo Nurmi and Ville Ritola established Finland as an athletic 'superpower'. Other countries had many theories to explain the amazing Finnish success. The Finns ate raw, dried fish, stone-hard rye bread and drank curdled milk, were directly descended from wild Mongolians, represented the triumph of a relatively poor society over soft, rich societies, whipped themselves and others in a sauna, bathed in ice-cold water and rolled in the snow, and were consequently tougher than most.[95] What all these theories had in common was a lack of scientific validity. Coubertin had been impressed by the Finns in Stockholm in 1912 and believed that the Finnish victories could be

TABLE 2
THE DISTRIBUTION OF OLYMPIC MEDALS FROM 1896 TO 1928 AMONG THE
NORDIC COUNTRIES

Number of participants from the four countries in brackets. Total number of medals distributed (TM), total number of countries participating (TC) and total number of participants (TP). (The Intermediate Games in Athens [1906] and Winter Games [1924 and 1928] included. Art competitions excluded.)[94]

	Denmark	Finland	Norway	Sweden	TM	TC	TP
1896	7 (3)	0 (0)	0 (0)	0 (1)	125	14	245
1900	6.5 (13)	0 (0)	5 (7)	1.5 (18)	265	26	1225
1904	0 (0)	0 (0)	0 (2)	0 (0)	280	13	687
1906	6 (53)	4 (6)	7 (40)	14 (44)	235	20	826
1908	5 (80)	5 (65)	8 (70)	25 (156)	326	22	2035
1912	12 (165)	26 (186)	10 (207)	64 (482)	309	28	2547
1920	13 (134)	34 (59)	31 (194)	64 (246)	437	29	2668
1924							
Summer	9 (65)	37 (105)	10 (59)	29 (159)	378	44	3092
Winter	0 (0)	9	7	1	51	16	258
1928							
Summer	9 (79)	25 (72)	4 (51)	25 (104)	327	46	3014
Winter	0 (0)	4	15	5	48	25	464
Total	67.5	144	107	228.5			

ascribed to nationalism: 'Finland without financial resources, without proper sports grounds, handicapped by its extremely severe winters, carried off an astonishing number of victories, simply because its athletes were determined to bring their country honour.'[96] This will to win observed by Coubertin to this day surprises the other Nordic countries. It is called 'the Finnish *sisu*' and seems to be an inherent characteristic of Finns. They simply refuse to be beaten.

In the early Olympic Games teams were sometimes formed from several countries. As early as 1896, a combined English-German tennis constellation won the doubles.[97] Denmark and Sweden shared a medal at the Olympic Games in Paris in 1900. It was in the tug-of-war, which the two countries won by chance. Because of one (of many) mix-ups by the organizers, the American team, who had qualified for the final against France, were prevented from taking part. A team was quickly formed consisting of three Danish and three Swedish sportsmen. It beat France. There were Norwegians available, but their Nordic brothers considered them too small. A true Nordic triumph was thus prevented.[98]

The Olympic movement has always been dominated by men. Initially, of course, women were absent. Coubertin believed simply that women should supply sons for the Games.[99] His Games were for men. In accordance with this belief, he once rewarded a Swedish woman with the IOC Olympic Medal because all her six sons were involved in one way or another in the Olympic Games in Stockholm in 1912.[100] His successors, Baillet-Latour, Edström and Brundage, did nothing to include women. Women became only slowly involved in the Olympic movement. In 1900 women participated in tennis. By 1912 they competed in archery, sailing and swimming. But matters still moved slowly. As late as 1948 women made up only nine per cent of the participants at the London Olympic Games.[101] And it was not until very recently that there were women on the IOC.

It was not until the women's organization Fédération Sportive Féminine Internationale was founded in 1921 that matters improved significantly. Edström, President of the International Amateur Athletic Federation, under pressure from the organization, reluctantly agreed that five athletic disciplines for women should be included in the Olympic programme of 1928.[102] From 1924 onwards the Winter Games eased the way for further female participation in the Olympic Games. Norwegian Sonja Heine, who won gold in the figure skating in 1928 and 1932, was the first great female media sports star and she widely popularized and publicized female participation in sport.[103]

However, if Sonja Heine was a female Nordic Olympic 'mega-star' she was the only one. In the Nordic countries, early political, economic and cultural equality between the sexes was a fact, but not in the Olympics. Women had only limited opportunities to participate in the Olympic Games but the Nordic countries did not take full advantage of even these! Nordic women were under-represented compared with women from other countries. Only Sweden achieved above average participation in the Olympic Games from 1896 to 1928 (see Table 3).

TABLE 3
NORDIC FEMALE PARTICIPATION IN OFFICIAL EVENTS OF ALL OLYMPIC GAMES 1896–1928 CALCULATED AS A PERCENTAGE OF MALE PARTICIPATION (EXCLUDING EXHIBITIONS, ART AND PRE-OLYMPIC COMPETITIONS)[104]

	Percentage female participation 1896–1928	Total female participants 1896–1928	First female appearance
Denmark	3.6	24	1920
Finland	1.1	6	1912
Norway	1.2	8	1912
Sweden	5.3	63*	1908
Olympic Games (overall)	4.1	666	1900

* Of the 63 Swedish women 35 per cent participated in Stockholm in 1912.

Nordic Co-operation and Obstruction

The Danish-Swedish tug-of-war team in Paris has been seen by posterity as an expression of Nordic fraternal feeling. This much-praised Nordic fraternalism, however, was occasionally put to the test.

When the repercussions of the Napoleonic Wars had died away, and Danes had got used to the fact that Norway had been ceded to Sweden, and Norwegians that they had not got their full freedom, and Swedes that Russia had got Finland, a feeling of 'Scandinavism' arose in Denmark, Norway and Sweden in the course of the nineteenth century. Its basic elements were a nostalgic belief that the Nordic countries had a common glorious past, that the Nordic peoples had a special moral quality and that a splendid future would result when the Nordic 'tribes' forgot the bickering and squabbling of former times and stood together, shoulder to shoulder.[105]

In sport this 'Scandinavism' was very apparent. It was primarily sporting co-operation in the form of innumerable inter-Nordic competitions, but efforts were made to co-operate on the organizational level too. Around the turn of the century there were even those who advocated the formation of a joint Nordic sports organization. The first effort came from a Swedish initiative, and the Centralkomiteen for the Skandinaviske Idrætsforbund (Central Committee of the Scandinavian Sports Federations) was formed in Gothenburg in 1901. The task of the Committee was 'to be a moral support for the Scandinavian sports federations' and an arbitration court for the respective countries' federations.[106] In fact much of the work involved making rules and arranging meetings.[107] However, the Committee failed to make an impact and was dissolved in 1903. It is interesting to note in passing that the later IOC president, Sigfred Edström, was chairman of the Committee.[108]

The next initiative for a joint Nordic sports organization came from the Danes in the autumn of 1904 and in the summer of 1905 Nordisk Centralkomite for Fællesskab i al Idræt (Nordic Central Committee for Fellowship in all Sports) was founded at a meeting in Copenhagen. Edström had a central position in this organization too. Another central figure was the Dane, Fritz Hansen, who became a member of the IOC in 1912. The purpose of the new organization was to draw up common rules and regulations. As previously mentioned, the Committee were mostly in agreement on the issue of amateur and non-amateur.

However, its decisions were never adopted in Sweden.[109] The Swedish political relationship with Norway rather got in the way. Norway wanted to have its own consular service. Sweden considered that this lay outside the Union agreement and refused. For the Norwegians, this became ostensibly the reason for rescinding the Union with Sweden in the autumn of 1905.[110]

Edström, who had actively worked for common amateurism rules, was attacked by Balck, who virtually accused him of being a traitor on account of his conciliatory attitude to Norway.[111] Edström and his fellow conciliators were in a minority on the question and in November 1907 Sweden formally terminated sports co-operation with Denmark and Norway, with the strong support of Balck.[112] Bitterness between Norway and Sweden was to last for some eight years. The Norwegians stayed away from the Nordiska Spelen (the Nordic 'Winter Olympics') in 1905. There was great antipathy in Sweden towards Norway in the following years and in 1909 Norway was not invited to the Nordiska Spelen. General Balck and his circle in particular were infuriated by Norwegian assertiveness and Balck himself was in favour of keeping Norway in the Union by armed force. Balck and his colleagues managed to maintain Sweden's sports boycott of Norway long after more peaceful political winds had begun to blow between the two countries.[113]

It was not the first time that the political relationship between Norway and Sweden had affected the world of sport. In 1895 the Norwegians had accused the Swedes of mixing sport and politics. Sweden had failed to enter a large gymnastics competition in Oslo. The Norwegians urged the Swedes to reconsider, since the gymnastics meeting 'has no politics in it, and the Swedes will be received here with the greatest friendliness'.[114]

For Sweden, the self-chosen isolation after 1905 resulted in a great step forward. Efforts were concentrated systematically and successfully on the international aspects of sport. In consequence, as early as the Olympic Games in Athens in 1906, Sweden was the third best nation, an achievement the country repeated at the Games in London in 1908, and, of course, then Sweden hosted the Olympic Games in Stockholm in 1912.[115] By the time of this last sporting *tour de force,* some years had passed since the dissolution of the Union, Sweden was now clearly the best Nordic sporting nation and a more mellow Swedish attitude to the disagreements of former times resulted. Nordic co-operation was resumed.

In the period 1906–12, for the reasons outlined above, Sweden had few official sports contacts with Norway and Denmark. However, there were occasions when the Nordic countries could not avoid meeting each other, in particular at the Olympic Games in Athens in 1906 and London in 1908. On both occasions there were problems.[116] In 1906 Denmark complained that the Swedes had obtained financial advantages from the Greeks. The Danes claimed this made the Swedes' stay in Athens much less expensive than their own. Furthermore, the Danes asserted the Swedes had influenced the composition of the official programme and the nature of the regulations. Seemingly the protest came to nothing.[117] Two years later, however, there were further problems.

London was a good Olympic Games for the Swedes, but a particularly bad one for Denmark. Posterity is more or less agreed that the English did a good job as regards organization but that the way the sports events were conducted, to put it mildly, was inadequate.[118] The Americans went so far as to talk of deliberate cheating by the English judges in their efforts to promote England at the expense of the United States – a harsh charge against the proprietor of the concepts of fair-play and 'gentlemanliness'. Nevertheless, the evidence was compelling. One of the consequences was that the IOC decided that at and after the Olympic Games in Stockholm in 1912 there would be an international panel of judges.[119] London had not been an isolated case of controversial judging. In Athens in 1906 there had been problems about the lack of neutrality of the fencing judges.[120] And in Paris in 1900 two clean and completely fresh Frenchmen had won the marathon ahead of the Swede, Ernst Fast, and a muddy and exhausted group of runners, several of whom claimed that they had overtaken the Frenchmen early in the race.[121]

There was also dissatisfaction in Denmark with the conduct of the competitions in 1908. But where the Americans found fault with English chauvinism, the Danes found fault with Swedish nationalism. Denmark had had high hopes of a good result in the team gymnastics competition but came only fourth. In his report after the Olympic Games, the chairman of the Danish Sports Federation, Fritz Hansen, pointed the finger at the Swedes. Hansen claimed that the three English gymnastics judges had studied gymnastics in Sweden at the institute directed by Viktor Balck. The same Balck, Fritz Hansen pointed out, was repeatedly seen in animated discussion with the judges during the voting. According to Hansen, this was the reason why Denmark was only fourth.[122]

Fritz Hansen and Viktor Balck were far from being good friends in these years. Hansen often complained, especially in private letters to another prominent Swedish sports leader and later IOC member, Edström, that Sweden, at Balck's instigation, had withdrawn from Nordic co-operation because of its relationship with Norway.[123] There was also a suspicion in Denmark that Balck had blocked the appointment of Fritz Hansen as an IOC member. This is difficult to prove, but Balck certainly had a say in the appointment of Nordic IOC members as in the case, for example, of the Norwegian, Heinrik Angell, in 1905.[124]

The London Games were characterized by other nationalistic problems during the entry parade. The flags of Finland, the United States and Sweden had not been hoisted in the stadium. In response, the American standard-bearer and shot-putter, Ralph Rose, refused to salute the English royal family with the standard, and some of the Swedish participants returned to Sweden.[125] The Finns stayed. For them, the Olympic Games were an opportunity to drew attention to the Finnish nation and nationalism. (Finland did not achieve its independence until 1917). The Finns had tried to obtain permission to enter the stadium under their own flag, as had been the case in 1906 in the Intermediate Games in Athens, where Finland participated in the Olympic Games for the first time, but the English, who had just signed a trade agreement with Russia, put pressure on Finland, who then agreed to march behind the Russian flag during the opening ceremony.[126] In the 1912 Games the Finns still did not have their own flag in the entry parade, but if the Finns won the Finnish colours were hoisted above the Russian flag.[127]

At the Stockholm Games of 1912 the quarrels between Norway and Sweden were on the way to being settled, but new Nordic conflicts arose this time between Denmark and Iceland, which was ruled by Denmark until 1944 and had had a participant in the Danish team in London in 1908. In 1912, however, Iceland wanted to participate in Stockholm under its own name with two participants and a team of wrestlers who were to demonstrate Icelandic wrestling, 'glimu', at the Games. The organizers gave Iceland permission to participate in the entry march on their own and behind their own sign, but Denmark protested and insisted that Iceland should march with its sign as part of the Danish team. The Icelanders refused, and boycotted the entry march. Iceland next took part in the Olympic Games in Berlin in 1936 as a nation. Arguably, Iceland participated in Antwerp in 1920 and won a medal into the bargain: seven of the eight players on the Canadian team that won the ice-hockey tournament were from Iceland and had dual citizenship![128]

The manner in which the Games were conducted in 1912 won much praise for the Swedish hosts. A few critical voices were heard. It was regrettable, some said, that boxing had to be cancelled because boxing was prohibited in Sweden,[129] and Coubertin thought the Swedes ill-advised to have arranged a church service in conjunction with the opening ceremony – not all the participants were Christian, much less Protestant.[130] However, Coubertin, who had considered Stockholm for the 1904 Olympic Games,[131] was pleased with the new art competitions for two reasons: he had insisted on them in the face of powerful Swedish opposition and he had won a gold medal for poetry.[132]

The Nordic Countries, Sport and Internationalism

Elite sport became increasingly international in the years after the First World War. Thus its problems also became international and had to be solved internationally. This influenced developments in the Nordic countries. The Nordic countries were neutral during the First World War. In consequence, inter-Nordic sport proliferated as international sport became difficult.

In December 1916 at a Nordic athletics congress in Stockholm Nordic co-operation at the administrative level commenced again after a break of more than ten years. Common regulations on amateurism were again an important issue.[133] There was no agreement. Denmark was positive, Norway half-hearted and Sweden negative on the issue. It became more and more difficult to find common ground both within and between the respective countries. In order to solve at least some of their problems, the Nordic nations considered a three-part division into 'amateur', 'non-amateur' and 'professional'[134] but could not even agree to this. A further joint meeting was held in Copenhagen in 1918 where attempts to establish joint-Nordic regulation on amateurism were abandoned.[135] A number of international sports federations had now been established, each with its own set of comparable but far from identical rules on amateurism. Those who decided such rules were neither the Nordic countries nor other countries, but the various associations gathered in international federations. Even attempts to make special Nordic rules on amateurism in specific sports disciplines, for example in soccer in 1921, had to be abandoned.[136]

Meanwhile, what had the greatest long-term importance was the establishment in 1918 of De nordiske Rigs-Idrætsforbunds Fælleskomite. There was no longer an attempt to achieve uniformity in sport and amateurism, still less a joint organization of all the Nordic countries – the original aim at the turn of the century. The purpose now was general co-operation and co-ordination among the Nordic counties in international sport. This time a viable organization had been established. Finland joined in 1925 and Iceland in 1929. In 1920, at the sixth Skandinaviske Idraetskongres (Scandinavian Athletics Congress), Finland became an informal participant in this Nordic co-operation.[137] Despite a desire for co-operation, there were some reservations in Finland about the other Nordic countries in the years after the First World War. In Finland's case, this had ended in a civil war, with 'the whites' defeating 'the reds' in 1918. The Swedish-speaking section of the Finnish population was strongly in favour of Nordic co-operation, but it was viewed with some suspicion by the Finnish nationalists who had come to power and saw *rapprochement* as a plot against hard-won Finnish independence.

Even though they gave up trying to agree about joint Nordic rules, on amateurism, there were other problems for the Joint Committee to tackle, many of which were associated with international sport and the IOC and were exacerbated by the end of the First World War. In the final years of the war, the Nordic countries had tried to agree on rules for foreign sports participation. It was decided, for example, that Nordic sportsmen could participate in competitions with foreign countries only with the permission of their associations.[138] This was a means of controlling sports relationships between the Nordic countries and the outside world. It was soon needed. After the First World War, Germany and the other losing countries were excluded from international sport. The victorious countries informed the world that countries which co-operated with the excluded would themselves risk exclusion. The Central Powers were excluded from participation at the Olympic Games in Antwerp in 1920.[139] As Coubertin stated: 'Common sense suggested that it would hardly be wise for a German team to appear in the Olympic stadium before 1924.'[140] The episode illustrates the fact that the IOC cannot remain above international politics. Coubertin and later presidents always claimed that the Olympic idea was above that sort of triviality. One of the presidents who most fervently maintained that sport and politics should not be mixed was the Swede, Edström. As early as 1923 he insisted that that 'the IOC must avoid all interference in the political sphere'.[141] Edström would attempt to move mountains to keep the Olympic movement out of politics. A striking example of this was his attitude to the international discussion about Jewish participation in the Olympic Games in Berlin in 1936. Edström's emphatic view was that what happened in Germany was no business of the IOC and the Olympic movement.[142]

The Joint Committee endorsed and implemented the neutrality to which the Nordic governments had adhered during the First World War. In November 1919 the Committee agreed to put on record for the world that the Nordic countries jointly would decide with whom they would co-operate: 'The Nordic countries' sports federations set their fraternal and harmonious co-operation in the field of sport so high, that if one of their special federations ... should be excluded from open international meetings, the other Scandinavian sports associations will support the party excluded.' The support included, it was declared, the Olympic Games.[143] Even Finland, which was not yet formally party to Nordic co-operation, agreed to the decision.[144] But the Nordic countries were obviously a little frightened of their joint decision. Denmark signed only after long internal discussions[145] having clarified that the boycott would apply to activities in Denmark only after government approval had been granted.[146] Norway was not wholly keen on the decision either. As in Denmark, there was far from common ground among the associations. It was decided to keep the decision secret. Making it public beyond the Nordic sports organizations might be provocative. The decision to keep the agreement confidential 'for as long as possible and preferably until after the Olympics in Antwerp' appears in a confidential letter sent with diplomatic dispatches to Paris to the Norwegian IOC member, Major Sverre, in January 1920.[147] A confidential letter to Norway from Denmark also emphasized that the agreement was secret.[148]

There was indeed a considerable risk that this policy might have to be implemented quickly and affect all the Nordic countries. In the summer of 1919 FIFA had threatened to exclude all countries which played soccer, including club games, with the Central Powers. The international gymnastics federation had sent a letter to its members excluding the German and Hungarian gymnastics associations and the exclusion threat was also heard within the rifle movement and swimming organizations. The situation in soccer became more critical when FIFA split after a meeting in December 1919. The Nordic countries stayed away from the meeting but had written to clarify their position. They reserved the right 'to maintain their right to continue connections with all countries'. Since Italy, Switzerland and Holland among others failed to back FIFA, the exclusion of the Central Powers and the countries that played soccer with them could not be enforced and England, France and Belgium then resigned from FIFA and for a time formed their own organization.[149]

However, the Nordic plan succeeded, even though there was manoeuvring in stormy political seas for some months. On the one hand the Nordic countries demonstrated that they were neutral. On the other the secret agreement and the decision that the Nordic sports men and women could not compete with foreign countries without permission ensured that problems could be headed off: 'According to this agreement, no invitations to open international meetings must be given, so that the risk of sportsmen from the Allies and the Central Powers meeting is avoided.'[150] The Nordic countries thus weathered the political storm. It was not necessary to implement the drastic decision about joint action. And even though Germany was not invited to the Olympic Games in 1920 *and* 1924, time as usual healed wounds. At the Olympic Games in 1928 the Olympic 'family', including the Central Powers, gathered again. There was one exception. Many years would pass before Russia in the form of the Soviet Union was again admitted to civilized circles. This did not happen until the Olympic Games in Helsinki in 1952.

The Olympic child grew rapidly to adolescence in the 1920s, to such an extent that there were voices raised about Olympic 'giantism'. These voices were heard especially after 1924, when the Winter Olympics had also become part of the programme. The Nordic countries had a common view of both the Winter Games and giantism. The Olympic Winter Games first took place in 1924 at Chamonix. Of course, there had been winter-sports elements at some previous summer Olympic Games – for instance, there had been ice-skating as early as 1908 in London. With a winter Olympics in place, the harvest of medals for Finland, Norway and Sweden at the Olympic Games increased considerably. In 1924 the three countries won more than half the total number of medals at the Winter Games and four years later in St Moritz in Switzerland they repeated their triumph. Norway won most (see Table 2). The Nordic nations were in favour of the innovation.

However, the Winter Games were adopted only after long discussion. The Nordic countries and England with its figure-skating tradition voted for its adoption.[151] The opposition was led by the later IOC president, Avery Brundage (1952–72). It claimed, with some justification, that the ancient Greeks had no winter sports. More to the point, it argued that winter sports could not unite the youth of the world as they had an extremely limited geographical distribution.[152] While the Nordic countries supported the new games there was not unmitigated enthusiasm for them in Scandinavia.

In 1925 the Nordic Joint Committee agreed to oppose the Winter Games: 'The congress decided that winter sports such as skating, skiing, ice-hockey etc., should not figure on the programme of the Olympic Games and that a separate Olympic Winter Games should not be introduced.'[153] The Winter Olympic Games, which had been a Nordic 'medal machine' in 1924, nevertheless were not of equal interest to all the Nordic countries. Denmark had no winter sports.[154]

The wish to discontinue the Winter Games was also connected with a wish to limit the size of the Olympic Games. In 1925 the view in the Nordic countries was that the Olympic Games had become too large and monopolized nations' sports interests as well as their financial and sporting resources. It was therefore decided to work 'for a sensible limitation of the Olympic Games programme'.[155] Only internationally organized sports disciplines should be on the Olympic Games programme, and new disciplines should not be admitted. The leaders of the four countries, however, could not agree about proposing a precise limitation on the number of participants in the individual disciplines.[156] Did the Nordic countries really want a reduction in the size of the Games? At the same meeting at which it was decided to work to limit the Olympic programme, Finland argued in favour of the Nordic countries *de facto* extending the programme by the inclusion of the ancient pentathlon.[157] Perhaps the truth was that a large part of the public and the sports movement were on guard against an insidious Olympic 'giantism', but that this fear was not wholeheartedly shared by all of those in positions of influence in the Nordic countries.

Conclusion

The Nordic countries took part in the Olympic movement from its inception. Sweden played a major role, Denmark a minor one. The Olympic movement for Finland, and for Norway to a certain extent, was a mechanism for the creation of a national identity. The sports organizations in the Nordic countries and the IOC suffered an early loss of power. The Nordic sports organizations had to hand over power to the national organizations; the IOC to the international associations.

The rules on amateurism were of great interest to the Nordic countries and the IOC alike. But whereas the Nordic countries, and to an extent, Denmark, tried to introduce both 'financial' and 'ethical' rules and categories of amateur and non-amateur, this was not the case with the IOC. Here the division was between amateur and professional, but in the Olympic movement, too, sportsmen were excluded for unethical behaviour. On the whole, the leadership in the Nordic countries as well as the leadership in the IOC were greatly interested in socialization through sport.

The Nordic countries often co-operated in the area of sports and also in relation to the IOC, where they acted as a block. Examples of this include the struggle for the national selection of IOC members, and opposition to the Winter Olympic Games and Olympic giantism. The Nordic countries' own Olympic Committees were controlled and dominated by the Nordic countries' sports organizations, not by the IOC. Local political interests, though, were often what decided the unity of the Nordic countries. The best example of this is the dissolution of the Union between Norway and Sweden, and the subsequent nationalistic repercussions which had an impact on the Nordic nations regionally and internationally on the IOC and on the Olympic Games of 1906 and 1908.

There was opposition to Olympism and the Olympic Games among the Nordic gymnastics advocates especially in Denmark and Sweden. But the perception of gymnastics as something special and better than sport was not just a Nordic phenomenon, it was also a European one. Nevertheless, Olympism does not seem to have played any major role in the Nordic countries up to 1928. However, its concepts were in place in the form of ethical expectations introduced by English-inspired ideas, the notion of fair play in particular.

In the Nordic nations, equality between the sexes was well advanced, but this was not the case in an Olympic context. In the period 1896–1928 women from the Nordic countries were under-represented at the Olympic Games, with the single exception of Sweden. In the case of Finland and Norway, they were very under-represented indeed.

The sports movement was organized from above in Finland, Norway and Sweden, while the state did not pay any particular attention to sport in Denmark until after the First World War. In contrast to the IOC, the Nordic countries tried to keep sport and politics separate, particularly after 1918 in relation to the Central Powers. This was probably a case of sport following the established policy of political neutrality in the Nordic states during the

First World War. For a time the Nordic sports organizations were frightened of their own decisiveness in the matter but all came out well eventually in the political wash.

In the final analysis what the Nordic nations in their relationship with the IOC, Olympism and the Olympic Games demonstrate is a complex, shifting pattern of individualistic, involved, indifferent, co-operative, confrontational, supportive, sectional, assertive, associations over time in which the Olympic concept proved to be a catalyst for many things – paradoxically, not least for a sense of regional and national identity.

NOTES

1. The Nordic countries traditionally include Denmark, Finland, Iceland, Norway and Sweden. The Faeroe Islands and the Oland Islands are often included in the term. This article, however, concentrates on Scandinavia, comprising Denmark, Norway and Sweden.
2. John J. MacAloon, *This Great Symbol: Pierre de Coubertin and the Origins of the Modern Olympic Games* (Chicago, 1981), p.ix.
3. Jeffrey O. Segrave and Donald Chu (eds.), *The Olympic Games in Transition* (Champaign, Illinois, 1988), pp.172–3.
4. Allen Guttmann, *The Olympics – A History of the Modern Games* (Illinois, 1992), pp.44–8.
5. David B. Kanin, *A Political History of the Olympic Games* (Boulder, 1981), pp.4–5.
6. Pierre de Coubertin, *Olympic Memoirs* (Lausanne, 1979), p.71. The term 'family concern' alludes to the official participant pictures from the IOC meetings in the early years. A good example is the meeting in Budapest (1911) where several of the IOC members had brought along their wives. Balck had both wife and daughter.
7. Coubertin, *Olympic Memoirs*, pp.5–6, 12–13.
8. Even before the congress in Paris, Balck wrote to Coubertin and gave him information about sports matters in Norway and Sweden. The IOC archives in Lausanne, Balck to Coubertin, 4 March 1894.
9. MacAloon, *This Great Symbol*, p.210.
10. Edström made a very good impression in the IOC, which regarded him as the principal person behind the holding of the Olympic Games in Stockholm in 1912. Guttmann (1992) op. cit., p.32. Coubertin refers to Edström in his memoirs with much veneration, after Edstrom had become an IOC member in 1920, and quickly attained a central position. Coubertin, *Olympic Memoirs*, p.109.
11. Today only Denmark has one IOC member; all other Nordic countries have two each.
12. Allen Guttmann, *The Games Must Go On* (New York, 1984), p.16.
13. MacAloon, p.199.
14. Jan Lindroth, *Idrottens väg till folkrörelse – Studier I svensk idrottsrörelse till 1915* (Uppsala, 1974) shows how Balck for many years was the strong man in Swedish sport.
15. Ibid., pp.182–3, 192.
16. Ibid., pp.253–4.
17. Hans Bonde, 'De olympiske leges værdigrundlag', in *Hurtigere, Højere og Stærkere, Idraetshistorisk Årbog* (DUO, 1988), pp.62–72.
18. In Sweden there was disagreement between Ling gymnastics and sport. This was also the case in Denmark, where the disagreement has actually been considered crucial to understanding the development of sport; see for example Ove Korsgaard, *Kampen om kroppen* (Copenhagen, 1984). But this is somewhat exaggerated. It was in particular the teachers of gymnastics in schools who had reservations about sport. Per Jørgensen, *Dansk Idrætsliv* (Copenhagen, 1995) bd.1, Per Jørgensen, *Ro, Renlighed, Regelmæssighed – Dansk Idræts – Forbund og sportens gennembrud ca. 1896–1918* (Odense, 1997) and

Lindroth, *Idrottens väg till folkrörelse.*
19. Coubertin, *Olympic Memoirs*, p.23.
20. MacAloon, p.169.
21. 'The gymnasts in Belgium are brothers', Per Jørgensen, 'Order, Discipline and Self-Control: The Breakthrough for the Danish Sports Federation and Sport 1896–1918', *International Journal of the History of Sport*, 13, 3 (Dec 1996), 340.
22. Jørgensen, *Ro Renlighed*, pp.116, 246–9.
23. Ibid., p.248.
24. Ibid., pp.261–2.
25. Jørgensen, 'Order, Discipline and Self-Control'.
26. Pierre de Coubertin, 'The Olympic Games of 1896' in Segrave and Chu, *The Olympic Games in Transition*, p.180.
27. John Hoberman, *The Olympic Crisis – Sports, Politics and the Moral Order* (New York, 1986), p.81.
28. Ibid., pp 81–5.
29. March L. Krotee, 'An organizational Analysis of the International Olympic Committee in Jeffrey O. Segrave and Donald Chu, *The Olympic Games in Transition*, pp.125–9. Karl Adolf Scherer, *100 Jahre Olympische Spiele* (Dortmund, 1995). Corrections have been made.
30. Danmarks Rigsarkiv (The Danish Record Office), R-10. 366-pk. 26-P. 109, letter of 24.4.1897.
31. Sveriges Riksarkiv (The Swedish Record Office) I-IIa (Balck's archive) vol 8. 17 Feb. 1900.
32. The IOC archives in Lausanne. Holbeck to Coubertin, 1 April, 10 April 1906.
33. The IOC archives in Lausanne. Letters from the military attaché in Copenhagen to Coubertin 2 Sept., 23 Oct., 15 Nov. 1906.
34. The IOC archives in Lausanne. Eugen S. Schmidt to Coubertin, 12 Feb. 1907 and *Revue Olympique*, janvier 1907, 197–9.
35. Coubertin, *Olympic Memoirs*, p.105.
36. Sveriges Riksarkiv, De nordiske Rigsidrætsforbunds Falleskomite Händlinger 1916–1950, July–Sept. 1925.
37. Norges Riksarkiv (Norwegian Record Office), PA-90-NIF; 3BO-7411; box 6 II, 10 Oct. 1926–19 Oct. 1926. Baillet-Latour asserted, though, that the representative who was chosen should be acceptable to the country he came from.
38. Guttmann, *The Games Must Go On*, p.12.
39. Lindroth, *Idrottens väg till folkrörelse*, pp.167–9 and 185–7.
40. The state played an active and interested role in the unification of the sports movements in Finland, Norway and Sweden. In Denmark the state was more or less uninterested in the sports movement before 1918. Jørgensen, *Ro, Renlighed*, p.264. Leif Yttergren, *Täflan Är Lifvet* (Stockholm, 1996). In Finland the gymnastics and sports movement was built up from above. Leena Laine, 'Idrött for alla men på olika villkor?' Idrott, samhälle och social kontroll i Finland 1856–1917', in *Idrott, Historia och Samhälle* (1988), 51.
41. In Denmark, rifle-shooting and gymnastics in the rural districts were controlled in one organization, founded in 1861, sport in another, founded in 1896. Until 1917 Finland was part of Russia and sport had four associations: gymnastics and sport (1900), football (1907), Swedish-oriented (1913) and working-class sport (1918). In Norway, sport was more or less collected under one umbrella organization in 1910 and in Sweden in 1904.
42. The early sports movement in the Nordic countries is described in: Jørgensen in *Dansk Idrætsliv*, 1 (1995) vol.1, Jørgensen, *Ro, Renlighed*, Finn Olstad, *Norsk Idretts Historie* (Oslo, 1986), vol.1, Matti Goksøyr, *Idrettsliv I borgerskabets by. En historisk undersökelse av idrettens utvikling og organisering I Bergen på 1800-tallet* (Oslo, 1991) and Leif Yttergren, *Täflan Är Lifvet*, p.134.
43. Riding as well as rowing and sailing became sports even earlier outside the Nordic countries than in them (Yttergren, *Täflan Är Lifvet*, pp.38 and 134, Jørn Hansen, *Dansk Idrætsliv*, 1 (1995), 29–30, Goksøyr, *Idrettsliv I borgerskabets*, pp.31–7). However, 'sportification' could have very different meanings from place to place, Yttergren, *Täflan*

Är Lifvet, p.134.
44. The term 'middle class' in the following is to be understood as the upper middle class.
45. Jørgensen, 'Order, Discipline and Self-Control', 341–51.
46. Jørgensen, *Ro, Renlighed*, p.290.
47. Sveriges Riksarkiv, Öfverstyrelsen, A-II-1, 25 Nov. 1905.
48. Ibid.
49. Sveriges Riksarkiv, Ö-II-b-1, July–Sept. 1925.
50. Jørgensen, 'Order, Discipline and Self-Control', 349–51.
51. Sveriges Riksarkiv, Ö-III-a-4, 1905–7
52. Andrew Strenk, 'Myth and Reality', in Segrave and Chu, *The Olympic Games in Transition*, p.321.
53. Coubertin, *Olympic Memoirs*, p.68.
54. Ibid., p.65.
55. It is not necessary to read many pages Coubertin's *Olympic Memoirs* to have this point of view confirmed. Ibid., pp.5–12.
56. Hoberman, *The Olympic Crisis*, p.29.
57. Guttmann, *The Games Must Go On*, p.21.
58. Danmarks Rigsarkiv, R-10.366-pk.-26, pp.420, 421. 3 and 4 Aug. 1900. The competition was held on 12 Aug.
59. Segrave and Chu, *Olympism*, p.37.
60. Guttmann, *The Olympics*, p.44
61. Andrew Strenk, 'Myth and Reality', in Segrave and Chu, *Olympism*, p.58.
62. Guttmann, *The Olympics*, p.40.
63. *Dansk Sportsleksikon* bd. 2 (Copenhagen,1945) pp.233–4 and Guttmann, *The Olympics*, p.51.
64. Strenk in Segrave and Chu, *The Olympic Games in Transition*, p.310.
65. Guttmann, *The Games Must Go On*, p.60.
66. Guttmann, *The Olympics*, p.44.
67. Kanin, *A Political History of the Olympic Games*, pp 38, 50.
68. Guttmann, *The Olympics*, p.44.
69. Sveriges Riksarkiv, 0-II-b-1, 23 Feb.–24 Feb. 1923, 7.9 May 1928.
70. Sveriges Riksarkiv A-I:7, 26 April 1925.
71. Glader, 'Restrictions Against "Broken-Time"', in Segrave and Chu, *Olympism*, pp.48–9.
72. The two notices were just a few lines long. Per Jørgensen, 'Da Coubertin kom i avisen', in *Hurtigere, Højere, Stærkere* (1988), p.80.
73. Ibid. pp.82–6.
74. No complete statistics have been collated on the social background of the Nordic sports leaders, but there is information from individual countries. Jørgensen, *Ro, Renlighed*, pp.246–55 and Lindroth, *Idrottens väg till folkrörelse*, pp.145–7.
75. The Olympic movement as an organization has always been dominated by Europe. With the exception of Avery Brundage, United States (1952–1972), the 7 presidents of the IOC have been from Europe. Europe has always been over-represented as regards IOC members, and the organization has always had its headquarters in Europe since 1915 in Lausanne, Switzerland. Krotee in Segrave and Chu, *The Olympic Games in Transition*, pp.117–48.
76. Problems of organization rather than ideology attached the Olympic Games to world exhibitions. The world exhibition concept was implicit in the actual Olympic Games idea. Jørn Hansen, 'Fra Crystal Palace til Athen' in *Hurtigere, Højere, Stærkere* (1988), p.15. On the Olympic Games and the world exhibition tradition, see MacAloon, pp 128–38.
77. Thus for example Guttmann, *The Games Must Go On*, pp.21–35.
78. MacAloon, p.269.
79. For a collected overview see Gerald Redmond, 'Toward Modern Revival of the Olympic Games: The Various 'Pseudo-Olympics' of the 19th Century' in Segrave and Chu, *The Olympic Games in Transition*, pp.86–7.
80. Åke Svahn, 'Olympska spelan i Helsingborg 1834 och 1836', in *Idrott, historia och samhälle* (1983), pp.77–8.

81. MacAloon, p.xii.
82. R.G. Osterhoudt, 'Modern *Olympism* in the conjunction of Nineteenth and Twentieth Century Civilization', Segrave and Chu, *Olympism*, p.353.
83. Jørgensen, *Ro, Renlighed*, pp.185–200.
84. MacAloon, pp.51–3.
85. Yttergren, *Täflan Är Lifvet*, p.53.
86. Jørn Hansen, '"Sport" og "dansk idræt"', in *Idrætshistorisk Arbog* (DUO, 1989) pp.73–90.
87. Many leading Danish sportsmen inclined to the English traditon of sport. Denmark had many top leaders who were oriented towards England. The best known is Eugen Stahl Schmidt, founder of the Danish Sports Federation. Jørgensen, *Ro, Renlighed*, pp.185–6. In Sweden, Balck had 'a generally Anglophile attitude'. Lindroth, *Idrottens väg till folkrörelse*, p.187.
88. J.M. Leiper, 'Political Problems in the Olympic Games' in Segrave and Chu, *Olympism*, p.109.
89. Coubertin, *Olympic Memoirs*, p.11.
90. Guttmann, *The Olympics*, p.19.
91. Leiper in Segrave and Chu, *Olympism*, p.109.
92. Lindroth, *Idrottens väg till folkrörelse*, p.186.
93. Guttmann, *The Games Must Go On*, p.54.
94. Erik Kamper, *Enzyklopaedie der Olympischen Spiele* (Stuttgart, 1972), *Lexikon der 12.000 Olympioniken* (Graz, 1975) and Erik Kamper and Bill Mallon, *Who's Who Der Olympischen Spiele 1896–1992* (Agon, 1992). In addition, specially for information about the Winter Olympics, Karl Adolf Scherer, *100 Jahre Olympische Spiele*.
95. Guttmann, *The Olympics*, pp.42–3.
96. Coubertin, *Olympic Memoirs*, p.80.
97. Guttmann, *The Games Must Go On*, pp.15–16.
98. Ture Widlund, 'Dragkamp vid Olympiska Spelen i Paris 1900', in *Idrott, Historia och Samhälle* (1981), pp.87–9.
99. John A. Lucas, *Future of the Olympic Games* (Champaign, Illinois, 1992), p.134.
100. Coubertin, *Olympic Memoirs*, p.80.
101. Spears, 'The IOC and Women's Sport' in Segrave and Chu, *The Olympic Games in Transition*, pp.368–9.
102. Guttmann, *The Games Must Go On*, pp.56–7.
103. Kanin, *A Political History of the Olympic Games*, p.49.
104. Kamper, *Enzyklopaedie der Olympischen Spiele*, Kamper, *Lexikon der 12.000 Olymploniken* and Kamper and Mallon, *Who's Who Der olympischen Spiele 1896–1992*. Scherer, *100 Jahre Olympische Spielet*. As mentioned only official competitions are included.
105. Jørgensen in *Dansk Idrætsliv* (1995), op. cit., 91–9.
106. Norges Riksarkiv, PA 90 NFF-3B0-8351, Protokol 1896–1901.
107. Sveriges Riksarkiv, Svenska Idrottsförbundet, Centralkomiteens kopibog.
108. Sveriges Riksarkiv, Ur-FriF; FXII:1 and Jørgensen in *Dansk Idrætsliv* (1995) op. cit., 95–6.
109. In 1814 Norway was forced into a union with Sweden with one King and one foreign policy.
110. Jan Lindroth, 'Unionsoplösningen 1905 och Idrotten – Den svenska idrotsörelsen i en utrikespolitisk krisstituation', in *Sveriges Centralförenings för Idrottens Främjande årsbok* (1977).
111. Sveriges Riksarkiv Ö-IIIa-4 op. cit. 1905–7. The letter from Balck starts with 'Brother Edström' and ends with 'Your friend Balck', but the content accuses Edström of treason.
112. Sveriges Riksarkiv, AII-vol-3 20 Nov. 1907, and Peeter Mark, '"Den eviga mumien", Amatörfrågans behandling i svensk Idrott 1880–1967', in *Idrott, Historia och Samhalle* (1989), 73–107.
113. Lindroth, 'Unionsoplösningen 1905 och Idrotten'.
114. Sveriges Riksarkiv 6-II-A;5, 19 April 1895 and 30 April 1895. Letters from Emil Petersen, The Norwegian Gymnastic Association (Det Norske Turn og Gymnastik Forbund).
115. Lindroth, 'Unionsoplösningen 1905 och Idrotten'.

98   THE NORDIC WORLD

116. Ibid., p.8. There was 'irritation between Swedish and Danish gymnasts' at the Olympic Games in 1906 and 1908.
117. Danmarks Rigsarkiv, R.10.366-pk9-p.191.
118. The preparation was otherwise good. The English collected the sports rules in a 200-page book, *The Rules of Sport*, in English, German and French. Ture Widlund, 'Det olympiska valspråoket - bakgrund och tillkomst' in *Idrott, Historia och Samhälle* (1982), 46.
119. Kanin, *A Political History of the Olympic Games*, pp.33–5. Guttmann, *The Games Must Go On*, pp.20–2.
120. Kanin, *A Political History of the Olympic Games*, p.39.
121. Guttmann, *The Games Must Go On*, p.18.
122. Danmarks Rigsarkiv, R-10.366-pk.2 p.153.
123. Lindroth, 'Unionsoplösningen 1905 och Idrotten' and Danmarks Rigsarkiv, R-10.366-pk.37. Letters to Edström no.113, 305, 361, 373, 374, and the letter of 11 March (333) to the Norwegian Lieutenant Colonel Seeberg: 'The worst of the whole bunch is our mutual friend Balck; I think the old fogey has become too old and indeed many of the sensible Swedes think so too.'
124. IOC archives in Lausanne. Letter from Balck to Coubertin, 29 Dec. 1905. Balck does not think Angell represents all Norwegian sport, but has nothing against his selection.
125. Kanin, *A Political History of the Olympic Games*, p.34.
126. Richard Gruneau and Hart Centelon, 'Capitalism, Commercialism, and the Olympics', in Segrave and Chu, *The Olympic Games*, p.352.
127. Coubertin, *Olympic Memoirs*, pp.76–7 and Kanin, *A Political History*, p.27.
128. Ingimar Jónsson, *Ólympíuleikar ad fornu og nyju* (Iceland, 1983), pp.75–8.
129. Guttmann, *The Games Must Go On*, p.22.
130. Coubertin, *Olympic Memoirs*, p.80. 'But I had a feeling we were exceeding our rights,' thought Coubertin about the very emotional church service.
131. IOC archives in Lausanne. Letter from Balck to Coubertin, 26 Nov. 1901. Coubertin had written to Balck suggesting that the Games in 1904 could be held in Stockholm, and that this would be in accordance with Balck's own wishes. Balck wrote back that he never wanted the Games in Stockholm in 1904, but rather in Berlin.
132. Hakan Sandblad, 'Kulturen och Stockholm-OS eller Så fick Coubertin sin guldmedalj', *Idrott, Historia och Samhälle* (1987), 89, 103.
133. Norges Riksarkiv, PA90-NIF-3B0-7411, Aeske I 1913–17.
134. Sveriges Riksarkiv d-II-b-l, 9–10 Dec. 1916.
135. Jørgensen in *Dansk Idrætsliv* (1995), 98.
136. Sveriges Riksarkiv, A-III-8, 15 March 1921.
137. Jørgensen in *Dansk Idraetsliv* (1995), 98 and Norges Riksarkiv PA-90-NIF; 3-B0-7411; Æske G I (1916–1921), 18 April 1920.
138. Norges Riksarkiv, PA-90 NIF; 3B0-7411; Æske 6-I (1916–1921).
139. Kanin, *A Political History*, pp.46–8. The Central Powers had the right to participate in the Olympic Games in 1920. The Olympic Games should of course stand above politics. Coubertin and the organisers however found a 'technicality' in the rules. It was not the IOC, but the host country, Belgium, who should send out the invitations. So the Belgians simply failed to invite the Central Powers and in addition, the communist regime in Russia, which shortly afterwards became the USSR.
140. Coubertin, *Olympic Memoirs*, p.100.
141. Leiper in Segrave and Chu, *Olympism*, p.112.
142. Reinhard Rürup (ed.), *Die olymplchen Spiele und der Nationalsozialismus* (Berlin, 1996) p.55. In world public opinion, there was growing anxiety about the situation of Jews in Germany after the Nazi takeover of power especially in the United States where there was vigorous agitation for a boycott of the Olympic Games in Berlin. Avery Brundage wrote to Erdström and presented the case. In his answer, Edström showed great understanding of Germany's treatment of the Jews. He found the American newspapers' treatment of the question exaggerated and pointed out that many sports clubs in the United States themselves denied admission to Jews.
143. Norges Riksarkiv, PA-90-NIF; 3-B0-7411; Æske 6 I, 22 Nov. 1919.

144. Ibid., 6 Dec. 1919–5 Jan. 1920.
145. In the course of December it transpired that Denmark had problems persuading the cyclists and the riflemen, among others, to hold back on the international work. Norges Riksarkiv, PA-90-NIF; 3BO-7411; Æske I. Letters of 30 Dec. 1919–5 Jan. 1920.
146. Jørgensen in *Dansk Idrætsliv* (1995), 99.
147. Norges Riksarkiv, PA-90-NIF; 3-B0-7411; Æske 6-I, 17 Jan. 1920.
148. Ibid., 12 Jan. 1920.
149. Ibid., 16 Jan. 1920.
150. Ibid., 17 Jan. 1920
151. Coubertin, *Olympic Memoirs*, pp.107, 128. It is interesting to read Coubertin's own memories of the course of events. According to these, it was he who slowly overcame the opposition to the winter games, not least in the Scandinavian countries themselves.
152. Guttmann, *The Games Must Go On*, p.53. Kanin, *A Political History*, pp.48–9.
153. Sveriges Riksarkiv, Ö-II-b-l, 7 Sept. 1925.
154. Norges Riksarkiv, PA-90-NIF; 3-B0-7411; Æske 6 II, 21 Feb. 1925–19 Sept. 1925. The initiative came from the Norwegian Ski Association.
155. Sveriges Riksarkiv, Ö-II-b-l, 21–23 Feb. 1925.
156. Sveriges Riksarkiv, Ö-II-b-l, 1916–1950, 7 Sept. 1925.
157. Sveriges Riksarkiv, ibid.

The Popular Sounding Board: Nationalism, 'the People' and Sport in Norway in the Inter-war Years

MATTI GOKSØYR

National identity as a subject for research has gained in popularity in the 1990s among historians both in Norway and world-wide.[1] However, the ever-increasing body of published literature on this subject takes little account of the importance of sport in the formation of national identity. At a more popular level the Norwegian media have also generally ignored nationalism in their coverage of large sports meetings in Norway, such as the 1994 winter Olympic Games in Lillehammer and the 1997 Skiing World Championships (Nordic branches) in Trondheim.

It is generally accepted that the end of the nineteenth century was the defining period for Norwegian national identity. From the 1880s on, political nationalism was strong. At the same time cultural nationalism grew. A national written language and the reconstruction of a 'Norwegian' past were important regenerative issues. Skiing acquired the status of a specifically Norwegian, or 'national', sport. The mountains, too, became national symbols.[2] Skiers, as arctic explorers, were the first national 'sports heroes'. Skiing heroes, especially Fridtjof Nansen and Roald Amundsen, strengthened an increasingly national self-awareness in a young, healthy nation capable of surviving on the edge of an icy waste.

Whilst the growth of national identity at the end of the nineteenth and the beginning of the twentieth centuries has been increasingly recorded by historians during the 1990s, in contrast the period between 1905 and 1940 has received only superficial attention. It is perhaps only natural that the creation of a national identity is of greater interest than its subsequent consolidation.[3] The purpose of this study is, above all, to draw attention to the subject in the inter-war years (1918–40).

After the break-up of the union with Sweden and the attainment of independence in 1905, Norway entered a new era in its construction of a national identity. The independent state of Norway had become a political reality and the country *inter alia* began to participate in international sports events in its own right. From 1906 it participated consistently in the Olympic Games, with financial support from the state.[4] As is often the case among newly independent states, the Olympic Games provided a means of demonstrating equality of status among nations and Norway was keen to take advantage of this.

The prevailing opinion among historians has been that the inter-war years were characterized by a relatively declining general and intellectual interest in 'the national question' in Norway. Interest among intellectuals – and hence nationalism itself – was subdued.[5] Nationalist fervour waned.[6] The old 'left-wing-nationalist' movement found fewer public issues to raise. It survived as a peripheral movement, based upon language wars and opposition to the metropolitan culture of the capital. A new right-wing national movement came into being. It was an alliance between townsmen and prominent farmers from south-east Norway (and Trøndelag), and the Frisinnede Venstre (liberal left) and the Bondepartiet (the agrarian party). After the 'Greenland issue'[7] in 1931, when the nationalist and imperialist interests of the Arctic Ocean lost – this political grouping moved more and more to the right. The national rhetoric was no less clear because of this. Now Nasjonal Samling (National Union), the apt name of the Norwegian Nazi Party, and Fedrelandslaget (the League of the Fatherland) were characterized more or less by marked fascist features, in keeping with general developments in Europe. It therefore became politically correct among intellectuals, especially those on the left, to distance themselves from nationalism and the ideal of the nation. But what happened at grassroots level? Did there exist another form of nationalism with more popular support?

The intellectual support for political nationalism in fact declined in the first decades after the political independence of 1905. However, a study of the development of popular activities such as sport could reveal a quite different situation as far as cultural nationalism is concerned. We may even be able to speak of sports nationalism as a cultural phenomenon. Research into 'the people' as indicators of cultural nationalism is certainly required.

Sport as an indicator of national identity is now an internationally important field of research.[8] According to Eric Hobsbawm, sport in nineteenth-century Europe 'provided a medium for national identification and factitious community'.[9] It is clear that sport can be both an arena and an instrument for establishing national identity.[10] In Norway further research on this topic is required. This essay, therefore, is concerned with the methodological and conceptual problems it may encounter.

In international historical research we can see from the selection and interpretation of cultural concepts like nationalism and national identity that they are determined by circumstance.[11] Particular expressions and experiences of nationalism and the associated preoccupations that lie behind the use of a concept, such as national identity, vary with time and place. This is certainly true of the Nordic nations. As mentioned above, this has been very noticeable in Norway.[12] In the 1970s and 1980s especially, interest in some of the Nordic countries in investigating national identity was limited. In the 1980s Aira Kemiläinen warned against investigating the historical phenomena of nationalism and national identity unless 'one has an impartial point of view'.[13]

Norwegian and Nordic Self-Esteem

There is an especially relevant article by the Norwegian historian Stein Tønnesson on the subject of Nordic self-esteem.[14] In 1993 he wrote 'Norden speiler seg: Identitetsdebatten 1986–93', dealing with Nordic self-esteem as seen in the textbooks and history syllabuses for what in Norway is called 'secondary education at advanced level'. The national identities of each of the Nordic countries were studied thoroughly, but space prevents their consideration here.[15] Tønnesson's work details the official self-perception of each country, rather than Norwegian perceptions of the other Nordic countries. Tønnesson finds the following stereotypes in these national self-presentations, or 'legends about oneself'. In the former Nordic Great Power, Sweden, until about 1990 there was a self-conception of being Nordic in Europe, and a diminution in the importance of a national identity. The saying was that 'to be Swedish is unSwedish'.[16] Only an established Great Power could take its own national identity for granted in this way. In Denmark they have for a long time been more European, and less Nordic; they are Danes in Europe. In Norway the syllabus stresses the importance of a consciousness of national characteristics. It is more openly national, and does not reject the view that one can be proud to be Norwegian. Finnish schoolchildren, according to Tønnesson, are provided with a more factually-oriented picture of the world. Finland sees itself as advocate for peace and human rights in the UN and the world. The fifth Nordic country, Iceland, appears in its schools textbooks as an island of thinkers and authors. The reasons for the different self-perceptions are, of course, historical.

Historically the most aggressive Norwegian nationalism has been left-wing oriented and relatively democratic, while the most aggressive Swedish nationalism has been strongly right-wing oriented and authoritarian. Despite Norwegian independence in 1905 and political developments in the inter-war years these different perceptions of nationalism did not change, perhaps because Norway continued to be subordinate to Sweden politically and economically. In the national-political disputes of the 1990s over membership of the European Union this difference is clearly evident.

'The People' as Indicators of Nationalism? Methodological Problems

The debt of the two main elements of Norwegian nationalism, the political and the cultural, to the liberal ideas of the French Revolution and German romanticism is considerable.[17] Nevertheless, the special historical circumstances of its formative years gave Norwegian nationalism in the nineteenth century its own character. Opposition to the union with Sweden, the fight for parliamentary democracy and extended suffrage merged in a national political movement. As in other countries that have striven for political independence, nationalism became associated with proud words like the peoples' sovereignty, democracy, freedom and independence. At the same time there was also talk of a cultural 're-awakening', of a retrieval of the original, 'proper' Norwegian culture, language and traditions. There was a search for the 'genuine' (that is non-urban) in the Norwegian provinces. The left wing successfully appropriated these national symbols. The right wing were the losers.[18] They had in part defended the union and power of the King and government. Øyvind Østerud calls Norwegian nationalism in its 'classical period' around the turn of the last century, 'a left liberal and progressive movement'. While the Swedish equivalent was a 'conservative elite manifestation'.[19]

It is therefore important to note that the key word 'folket' (the people) existed from the start in Norwegian nationalism. It has since been used as a legitimating factor in the whole Norwegian debate on nationalism. The democratic element, in keeping with the earlier French republican ideas that the nation was created by the people, has been an inevitable precondition for discussion of the meaning of nation, national or nationalism. The idea that the people are fundamental to the concept of the nation is essential for the following discussion. When broad popular support for the politically 'nationalist' behaviour and viewpoints began to disappear, after the First World War, legitimization of these views became noticeably weaker and nationalism became a more marginal phenomenon. As a concept it acquired a decisively negative connotation before and during the Second World War. The term was monopolized by the fascists and was thus stigmatized for many decades to come. On the other hand to be truly Norwegian and 'national' was to be against the German occupiers and their Nazi sympathizers. Thus since the Second World War the term 'nationalism' in Norway has been considered an obscenity that few want to use, many have preferred the expression 'national attitude'.[20]

Historical research into such phenomena raises difficult methodological questions. National identity and nationalism as historical phenomena rather than constructs of the history of ideas require investigation of more than written expressions of national feeling. Further, the emotive nature of the concepts makes it difficult to interpret the significance of the sources. What counts as historical evidence of the importance of nationalism to the people rather than individual politicians and writers well able to express themselves? How can the voice of the people, the popular soundboard, be measured?

To answer this question an attempt must be made to separate actual historical actions from rhetoric. The comparison of support for 'nationalist' parties in elections and the study of changes in the electoral programmes of the political parties has been a traditional way of measuring shifts in the people's preoccupation with national questions. Both these 'techniques' can lead to faulty conclusions. The contents of a party programme can overlook or ignore genuine concerns. The same thing is true of the support for political parties at elections. It may be better therefore to view popular nationalism from another angle. One such possible angle is the people's interest in sport and sports events in the inter-war years. Such a study would not be without methodological pitfalls and weaknesses but may well be worth the effort.

Historical studies of this kind in a Norwegian and indeed a wider setting could attempt, in spite of obvious methodological problems, to broaden the scope of investigation beyond the intellectuals' perceptions of reality. The challenging task is to study popular involvement and popular commitment. Indeed this is what makes terms like nation and national meaningful at all. There must exist a genuine 'popular resonance', as Hobsbawm puts it,[21] for such expressions to be something other than facile or substitutional conjuring. This popular resonance can therefore be taken as the research concern here. This may usefully complement the emphasis other students of nationalism have put on the ways in which national identity has been imagined, invented or constructed.[22]

The close connection between 'people' and nation evident in French liberal thinking and in Norwegian political practice has not been inevitable. The stress on the people as 'demos' (people) rather than people as 'ethnos' (race) is, *inter alia*, a major difference between Norwegian and German nationalism.[23] In more recent Norwegian history, despite attempts from the extreme right wing in the inter-war years to introduce an ethnic and almost racist variation, 'the people' as a concept has coincided with the all-prevailing democratic view as to what a nation is and consists of.[24]

Who Are the People?

It is a truism that most historical sources have come from society's middle and social upper classes, since the working class, for the most part, only very rarely had occasion to or considered it worth while to record their own thoughts and experiences for coming generations. In any analysis of the people's nationalism, does it mean that we must refer only to those commentators who have given written expression to popular feeling? The questions become: where and how is such feeling expressed elsewhere; is it possible to operationalize 'true' national feeling as popular participation; what about the difference between volume and tension in national expressions; even if popular support is of relatively measurable extent, how shall historians record, interpret and compare such feelings, emotions, sensations; what kind of means and scales of comparison should be used; are the studies of nationalism reduced to questions about counting flags, perhaps supplemented by the number of spectators and a decibel analysis of how loudly the national anthem was sung; are these things relevant; are there nuances in popular nationalism; and how can one then distinguish between an elite's and 'the people's' evocation of nationalism?[25]

The sources become one of the problems here. Recent times have seen a renaissance of popular expressions of forms of identity and association that may just make this kind of interpretation that we are seeking, possible. These are especially to be found at local and regional levels, as for example, football fans' and other sports supporters slogans, 'war songs' and chants. Such popular expressions of identity from the inter-war years are to be found for the most part in peoples' memories, and to a lesser extent in the press. We must look more to 'popular' historical sources for the experience of fellowship, to oral history and to newspaper records rather than to traditional academic and intellectual sources.

Benedict Anderson's concept 'imagined communities' is useful in any consideration of national identity.[26] Sport as a cultural phenomenon, however, suggests a conceptual adaptation – 'experienced communities'. The roots of, and preconditions for, this common experience lie in experiences of body and soul, even if for only 90 minutes.[27] Through sport, as is frequently demonstrated, intense feelings of nationalism can be experienced. The modern history of sport records frequent instances of so-called 90 minutes nationalism.[28] It is worth mentioning how neatly adapted this form of national feeling is to modern society and the demand for short-term and not deeply felt responsibilities and loyalties. The feelings of belonging that are expressed in the response to national symbols, rituals and efforts at a football match, at a winter Olympic Games or at the Skiing World Championships, do not have to last longer than the event itself. Nor is it necessary to take any position in relation to more extensive national or political matters – a truly perfect form of belonging in Europe at a time when traditional identities, bound to class and even to nation, are perhaps diminishing.[29] What of sport in the inter-war years? Was it a potent arena for experiencing national community – long term or short term?

The Inter-War Years and National Sports

The period between the two world wars has been 'de-nationalized' by most Norwegian historians. In party politics most of Det Norske Arbeiderparti's (the Norwegian Labour Party; DNA) bourgeois opponents defined themselves as 'national', as a counterweight to the 'revolutionary internationalism' supposedly implicit in the DNA. The use of such expressions demonstrates the need to define terms in studies of national attitudes in order to distinguish between rhetoric and reality.

Until the mid-1930s, when the Labour government took office, in the worker's movement the 'tone' was international. The red flag flew on 1 May, Labour Day. Socialist ideologues called 17 May (Norway's national day), when Norwegian flags flew, the bourgeoisie's day. Confrontation was thus apparent in both symbol and rhetoric. In 1935, according to Øyvind Østerud and Hans Fredrik Dahl, the Labour Party leaders 'overcame their aversion to national symbolism and accepted both the flag and the constitutional celebrations'.[30] Tore Pryser has also touched on this in his volume on the history of the Norwegian workers' movement.[31] Is it possible that the Labour Party's change in policy was a response to popular latent nationalism? A 'popular resonance' may have predated and produced the change.

According to Hans Fredrik Dahl, who has made a thorough study of the Labour Party's ideological discussions, the party was not much concerned with 'the national question'. In contrast, the political right was inclined to use the concept 'national' as an honourable word and as a political weapon against the 'non-national' socialist party. In the 1930s the DNA used the term 'the people' as a synonym for 'the nation', which was more suspect. There are echoes here of the 1890s struggle over proper symbols. At that time, of course, it was the left who managed to portray their opponents on the right as 'non-national', while the right protested their patriotism. In the 1930s this was reversed; the workers' movement was considered 'non-national', preferring to refer to 'the people'.

The Labour Party's Foreign Secretary, historian Halvdan Koht, tried to reconcile the socialist with the nationalist perspective, in a way hardly representative of the DNA's view of nationalism before 1935. He belonged to the so-called Lysakerkretsen (the Lysaker group) together with Fridtjof Nansen and many 'national-minded' artists.[32] Koht claimed a socialist concern with the 'national question' and accused the bourgeois of being 'supposedly national', only so far as they pressed their own interests.[33] Other nationalistic forms of expression existed. Agrarian culture was considered by the remnants of the old left-national tradition more Norwegian than that of the towns.[34] In lifestyle, language and culture the farmer was more 'genuinely rooted' than the townsman. The practice of national folk dances, games and folk music gave abundant opportunity for expressing national 'traditions', well before the advent of the workers' movement. While opposition to the union with Sweden was no longer a unifying political force, the old nationalistic conflicts with neighbouring countries still existed 'as mythology in the collective present consciousness' through the medium of sport.[35]

Was sport in the inter-war years, then, an area where nationalist behaviour, although politically incorrect, could be indulged? Was sport a new and necessary symbol of nationalism? There had been national heroes long before the inter-war years, in the fields of arctic exploration, outdoor life and sport. The skaters, Axel Paulsen and Oscar Mathiesen, were, for example, household names in the 1880s and during the First World War, respectively. Did the sports heroes of the inter-war period represent something new and more national in comparison with the earlier ones, or had historical change given sport an increased significance? Certainly sport became a more important feature of society at a time when other 'national' arenas were declining or discouraged. Large sports gatherings now acquired acute symbolic significance as new manifestations of old impulses.

'Nation Building' through Sport?

The sports arena was now a place where national myths were increasingly constructed and where national stereotypes could find endorsement. International matches, international championships and similar events were organized in such a way that the national component was highlighted. The expressions 'representation' and 'representatives' echoed around these gatherings in a patriotic polarization between 'us' and 'them'. Sportsmen became national icons. On certain occasions their function as objects of association could be very clear, as the example of the so-called 'bronze medal team' of the 1936 Olympic Games football tournament shows. Did this team symbolize something new concerning national identity?

Quantitatively, it is clear that interest in football's national teams increased during the inter-war years. In 1913 the Bislet stadium had to close its gates before the international matches against Sweden.[36] Later the Frogner stadium in Kristiania (Oslo) became the national ground for a time. It was larger and could house 12,000 spectators, yet as a rule it was packed for international matches against the traditional enemies and old rivals, Sweden and Denmark. In short, in the inter-war years the number of spectators increased considerably. In response the Norwegian Football Association created new facilities. In 1923 the match against Sweden had a record 14,000 spectators. In 1926, against Denmark the number increased to

20,000. In 1929 there were 24,000 for Norway versus Sweden. In 1931 the match against 'dear brother' Sweden produced a new Scandinavian ground record with 29,400. Some 5,000 were turned away. In 1935 the match against Sweden again kicked off before a new record gate of 34,000 spectators, the maximum for the Ullevaal stadium.

All in all there was a clear increase in public interest in the national soccer team from around 1930. The 1930s were also the most successful period for the Norwegian team, providing a string of Nordic triumphs and a bronze medal in the Olympic Games in 1936. Participation in the World Championships in 1938 resulted in the narrowest of defeats by the new World Champions, Italy.[37] Public interest grew with Norway's success, but it is noteworthy that the greatest increase came before the big successes. Supporters who only follow successful teams can hardly be counted as proof that the national element did play a greater role in the 1930s than before, nor can the attendance of those who only came to experience football at a high level. The intensity of the feeling at the matches and in the newspaper reports afterwards was certainly evidence of considerable national pride. It proved that little Norway could eat 'cherries with the great'. Most important of all, the attendance record was constantly adjusted upwards when Norway played its traditional Nordic enemies. In spite of home matches against the big European teams of the time such as England, Italy and Germany, it was at the matches against the Nordic rivals that national identity could really be expressed. At these encounters it became increasingly important to be present, and take part, as a spectator.

The national football team played the greater number of their most important matches in the capital, Oslo. What interest in it was there in the rest of Norway? International matches outside Oslo attracted fewer spectators than in the capital, not unexpectedly, since these venues were in smaller cities. However, in general, a growing interest in following national teams against Sweden and Denmark and also in the Olympic Games and World Championships was apparent both in Oslo and in the rest of the country. Local newspaper coverage of national teams increased markedly, and the new radio broadcasts attracted a completely new football public throughout the country.

All national teams are by definition national representatives. However, the degree of representativeness and its role require consideration. When Norway played its first international match in 1908, it was 'inevitable' that most of the players came from the best club in the capital, Mercantile. The previous year Mercantile had been Norwegian champions. Moreover, participation in football was limited, both socially and geographically. The game grew quite quickly during and after the First World War, but the national team was mainly chosen from the central football areas: Oslo, plus the areas of lower Telemark, Vestfold and eventually Østfold. In the first match against Sweden in 1908 the national team played its role both iconically and emotionally. In 1908 memories of the battle for the dissolution of the union were still vivid. Sweden had a running boycott of Norwegian winter sportsmen and in Norway, in response, there were those who were reluctant to travel to Sweden to play against the former 'brother people'. That year Norway lost 11–3 – a confrontation with reality that led to the Football Association cancelling their planned participation in the London Olympic Games of the same year. During the match the Norwegian players saw a spectator lower the Norwegian flag. According to the memories of the team captain Hans Endrerud, 'our left winger ran to the stand and hoisted it again'[38] – in the middle of the match!

The later 'bronze team' of 1936 was called 'the people's team', mainly because of the massive public support and interest the team enjoyed. But also because the composition of the team was more representative of the country as a whole. The players came not only from the area around Oslofjorden, but also from Stavanger, Bergen and Kristiansund. And interest in the team by now was correspondingly widespread. Furthermore, the development of radio made it possible for 'the people' to take part in the celebrations to mark the surprise victory over Germany more completely and extensively than earlier. This time spontaneous festivities erupted in many parts of the country.

Workers' sports differed organizationally from that of the bourgeois. They were organized in national workers' sports associations. Nevertheless, Arbeidernes Idrettsforbund (the Workers' Sports Association) arranged international matches, sent national teams and representatives to worker 'Olympiads', and stressed strongly and repeatedly that the workers were representing 'Norway' when they took part in international competitions. This kind of nationalism was emphasized, even during the workers' movement's more revolutionary period. In addition, the movement organized children's games in Norwegian national costume, without this creating as much debate as the controversies over the Norwegian flag and 17 May. And the crowds which gathered outside the newspaper offices when the results came in from the bigger sports events in the 1930s appeared to be as large outside the office's of the workers' newspapers as outside those of other papers.

The search for national identity that had been so clear in the period 1880–1905 was in the inter-war years succeeded by a concern to consolidate that identity by integrating ever larger sections of the population or 'people' into a common culture that functioned at a more popular level. The popular interest in sport clearly consolidated a sense of national identity. International matches and skating competitions attracted large numbers of spectators, who came to see 'our Oscar' (Mathiesen) and 'our boys'.[39] Sports stars became national heroes. The achievements of Oscar Mathiesen, a surviving star from the First World War, Johan Grøttumsbråten and Thorleif Haug from the 1920s and the new heroes from the 1930s stimulated an unprecedented common national interest. From a participator's or an organizer's perspective, this was the time when the country formed club leagues and other sports networks. Governmental support for such 'nation building' did not develop until after 1945,[40] but the 'voluntary' nation building through sports networks was born and grew up in the inter-war years. In 1933, for example, Norway's Football Association organized its first 'nation-wide' club league.[41]

Even more visible as national events were the 'invented traditions'.[42] The 'Birkebeiner' (birchleg) cross-country skiing race, for example, had an obvious national-mythical origin. It was supposed to take place on the same route as the mythological journey the young prince Håkon Håkonsson took at the age of two, with two 'Birkebeiners' as companions over the mountain between Lillehammer in Gudbrandsdalen and Østerdalen in 1206, as he fled from the 'baglers'.[43] Håkon became the medieval Norwegian King (1217–63) who created the Norwegian Empire and made Norway a great power in north-west Europe, ruling over Iceland, Greenland, the Faeroes, Shetland and parts of Ireland and England. The term 'birkebeiner' has in modern times become a strong nationalist symbol. History has marked the greatest 'birkebeiner' king, Sverre Sigurdsson (1184–1202) as the Norwegian king who dared oppose the papacy and the papal envoy 'by contradicting Rome'.[44] In 1932 the first 'Birkebeiner' race was thus arranged on a solid national-historical basis, but it should be observed that the model for the Birkebeiner race came from Sweden. In 1922 the Swedes founded the 'Vasaloppet' (the Vasa race) in memory of their national hero, Gustav Vasa, and his journey from Mora to Sälen.

'The People' as Participants?

Whether the enthusiasm documented so extensively for Birger Ruud and other skiers, for Ivar Ballangrud and other skaters and for the 'bronze team', was essentially national or whether it was based on a general enthusiasm for increasingly available and publicized sports is difficult to determine unequivocally from existing sources. Was popular involvement especially strong in the inter-war years? If the Norwegians also valued foreign sportsmen and their achievements, then perhaps this could be taken to show that nationalism did not preoccupy 'the people'. The accounts of workers' sports certainly stressed intra-national 'solidarity', 'friendship' and 'internationalism'.[45] Perhaps 'the people's' interest in, and wish to spend time and money on, national rituals, symbols and other expressions of patriotism is not an entirely unambiguous indicator of growing national identity. At the same time, how sincere was socialist rhetoric?

It is a fact that sports meetings before the turn of the century had also attracted relatively large crowds of spectators. What was it, then, that was new in sport in the inter-war years? It seems there was no more flag-waving than among earlier sports spectators – in reality equally little. Exaggerated flag-waving seems to be a modern phenomenon of 90 minutes nationalism, and most noticeable in these later decades of the twentieth century.[46] Whether the sports spectators during the inter-war years attached themselves to or used other kinds of symbols is difficult to say, but the available evidence reveals few signs of this.[47]

What seems true is that the interest in such symbols increased during crises. In the decade before 1905 and around 1905 the Norwegian flag and Norwegian names were especially unifying symbols much used in sports.[48] The leader of the Norwegian team at the extra Olympic Games in Athens in 1906, Major Johan Sverre, for example, narrated the following when Norway won its first 'Olympic' gold medal: 'Our beautiful flag rose to the top of the middle pole, the winners pole, and the colours we had fought for waved over this wonderful stadium, while the Norwegian national anthem sounded over this historical site.'[49]

In Sweden during the first years after the dissolution of the Union and the Norwegian sports boycott of the Nordic Games in Stockholm in 1905, the Norwegian flag could still act as a 'red rag'. One example was the international football match in 1908, and another the skating World Championships in Østersund in 1907, when it was only with extreme reluctance that the Swedish organizers hoisted the flag for the world champion Oscar Mathiesen from Norway.

In 1940 the flag, the national anthem and the King, were all symbols of opposition to the German occupiers. At the football cup-final in the autumn of 1940 – one of the last official football matches organized by the Football Association as the country's sportsmen began a five-year sports strike shortly afterwards – some of the spectators started spontaneously to sing the national anthem, as a clear protest against the Germans who were in the stand.[50]

What was different in the inter-war years? They seem to have shown an actual diminishing use of visible symbols like flags. Yet, they seem to have developed a qualitatively different form of nation building through sport than the earlier decades. Among other things the national football team, including players from many parts of the country, was to an increasing degree a national symbol, to a greater extent than individual sportsmen, although stars and heroes such as Oscar Mathiesen and Birger Ruud also contributed enormously to establish an interest in sport that was nationalistic.

The importance of the modern media in the formation of national identity through sport cannot be stressed enough. They created a new way of taking part in and experiencing sport that did not require a physical presence at the arena. They are responsible for the ever-increasing interest in national representatives during the inter-war period. Technological developments enabled participation in events nation-wide. The problematic question of whether it was the national honour or interest in sport that weighed most in 'the peoples' minds, however, cannot be accurately ascertained. The imperatives of national honour, as in the Nordic 'brothers' settling of scores on the football field, meant that modern sport as it developed became a new means of expressing long-established antagonisms and antipathies on a public scale and in a public way previously not possible.

Extensive participation in international and national competitions of course became commonplace. On these occasions following 'our' representatives, witnessing the matches between 'us' and 'them' either on the spot or by means of new technology as history unfolded was a decisive qualitative difference from past 'experienced communities'. It is this that transformed sport into a compelling part of a nationalistic popular culture of 'the people'. The shared feeling of participation 'of the body' and 'in the heart and in the soul', on track and field as well as in the stands and via the radio, gave the sometimes elusive concept of national identity a new dimension.

NOTES

1. A Norwegian state-supported project called 'Utviklingen av en norsk nasjonal identitet på 1800-tallet' (The development of a Norwegian national identity in the 19th century) has published 17 titles on the topic between 1993 and 1997; for example, Øystein Sørensen (ed.), *Nasjonal identitet - et kunstprodukt?* (Oslo: NFR, 1994).
2. Matti Goksøyr, 'Nasjonal identitetsbygging gjennom idrett og friluftsliv', *Nytt Norsk Tidsskrift*, 2 (1994), 182–93.
3. See Miroslaw Hroch's phases of development of national identities. M. Hroch, *Social Preconditions of National Revival in Europe* (Cambridge, 1985).
4. Norway did take part with a small troupe in Paris 1900, another historical example of the IOC's lack of clarity in dealing with the concepts of sports nations as opposed to political nations.
5. Stein Tønnesson, 'Norden speiler seg. Identitetsdebatten 1986–93', *(Norsk) Historisk Tidsskrift*, 3 (1993), 360–97:
6. Ø. Østerud, *Hva er nasjonalisme?* (Oslo, 1994), p.43.
7. 'Arctic imperialist' interests in Norway tried to occupy parts of eastern Greenland, claiming this was old Norwegian territory. The new colonial power in Greenland, Denmark naturally disliked this. The two agreed to bring the case before the international court in the Hague, which ruled against Norway on all issues.

8. There have been a number of studies in the 1990s. See, for example, J.A. Mangan (ed.), *Tribal Identities: Nationalism, Europe, Sport* (London and Portland: Frank Cass, 1996), V. Duke and L. Crolley, *Football, Nationality and the State* (Harlow: Longman, 1996) and Derek Birley, *Sport and the Making of Britain* (Manchester: Manchester University Press, 1993). Birley's book is one of a trilogy, the other volumes being *Land of Sport and Glory* (1995) and *Playing the Game* (1995), which update previous studies.

9. Eric Hobsbawm and Terence Ranger (eds.), *The Invention of Tradition* (Cambridge, 1984), p.300.

10. See M. Goksøyr, *Vi gir alt for Norge: Om nasjonal reisning og kulturell tilhørighet* (Oslo, 1996).

11. Østerud gives an informative picture of the representations of the nation on the scale between a political-civic and a ethnic-cultural apprehension (1994), pp.19–58.

12. Ibid., pp.42–5.

13. Kemiläinen reported suspicions and allegations of being a nationalist in disguise if one took interest in the topic of nationalism in the early 1980s. Aira Kemiläinen, 'The Idea of Nationalism', *Scandinavian Journal of History*, 9, 1 (1984), 39. One is reminded of Hobsbawm's statement that 'no serious historian of nations and nationalism can be a committed political nationalist ... Nationalism requires too much belief in what is patently not so'. Eric Hobsbawm, *Nations and Nationalism since 1789* (Cambridge, 1991), p.12.

14. S.Tønnesson, 'Norden speiler seg: Identitetsdebatten 1986–93' (*Norsk) Historisk Tidsskrift*, 3 (1993), pp.360–97. See also Tønnesson, 'History and National Identity in Scandinavia: The Contemporary Debate' (unpublished doctoral thesis, University of Oslo, 1991).

15. For example, Ole Feldbæk (ed.), *Dansk identitetshistorie*, vols.1–4 (Copenhagen, 1991–92). A. Linde-Laursen and J.O. Nilsson (eds.), *Nationella identiteter i Norden – ett fullbordat prosjekt?* (Stockholm, 1991).

16. Linde-Laursen and Nilsson, p.9, Tønnesson (1993), p.365.

17. The political and cultural dimensions of the concept of nationalism are otherwise thoroughly dealt with in several studies: Anthony D. Smith, *National identity* (London, 1991), Ernest Gellner, *Nations and Nationalism* (Oxford, 1983), Eric Hobsbawm, *Nations and Nationalism since 1789*, Benedict Anderson, *Imagined Communities* (London, 1991), Liah Greenfeld, *Nationalism: Five Roads to Modernity* (Harvard, 1993), John Hutchinson, *Modern Nationalism* (London, 1994). Smith's definition of nationalism as a 'political ideology with a cultural doctrine at its centre' (p.74) in this way does not imply elements of chauvinism or racism.

18. Helge Danielsen discusses the tenability of this statement in, *'Rakrygget og selvtillidsfuldt Fædrelandssind': Om holdninger til det nasjonale i Aftenpostens redaksjonsmiljø i siste del av unionstiden* (Oslo, 1997).

19. Østerud, p.42.

20. Ibid., p.44.

21. Hobsbawm and Ranger, *The Invention of Tradition*, p.264.

22. Anderson, op.cit.; Hobsbawm and Ranger, op.cit.; Gellner, op.cit.; Smith, op.cit.

23. See Lars Christian Trägårdh, *The Concept of the People and the Construction of Popular Political Culture in Germany and Sweden: 1848–1933* (Berkeley: University of California, 1993), for a further discussion realting to German and Swedish history.

24. Perhaps because the Norwegian nation was perceived as ethnically very homogenous, partly as a consequence of an efficient assimilation policy towards the Sami population in the north of Norway.

25. See Jens Arup Seip, 'Nasjonalisme som vikarierende motiv', in Seip, *Fra embetsmannsstat til ettpartistat og andre essays* (Oslo, 1963).

26. Anderson, op.cit.

27. About the term '90 minutes nationalism' and modernity, see M.Goksøyr, 'Norway and the World Cup: Cultural diffusion, sportification and sport as a vehicle for nationalism', in John Sugden and Alan Tomlinson (eds.), *Hosts and Champions: Soccer Cultures, National Identities and the USA World Cup* (Arena, 1994), pp.189–90.

28. Since this is originally a Scottish expression, examples from here are the most known. However, the term can be applied universally. Grant Jarvie and Graham Walker (eds.),

Scottish Sport in the Making of the Nation: Ninety Minutes Patriots? (Leicester, 1994).

29. For a discussion of this issue see Mangan, Tribal Identities, pp.8–9.
30. Hans Fredrik Dahl, Fra klassekamp til nasjonal samling (Oslo, 1969). Østerud, p.44.
31. Tore Pryser, Klassen og nasjonen 1935–1946: Arbeiderbevegelsens historie i Norge, Vol.4 (Oslo, 1988).
32. Bodil Stenseth, En norsk elite: Nasjonsbyggerne på Lysaker 1890–1940 (Oslo, 1993).
33. Halvdan Koht, Norsk vilje (Oslo Noregs Boklag, 1933).
34. Jostein Nerbøvik, 'Den norske kulturnasjonalismen' and Bodil Stenseth, 'Borgerlig nasjonalisme og bygdenasjonalisme', in Øystein Sørensen (ed.), Nasjonal identitet – et kunstprodukt? (Oslo: KULT 30, 1994).
35. Berge Furre, Vårt hundreår: Norsk historie 1905–1990 (Oslo, 1991), p.139.
36. Asbjørn Halvorsen (ed.), Norges fotball leksikon, Vol.1 (Oslo, 1947). Figures in this section are from this source.
37. Through a very dubious refereeing decision (according to Norwegian journalists) when a Norwegian goal was disallowed for offside. 'It was never an offside' were the words of the Norwegian Broadcasting Corporation's (NRK) man on the spot, Per Christian Andersen (NRK, radiotape 5/6–1938).
38. Hans Endrerud, 'Vår første landskamp', in Kristian Henriksen and Bjørn Storberget (eds.), På tokt med Norges landslag (Oslo, 1951), p.19.
39. Finn Olstad, 'Idrett – en del av historien?', in K.Kjeldstadli, J.E.Myhre and T.Pryser (eds.), Valg og vitenskap: Festskrift til Sivert Langholm (Otta, 1997), p.172. However, Olstad suggests that skating stars also created national interest before this period.
40. E. Andersen and K. Asdal in M. Goksøyr (ed.), Kropp, kultur og tippekamp: Statens idrettskontor, STUI og Idrettsavdelingen 1946–1996 (Oslo, 1996).
41. Although nation-wide might be too strong a word for a league that did not cover the country's three northern counties as well as Sogn og Fjordane in the West.
42. Hobsbawm and Ranger, The Invention of Tradition.
43. Members of the antagonists, the Bishop's Party in the Norwegian civil wars.
44. A saying that slightly rewritten was taken into the national anthem's lyrics by Bjørnstjerne Bjørnson in 1859.
45. Petter Larsen, Med AIF-stjerna på brystet: Glimt fra norsk arbeideridrett (Oslo, 1979).
46. M.Goksøyr, 'Nasjonal identitetsbygging gjennom idrett og friluftsliv'. Also. M. Goksøyr, 'Football; development and identity in a little nation. A historical outline of football culture, spectator interest and playing styles around the Norwegian national team in the 20th century', Paper for the international conference 'Football and Identities' Brisbane, Australia, 21–23 March 1997.
47. When, for example, Norwegian rowers carried a Norwegian flag into the Olympic Stadium in Berlin 1936, both the rowers themselves and other spectators thought it unusual. Aftenposten 1993.
48. Henrik Angell, Norway's first IOC member, gives a similar impression in his report from the Olympic Congress in Brüssels 1905. Revue Olympique (1905).
49. Johan Sverre, 'Athenerfærden 1906', in Idrætsminder: Fortalt af idrætsmænd (Oslo, 1924), p.39.
50. Stein Tønnesson, Norsk idrettshistorie, vol.2: Folkehelse, trim, stjerner (Oslo, 1986), p.30.

A Mutual Dependency:
Nordic Sports Organizations and the State

JOHAN R. NORBERG

Nordic Sports Organizations' Two Functions in Society

The political situation in the Nordic countries has been summarized, not least by foreign observers, under the heading 'the Nordic model'. What has tended above all to be seen as typically Nordic is how different social groups through co-operation and mutual compromise have managed to build up modern welfare states and, in an international context, a high standard of living. More precisely, the occurrence of a dialogue and a *feeling of mutual understanding* in Nordic political culture has been seen, from an international perspective, as exceptional. The Nordic model has become synonymous with 'the politics of compromise'.[1]

The essentially voluntary nature of organizations constitutes a central part of the Nordic model. These organizations take part in Nordic politics through direct discussion with the representatives of the political parties in power; they co-operate in official inquiries and constitute important bodies of reference. Sometimes even independent groupings of citizens carry out public tasks. According to the most basic pattern of government, official policy is formulated and decided by parliament, while its implementation is executed by the civil service and public boards. When in different ways the state allows non-governmental organizations to take part in the political process, the much discussed concept of *corporatism* tends to be used. The characteristics for corporative arrangements are that there is only one strong organization within a specific field of interest, and that that organization has received a government-sanctioned monopoly to represent the citizens in this field.[2]

Even if it rarely happens, Nordic sport can be appropriately described by concepts such as 'the Nordic model' and incorporatism. In the main, sport has been developed and organized on a voluntary basis. Its scope, its geographical spread and its democratic organizational structure justify consideration of the 'sports movement' – a collective term for the voluntarily organized activity – on an equal footing with other Nordic *popular movements*. But although the sports movement appears in a number of ways as the prototype for voluntary organizations, the activity has developed through an intimate co-operation with public institutions. That the state has considered sport as good for the community has resulted in both extensive economic support and an influential role for sports institutions in the sports-political process. This corporative co-operation has with time led to the sports movement's central organizations having *double community roles*: they are today both the *highest instance of the popular movement* and also *quasi-authorities* in their respective countries.[3]

The participation of voluntary organizations in the political process and the corporative administrative model have for long been central areas of research in both political science and modern political history. Interest has centred mainly on the connections between the economic interests of organizations and the state. The relations between political power and other forms of citizens' groupings, including the sports movement, have been greatly neglected. Not even Nordic research into the history of sport has paid much attention to corporative arrangements in sport. Not one extensive work has been published, nor have comparative studies been attempted, although in the Nordic countries there are both interesting similarities and significant differences.

There is, however, reason to study the sports movement's double role in society. By focusing our attention on how the Nordic sports organizations have been given rights to act 'in place of authority' we can then both vary the picture of the sports movement's non-governmental and autonomous character, and at the same time deepen our knowledge of the dual power base and the unique function that the Nordic sports movement has in modern society. In addition, the corporative arrangements between the state and the sports movement's own institutions differ in essential ways from the area of policy that has been studied in more traditional corporative research. To study Nordic sports from a corporative angle can also contribute to more broadly based research on 'the Nordic model' in Nordic politics.[4]

The aim of this study is as follows. First, the relationship between the Nordic sports organizations and the state will be discussed in the light of the established research on corporatism. Then the historical background to the introduction of corporative arrangements in Nordic sport will be outlined. Corporative political arrangements and administrative solutions often occur in the Nordic political culture, as mentioned above. This means that the development of corporatism in Nordic sport must be studied from the standpoint of its historical and political connections. Purely organizational conditions in sport must be seen in relation to the Nordic political system and the development of society in general. Corporate arrangements in sport are closely connected with the creation of the Nordic welfare state. They are the consequence of a process whereby sport developed from a autonomous part of the civil society into a socio-political concern. This important change in the role of sport in society will be described and then followed by a short description of the development of different forms of corporative structures in Nordic sport. On the basis of these examples, and by way of conclusion, a number of common 'Nordic' lines of development will be shown in the relations between voluntarily organized sports and the state.

Unfortunately Finland will be omitted. Although Finnish research on the history of sport is substantial, the language barrier impedes a comparative study. In this connection the 'Nordic' concept refers only to Sweden, Norway and Denmark.

The Influence of Sports Organizations on the Political System: A Dilemma

Voluntary organizations are both necessary and potentially dangerous in all democratic systems. Consequently, the participation of voluntary organizations in the political process and corporative models of administration have attracted both supporters and critics. Supporters tend to point out that the right of the individual to organize himself is an essential part of political life and that to restrict this right would be in breach of basic democratic principle. In addition, it is contended that organizations are necessary to a functioning democratic process since they act as important complementary channels between the state and the citizen. It follows from this that parliamentary elections are in themselves not enough to guarantee a functioning democratic system, and individual citizens themselves must be active in political life in order to strengthen and clarify their demands on elected representatives. 'Participative democracy' is a common term used to express this point of view. Furthermore, corporative arrangements give different interest groups the opportunity to meet, discuss and agree upon solutions that all can accept. This makes other and more conflict-charged forms of action superfluous. In this way corporatism generates a 'calmer' political climate.

The critics of corporatism, nevertheless, tend to object to this reasoning and instead stress that individuals should use their political influence in parliamentary elections. If organizations are allowed to influence the political process then parliamentary power will diminish. Those citizens who belong to strong organizations will receive something like a 'double' vote. Those citizens who belong to organizations with fewer resources – or those who are not organized at all – thus have less chance to defend their interests.[5]

Another problem concerns the question of responsibility. If non-governmental organizations participate in political decision-making then individuals can no longer hold politicians and civil servants wholly responsible for the political decisions made. Nor will citizens in general be able to influence the choice of individuals who represent the free organizations, because these representatives cannot be elected in general elections.[6]

For public institutions as well as free organizations corporative arrangements mean both *opportunity and risk*. Close co-operation with organizations provides the state with information on the wishes of large groups of people. A decision that has the broad backing of important organizations has, therefore, a high degree of legitimacy and is easy to execute. As the state allows organizations a certain amount of influence in the decision-making process then potential opposition groups are by the same token bound by the decisions taken. At the same time the state takes a risk when it gives non-governmental organizations influence over the formation of policies. The risk is one of domination by organizations which are too strong, with the result that influential special interests change the political process to the detriment of the interests of society as a whole.

The same risk arises for the organizations. Close co-operation with the state can give the organizations governmental legitimacy, political influence and often economic support. In other words, an organization can gain much by developing a close relationship with public decision-makers. The risk is that the organization will be co-opted by the state: that it develops a dependence on the state and that its representative in the administration becomes the administration's representative in the organization. The organization's autonomy is, therefore, threatened, members' support for their own representative is undermined and internal unity weakened. At worst the future of the organization is threatened. Corporative arrangements thus always lead to ambiguity in the division of power and responsibility as between the state and the free organizations.[7]

Corporative research has concentrated more or less exclusively on the economic and political interest groups' influence on the public political process. There are certain problems with using this model in a study of the sports movements' relationship to the state. While the interest groups' activities are geared to influencing the way society and public politics develop, the sports movements have had only minor political ambitions. The *raison d'être* of the sports movements' institutions has always been to organize an activity – to practise sport. Certainly the sports movements have wished their activities to be seen as useful to society – a precondition for public support – but otherwise their main aim has always been organizational autonomy. The basic problem for the sports movements has been how to combine their wish to organize independently and run their sporting activities in relation to the society around them, and at the same time persuade the public institutions to support them financially, but not to control them.[8]

Consequently, what must be studied is the relationship between the sports movements and the state. A topic not considered by traditional corporative research. The main question is not to what extent the sports' own institutions have influenced public sports policies, but instead to what degree the public institutions have influenced non-governmental and voluntarily organized activities. This does not mean that the corporative perspective lacks relevance. What is to be considered is *de facto* the interplay between extensive voluntary citizen associations and the public authority. A great deal can be learned from traditional corporative research, but it must also be borne in mind that sports organizations differ in important ways from organizations with explicit political ambitions.

Historical Background: Prospects for Corporative Administration Models

The presence of numerous voluntary organizations in the Nordic countries can be traced back to the nineteenth century. Before this period there were no voluntary society activities as understood today. Instead Nordic citizens were forced into a number of spiritual as well as worldly communities. It is true that there were corporations in the form of guilds and village communities, but these can in no way be compared in quantity or importance with the character of the organizations that now made their appearance. Groupings of citizens came into being as a reaction to the new shape of society. As state and church increasingly lost their hold over the citizen a vacuum was created in which individuals could join together and influence the development of the community.[9]

In Swedish historical research on the development of modern organizations, a distinction is made between two separate types of organization: associations and popular movements.[10] The associations were a mainly middle-class organizational model, the origins of which can be traced back to the clubs and closed communities of the eighteenth century. Even though the associations were in principle open to everybody, the upper classes dominated with patriarchal concern they worked mostly in the social field in, *inter alia*, philanthropy, teetotalism and education. Often these associations worked in conjunction with the state and the church and even provided services the state was unable to provide at that time. Not only socio-economically but also organizationally the associations were distinguished by a 'top-down' structure where power and influence were concentrated in independent and powerful committees. Meetings were normally restricted and advanced organizational structures with regional and local organizations were lacking.[11]

The popular movements in many ways contradicted the associations.

While the associations usually worked in harmony with the state, the popular movements protested against the existing state of society. While the associations tried to retain the existing order in society, the popular movements wanted to change it. Furthermore, this latter organizational form was built literally on 'people in movement': it was through the active participation of many citizens that the movements generated strength. They had a marked 'bottom-up' character which was also mirrored in their complex pyramid-like organizational structure. At the bottom were the individual members, belonging to local societies. These societies were in turn connected to district organizations which were bound together in a common national governing board.[12]

The importance of the popular movements for the development of society in the Nordic countries cannot be exaggerated. With these movements voluntary societies and horizontal structures of loyalty came to replace the more vertical solidarity structures of the old society. A democratic and equal work environment was developed which then was taken over by succeeding movements. This form of organization also meant that citizens looked for dialogue with the opposition: it was a path of non-violence. The early popular movements contributed indirectly to a less turbulent political climate in the Nordic countries.[13]

The Organization of Voluntary Sports

The earliest national organization of Nordic sport was in organizations of a clearly association character. It started with the rifle association. In Norway, the 'Centralforeningen for Udbredelse af Legemsøvelser og Vaabenbrug' was founded in 1861. In Denmark, the 'Centralkomiteen for oprettelse af skytteforeninger' was founded in the same year. The purpose of these groupings was to strengthen on a voluntary basis their country's willingness and ability to defend itself. Although the main activity of the clubs was shooting, gymnastics were also practised. Soon other associations were founded and can be seen as pioneers of Nordic sport. In Norway and Sweden societies for promoting, among other things, skiing, tourism and outdoor activities appeared. The first such society which concentrated simply on sport was founded in Norway in 1893 when, because of reorganization in the Norwegian rifle association, the Centralforeningen lost its place at the head of the movement and had to find a new role. With the same military purpose in mind, it chose to support 'other' sports, under the name of 'Centralforeningen for Udbredelse af Idraet'.[14]

It was a characteristic of the early sports organizations in the Nordic countries to use sport as a means to achieve improved national defence, a stronger feeling of national identity and better general health. It was the upper classes of society who initiated and organized the activities. The aims of sport as well as its socio-economic exclusive leadership meant there were close contacts with the political power. In connection with other voluntary activities these pioneer sports organizations were early given state support. The Nordic sports movements did not emerge from the lower and middle strata of the population. The initiative, mobilization and finance came from the upper stratum.[15]

Interest in sports increased markedly during the last decade of the nineteenth century, as can be seen from, *inter alia*, the rapid increase in the formation of societies and competitive activities and a greater interest on the part of the general public. During this period the first specialized leagues for particular sports came into being at a national level. In these leagues and in the local sports clubs, sport was played for sport's sake. The rise of new societies and the dawn of national and international competitions gave rise to a need for common popular organizations, which could prepare for competitions, work out standardized competitive rules and solve possible points of dispute. The turn of the century saw an organizational renewal in Nordic sport. The centrally governed associations, already established, had been effective in creating an interest in sport but less effective as leaders of the actual activities. They became an organizational model and were overtaken by a more democratic organizational model.

The ways in which the new popular leagues were organized in the Nordic countries were so similar that it is possible to speak of the rise of a 'Nordic' organizational model. It was distinguished by the way it solved the problems of conflicting interests: those of the single sports clubs as against the multi-sports clubs; those of the national interest as against provincial and district interests. The result was an organizational structure which included a horizontal structure where the national organizations constituted an umbrella organization for relatively autonomous specialized leagues and a more traditional vertical and pyramid-like structure of clubs and district leagues under a central national leadership.

The 'Nordic' model of organization was first established in Sweden. 'Svenska gymnastik- och idrottsforeningars riksforbund' (since 1947 'Sveriges riksidrottsförbund', RF) was founded in 1903 and developed the organizational structure described above during its first years. Very soon RF also became the central controlling institution for sport in the country. All clubs wishing to conduct serious competitions were obliged to join. In other words RF quickly gained control over the voluntary organized sport in Sweden – and maintains this position to this day. At the side of RF until the early 1930s 'Sveriges centralforening för idrottens främjände' was responsible for the sports movements' financial and publicity activities.[16]

In Norway, the first umbrella organization of independent specialized leagues was founded in 1910 under the name of 'Norges Riksforbund for Idraet'.[17] In contrast to the Swedish RF the Norwegian equivalent was not divided into districts at first and all power was concentrated in the specialized leagues. For various reasons the organization experienced internal disagreements. Not until 1919 did the league settle into a more 'Nordic' model with a vertical as well as a horizontal organizational structure – this time under the name of 'Norges Landsforbund for Idrett' (since 1945 'Norges Idrettsforbund', NIF, after a merger with 'Arbeidernes Idrettsforbund'.[18]

In Denmark the development of the sports movements took other interesting patterns. The competitively oriented sports were concentrated in the big cities and organized in 'Dansk IdrætsForbund', DIF, which was founded in 1896. As in Norway, this league became early on, in 1904, an umbrella organization for autonomous specialized leagues. A common division into districts took place in the 1940s. In the Danish rural areas, and with roots in the rifle association, there developed simultaneously with competitive sport a 'popular' sports movement without the same focus on performance and results. The central leagues for this activity became 'De Danske Skytteforeninger' (since 1919 'De Danske Skytte og Gymnastikforeninger, 1930 De Danske Skytte, Gymnastlk og Idraetsforeninger') and 'De Danske Gymnastikforeninger' (since 1965 'De Danske Gymnastik og Ungdomsforeninger'). In 1992 the two organizations merged to form 'Danske Gymnastlk- og Idrætsforeninger', DGI.[19]

The Early Sports Movement: A Popular Movement Mobilized by the Middle Class

From the turn of the century, voluntarily organized sports in the Nordic countries began increasingly to take the form of a popular movement. The earlier centrally governed leading bodies were replaced by democratically constituted popular leagues. At the same time the geographical expansion of activities and the extensive recruitment of members started in earnest. But although the sports movement took the form of a popular movement, it diverged in important ways from other popular movements. Above all, the sports movement organized a straightforward activity. Voluntarily organized sport did not arise from the general population as a protest and reaction against the existing state of society. It was instead the upper classes who initiated and organized sport. Even after the reorganization at the turn of the century, the sports movement's exclusive leadership continued in power.[20]

The sports ideology put forward by the representatives of the sports movement, particularly in connection with their applications for state support, was noticeably conservative. They maintained that sport furthered defence capability and willingness, strengthened national identity and improved general physical well-being. They also argued that international competitions created an international feeling of brotherhood and that sport in general reduced antagonism between the classes. This was an ideology aimed at preserving, not challenging, the *status quo*.[21]

It is difficult to analyse the sports movement that began to be institutionalized at the turn of the century. Simply put, it had the form of a popular movement, but its content – its historical origins, ideology and social structure – retained many of the characteristics of the earlier associations. It may be described as a popular movement mobilised by the middle class. This somewhat contradictory wording hints at two important points: that sport had become a broadly based movement and that its origin was very different from, for example, the workers movement and other popular movements of socio-political protest.[22]

It is important to emphasize the sports movement's unique position as a popular movement and its position *vis-à-vis* the state. This explains both why the sports movement applied for support from public institutions and why its activities were quickly favoured by the state. It explains also why the sports movement, in comparison with other popular movements, speedily received both state grants and official status. By supporting sport the state could promote, at low cost, both idealism and patriotism.

Already during the first two decades of the century all the Nordic popular sports leagues received regular and annual state grants.[23] For the voluntarily organized sports this created the opportunity to develop their activities. At the same time the state grants entailed certain limitations on the organizations' independence and freedom of action. Particularly in Norway, on several occasions the state used the influence that comes with state support to ensure that sport took a form favourable to the state. The most obvious way in which the state exercised its influence was its active participation in the organizational changes in the Norwegian sports movement during the first decade of the century. The availability of state grants meant that, at least formally, non-governmental matters became the object of parliamentary decisions.[24]

In Denmark the state chose mainly to support the 'popular' sports organizations. This is perhaps not surprising bearing in mind that the activity grew out of the rifle association and in this way was connected to the military. Competitive sports in DIF did not receive the same official status and were given fewer grants. The league was, therefore, more independent *vis-à-vis* the state than its equivalents in the neighbouring countries. At the same time the league became dependent to a greater extent on other sources of finance, mainly on membership fees and donations from the business world.[25]

It is debatable whether the presence of state grants can be considered as a form of corporatism. In the sense of straight grant-giving it can be seen as such. State grants mean *de facto* that non-governmental organizations pursue an activity acceptable to the government and partly funded by public money. At the same time this is almost to misunderstand 'corporatism' as a concept. The Nordic sports movement came into being in the civil society. Sport was a leisure activity based on idealistic efforts unrelated to the main fields of public politics. Sport was not primarily a field of governmental responsibility or a socio-political matter. What we see here is how the state encouraged, and influenced, a voluntary, private activity. This should not be confused with the situation where voluntary organizations have an authoritative role or enjoy an influence legitimized by government through the political process. Sport was an activity mainly exercised outside the arena of public politics.

The Development of the Modern Welfare States

In socio-historical research there is a clear consensus that the 1930s was an important decade for the subsequent development of Nordic politics. During this period social democracy developed as a political force which was long to dominate the governments of all the Nordic countries. Welfare state thinking took root. At the same time, when the social democrats assumed power their traditional national politics were replaced by consensus politics. Their programme of economic and social reform had as its goal greater equality and well-being for the whole nation, to be achieved through co-operation and understanding across the political barriers.[26]

These ideas manifested themselves in similar ways in all the Nordic countries. To win support for their economic policy and to reduce the high rate of unemployment the social democratic governments concluded agreements with the farmers' parties. The importance of these 'historical compromises' between workers and farmers cannot be overestimated. A more stable parliamentary base permitted the adoption of a more long-term political programme and created the political climate in which the Nordic welfare states could develop. These compromises also showed that political co-operation was possible. Thus from the beginning of the 1930s a long period of consensus politics commenced.[27]

At the same time, and partly as a consequence of this new political climate, the state's attitude to voluntary organizations changed. It became clear that the development of society could be guided effectively and thoroughly by co-operation and to a certain extent through voluntary organizations. These were now seen more as a means and less as a threat. Corporative arrangements became a method of solving political problems.

In short, the development of society in the 1930s went from class struggle to class co-operation – from conflict to consensus. 'The Nordic model' was being developed.[28]

Sport: From Leisure Pursuit to Society Concern

The political development of the 1930s influenced the relationship between the state and the sports movement. The political advance of the social democrats might have been a setback for the established organizations of the 'middle class' sports movements. Already in the 1920s workers' sport was beginning to develop in the Nordic countries. Especially in Norway the organization of sport based on the ideology of class struggle was a real challenge to the Norwegian middle-class sports movement. For the reform-minded social democrats, however, a separate workers' sports movement was not the best possible alternative. Social democratic policy was not concerned with replacing the *status quo* with a socialist alternative. Its aim was to work within society and to transform the already established middle-class institutions. For the Nordic sports movements this meant taking a political stand against workers' sport to the advantage of the already established leagues. Thus the 'middle-class' sports movement also became a social democratic project.[29]

What did affect the relationship between the sports movement and the state, however, was the development of the welfare state.[30] Social democratic welfare state ideology and social welfare reforms broadened the scope of public politics. In the spirit of social engineering many aspects of social life became the objects of political concern. Questions that earlier were not primarily matters for state interference became the concern of national politics. Not least, leisure time and the situation of young people were politicized. Indirectly this affected the state's attitude to sport, which with its physical and moral enhancing qualities was perceived to a greater extent than before as serving the common good. Sport promoted the physical well-being of the people. Further, the usual activities and the accompanying club life were very suitable as leisure activities for young people. With the development of the welfare state sport became a question of national politics and an area of public concern. In short, sport became a part of the social democratic welfare state project.[31]

Welfare politics were accompanied by 'the concept of the strong society'. Central to this concept is the belief that direct state intervention results in the most effective collective activities.[32] This also influenced the relationship between the state and voluntarily organized sport. That sport even in the future should be run by non-governmental organizations on a voluntary basis was never questioned. But as a consequence of sport becoming a matter of national politics at the same time as trust: in the capabilities of national politicians increased, politicians be came more interested in the use of public funds. To present a somewhat simplified argument, during the period up to the Second World War it can be said that the sports movements attempted to extend state responsibility for sport – first and foremost by obtaining larger and larger state grants. It was now questionable whether the sports movement, despite the increase in public support, could retain its independence. The central issue for the state now was whether there should be a state bureaucracy for the preparation and use of public grants, or whether these tasks in the future should be allotted to the independent organizations.

The issue of the responsibility of the state and the independence of organizations in sport was discussed and debated extensively after the Second World War. Now the voluntary organizations were considered a possible administrative solution of a political problem. Thus for the first time it is possible to talk about corporatism in sport. The following examples will demonstrate three different solutions to the allocation of authority.

Three Examples of Corporative Structures in Nordic Sporting Activities

The Swedish Model[3]

In Sweden, corporative administration of relations between the sports movements and the state was established earlier than in the other neighbouring Nordic countries. RF was first given its task as the administrative guardian in the early 1930s. In practice the league included all the organized sports movements, and the state thus delegated administrative duties to the movement's own central body. Not least of the administrative tasks was the administration of state grants for sports. RF became the central body under the government for administering these grants. It estimated the needs of all the sports organizations for state funding. This applied to organizations within its own league as well as to other organizations. Even applications from municipalities for state aid – for example, the building of sports grounds –were dealt with by the RF. Its role in the matter of state grants expanded with experience. There was never any formal parliamentary decision giving RF the right to act 'in place of authority'.

Sweden led the way in state financing of sports, but the sports movement maintained that the aid was not adequate and various suggestions for financial help from outside the state budget were discussed. The suggestion that was finally tried out was to establish a state-controlled betting office. In 1934, following a government decision, a joint-stock company was launched to organize betting in connection with sports competitions. The company's profits, after certain deductions, were to go to the sports organizations. The enterprise was successful and the sports movement's finances improved greatly during the 1930s. Unfortunately the scheme turned out to be rather too lucrative. At the outbreak of war in 1939 grants for sport were reduced appreciably. After the war all estimates for sports funding again exceeded the state budget. The state was no longer in favour of funding sport from betting.[34]

Between 1945 and 1955 decisive organizational changes took place in the sports movement. In 1945 the 'Svenska korporations-idrottsförbundet' (Korpen) was founded and in 1955 'Skid- och friluftsfrämjandet' (Främjandet) left the RF league. The movement, therefore, consisted of three major national organizations; and conflict between RF and the separate leagues ensued. At issue was RF's monopoly of financial control. Korpen and Främjandet argued that the sports movement consisted of three completely separate national organizations. RF was the main organization for competition-oriented sports, while Korpen and Främjandet were responsible respectively for non-competitive exercise and outdoor activities. That the state allowed one of the three branches of the sports movement, RF, to exercise straightforward control over the others was seen by Korpen and Främjandet as a direct threat to their own leagues. They also maintained that RF, when allocating grants, supported its own specialized leagues and favoured competitions at the expense of other organizations. According to Korpen and Främjandet, this was partly because RF was competition-oriented and had too little sympathy for non-competitive exercise and outdoor activities. They also suspected that RF 'starved' the other leagues in order to incorporate them into its own organization.

The criticism of RF's exercise of its official duties impressed the state. RF's domination no longer had credibility in the collected sports movement. At the same time the range of state support for sport was not settled. The time was ripe for a thorough investigation of the future shape of Swedish sport.

From 1955 to 1970 the 'guardianship' issue was at the heart of what can be called the Swedish 'sports war'. Three state commissions tried to solve the problem. The first commission proposed a permanent government board for sports issues.[35] This administrative solution would ensure equal treatments for all three leagues. At the same time the state could, by this administrative solution, have greater influence over the use of public funds. Unsurprisingly this solution was strongly opposed by the greater part of the sports movement, led by RF. It was seen as unwelcome state *dirigisme* of voluntary sport and above all, as a threat to the whole future existence of the sports movement as an independent popular movement. Consequently no official sports board was established.

The task of the second commission was to bring about the unification of the different 'branches' of the sports movement. From the state point of view unification would have been an ideal solution. If the sports movement could have been reunited in one national organization then the corporate arrangements could have been reinstated. With only one league no organization could have been considered as having a favoured status. Conflict between RF and the other leagues, however, was too great to bring about unification and the commission achieved no noticeable result.[36]

A third and final solution was presented by the sports commission of 1965 which proposed that RF, in spite of criticism from the other leagues, should be given guardianship.[37] This solution was accepted by a large majority in the Swedish parliament. Why the state opted for a solution which it knew to be disliked by parts of the Swedish sports movement is unclear. It may be that there was simply no other alternative, particularly as there was such strong opposition to anything that could be interpreted as state *dirigisme*. Nevertheless the decision can also be seen as a conscious attempt by the state to unite the different leagues of the sports movement. By giving RF a 'most favoured' position the state created a strong incentive for the other leagues to join the RF-league. The outcome of the 1965 commission is, in other words, an example of state intervention in matters which were formally an internal matter for free organizations. The decision is also a clear example of how a structure of free organizations can be affected by a political decision. In 1975 Korpen chose to join the RF-league. RF's guardianship role and its 'most favoured' position *vis-à-vis* the state played a part in this development.

The Norwegian Model[38]

The origins of the Norwegian model go back to the German occupation of Norway during the Second World War. The Norwegian sports movement had early demonstrated its dislike of German attempts to strengthen state influence on sport. The sports movement argued that it was a non-governmental popular movement and took neither orders nor guidelines from the German authorities. This opposition was demonstrated by the cessation of all voluntary sporting activities in the so-called 'idrettsfronten'. At the end of the war the sports movement also played an important part in the Norwegian home guard. Unfortunately the sports strike and the German occupation led to an extensive destruction of the existing sports grounds and at the end of the war there was need for public financial support for the reconstruction of Norwegian sport. The independent patriotic action of the sports movement during the occupation strongly enhanced the legitimacy of its claims for support.

The Norwegian state was willing to offer extensive financial sponsorship of sport. At the same time the economy was hard pressed because of the war. The solution was following the Swedish model, to establish a betting office, where part of the profits were reserved by statute for sport. This funding together with government grants soon exceeded all expectations. However, questions remained: which institution would be responsible for the division of these new funds; and which sporting activities should be given priority? The state had to choose between corporative co-operation with the central organization of sports, NIF, or the establishment of its own state sports bureaucracy. It chose the latter.

At the same time as the establishment of the betting office in 1946 'Statens Idrettskontor' (from 1950, 'Statens Ungdoms- och Idrettskontor', STUI) were founded. Rolf Hofmo, a rather controversial social democrat, who had earlier led the workers' sport movement was chosen to head it. Although the sports movement now received more state funding, the chosen administrative solution meant that the state strengthened its influence over sports policy. All applications for grants from the betting-profits were handled by STUI, which reviewed them and made recommendations for the distribution of funds, which then went to the state for a final decision. Although NIF were consulted about the grant distribution, in reality the league had no direct channel to the political power. In other words, the establishment of a public sports bureaucracy meant that the position of voluntarily organized sports was weakened. Not surprisingly conflict arose between STUI and NIF, which resulted in a Norwegian 'sportswar' for much of the 1950s and 1960s.

As in Sweden, the Norwegian sports war was about the dichotomy of the state determining sports policies and the sports movement's freedom to make its own decisions. Hofmo's and STUI's stated policy was that the sports share of the betting income should be used for building sportsgrounds. Other areas of activity – such as NIF's administration and training activities – should, on the other hand, be financed by state grants and their own membership fees. NIF, and especially its leader Arthur Ruud, argued that money from the betting surplus also should be used for sports activities and for the league's administration. At the same time the league wanted more freedom to use the funds as they wished. The conflict was further complicated by other factors – not least by the personal antagonism between Hofmo and Ruud.

NIF finally won. In 1957 'Statens ldrettsråd' was established with representatives both from NIF and the state. The aim was to create a buffer between STUI and NIF. In practice it meant an essential change in the preparation of the public financing of sports. According to the new arrangements STUI's distribution of grants had to be considered by 'Statens idrettsråd' before a political decision were taken. This was what NIF wanted. It now got ever larger grants than STUI recommended and more freedom to decide on their use. In practice the new arrangement meant that the voluntary organizations were placed above state authority.

The Danish Model[39]

Naturally the concept 'the Nordic model' describes the political systems of some countries better than of others. While Swedish politics most closely resemble the Nordic model, Danish politics differ in many ways. The scope of the state has been somewhat more restricted than in the other Nordic countries. Social democrats have never had such a dominant position. Nor have corporative solutions been used to the same extent.[40] Sport also, interestingly enough, diverges in many ways.

Most importantly, Danish sport has never been concentrated in a single unified national organization. While competitive sports have been concentrated in the cities and organized within DIF, parallel 'popular sports' have been organized in the country. This pluralism has made it more difficult to use corporative arrangements. When different organizations lay claim to represent the interests of sportsmen, the state has difficulty in giving one organization a monopoly. Further, voluntary sport has been more independent of the state in Denmark than in the other Nordic countries. The sports organizations have in general opposed any kind of state meddling in what they considered to be their own affairs. Even the public authority has noted and stresses the independence of the organizations. Public sports policies have been, and remain, little developed. No real state bureaucracy has been established. Even after the creation of the welfare state, sport has remained clearly anchored in the private sphere.

On the other hand the Danish government, as in the other Nordic countries, has given substantial financial support to sport. The form of this support clearly shows the special characteristics of Danish sports policies. In Denmark, too, a state-owned betting office was established in 1948 where a part of the surplus was earmarked for the encouragement of sport. In contrast with Norway, however, most of these funds were given untouched to the sports leagues as of right. The state made no demands as to how the funds should be used nor did it impose any auditing requirements. Support for sport was not distributed but enacted. This policy gave the sports leagues great freedom of action and enhanced their autonomy. At the same time the method of financing helped pave the way for the present organizational structure. As the organizations knew that the amount of state support was fixed, a certain restraint on increasing their activities was imposed. For example, each new member of DIF meant more demands on a fixed sum of money. To be selective in choosing the new specialized leagues meant, in turn, a conflict with DIF's desire to be the umbrella organization for all Danish sports.

Nevertheless, different forms of corporative arrangements between the sports movement and the state were established. Now among politicians there is increasing interest in sport and its future direction. Contacts between the sports bodies and political institutions have increased. 'Idrettens fællesråd' was established in 1976 as a link between the sports leagues. At the same time a committee of representatives of the sports movement and the ministry that deals with sports issues was set up. Through these joint bodies the different leagues have the chance to discuss and co-ordinate their demands on the public institutions. So, too, the state has acquired legally recognized bodies in which issues of common interest can be discussed. During the 1980s the state began to place certain, if only vaguely formulated, conditions on how sports grants should be used.

Conclusion: The Nordic Model

Voluntarily organized sport in the Nordic countries came into being in the private sphere. It was a leisure activity organized on ideological principles, unconnected with the main preoccupations of public politics. Early organization took the form of associations. The associations co-operated with the state but in areas which the state did not fund and could not influence. Sport was partly a voluntary, idealistic and non-governmental activity, partly a phenomenon thought by the government to be good for society and therefore worthy of state support and encouragement. Although sport underwent certain fundamental organizational changes at the turn of the century and became a popular movement, the position of sport in society did not change, nor did its relationship with the state. The sports movement became a popular movement mobilized by the middle class. This explains why the sports movement in comparison with many other popular movements was privileged and acquired official status.

With the creation of the Nordic welfare states, sport acquired a new status in society. The scope of public policy-making grew with the social democratic welfare reforms. Matters that had not earlier been primarily state responsibilities became politicized, not least leisure time, issues concerning young people and sport. With its physical and moral enhancing qualities sport became a matter of public politics and moved into the public sphere of responsibility. This led, on the one hand, to more financial support – from the 1930s state grants for sports increased sharply in all the Nordic countries – and on the other to greater political interest in sport. Above all, the state authorities became interested in controlling the use of steadily increasing public funds. Friction between the state and the voluntary bodies followed. The sports movement, which had indeed gratefully accepted increased state funding, now saw its non-governmental character and independence threatened. Although solutions to this problem varied in the Nordic countries, it is possible to talk about a common 'Nordic' model. The increase in political interest became a problem for the state. Certainly the state had ambitions to increase its influence over the shaping of sport, but this also meant a challenge to the ideological freedom and voluntary character of the sports movement. This was not desirable. The solution was for governments to involve the voluntarily organizations and use their competence and administrative apparatus – to further sports policies through the sports movement's own organizations and to persuade the specialized sports interests to take on public responsibility – in other words to establish corporative arrangements with the voluntary organizations. Outwardly, the sharing of responsibilities between the state and the sports movement that had already existed before the welfare state came into being remained. The state chose to take responsibility for the general financial framework while the voluntary organizations looked after the sports activities. The decisive difference was that sports now became a public responsibility and a public obligation – although mainly organized by non-governmental organizations.

In other words, the sports movement's own bodies have been partly incorporated in the state apparatus. The private and the public have been woven together into a complex network of formal and informal relationships, manifested in different forms of corporative arrangements. A mutual dependence has been created. The Nordic sports movements of today are dependent on public funds and are thus affected by state decisions and guidelines. The state is dependent on the competence and administrative apparatus of the voluntary organizations and therefore influenced by them. Further research will show to what extent these collaborative arrangements have influenced the development of the Nordic sports movement, to what extent the representatives of the sports movements have influenced national sports policies and to what extent, in turn, the representatives of the state have influenced voluntary organizations. These organizations have been given a strong formal position in Nordic sport. They have developed a dual power base as a popular movement and as a public authority. However, what form policy actually took in practice and how public and private resources were infused are still open questions which deserve closer study.

NOTES

This essay develops and compares information discussed in Johan R. Norberg, 'I myndighets ställe: en analys av Sveriges riksidrottsförbunds utveckling till partiell myndighet 1955–1970' (unpublished essay, University of Stockholm, 1995).

1. Olof Petersson, *Nordisk politik* (Stockholm, 1992), pp.22–6, 109–12.
2. Ibid., pp.109–12. One should stress that the study of corporatism is unusually controversial and that a commonly accepted definition of the concept is lacking. To make it clear that the concept should not be connected with fascist Italy, some researchers use terms such as 'neo-corporatism' (Colin Crouch) and 'democratic corporatism' (Peter J. Katzenstein). For a summary of this research see Peter J. Williamson, *Corporatism in Perspective: An Introductory Guide to Corporatist Theory* (London, 1989).
3. Jan Lindroth chooses to speak of four community roles by discussing the concepts of competitive sports and exercise sports. See Jan Lindroth, 'Idrottens fyra samhällsroller. Ett diskussionsunderlag', in *Fritidspolitiska studier* 7, Institutet för Fritidsvetenskapliga studier (Stockholm, 1994).
4. It is clearly characteristic of the state of research that the relationship between sport and the state is studied mostly on the initiative of the public institutions, see for example SOU 1969: 29: *Idrott åt alla*, Matti Goksøyr, *Staten og Idretten 1861–1991* (Oslo, 1992); Matti Goksøyr (ed.), *Kropp, kultur og tippekamp: Statens idrettskontor, STUI og Idrettsavdelingen 1946–1996* (Oslo, 1996); Claus Bøje and Henning Eichberg, *Idrættens tredje vej – om idrætten i kultur-politikken* (Aarhus, 1994).
5. A classic work on the dilemma of democracies is Robert A. Dahl, *Dilemmas of Pluralist Democracies – Autonomy vs. Control* (New Haven, 1982). For important works on corporatism see Philippe Schmitter, 'Still the Century of Corporatism?' in Fredrick B. Pike and Thomas Stritch (eds.), *The New Corporatism* (London, 1974); Alan Cawson, *Corporatism and Political Theory* (Oxford, 1986). For Nordic conditions, see Peter J. Katzenstein, *Small States in World Markets – Industrial Policy in Europe* (New York, 1985).
6. Torbjörn Larsson, *Det svenska statsskicket* (Lund, 1993), pp.307–9, 329–31; Michele Micheletti, *Det civila samhället och staten: medborgar-sammanslutningarnas roll 1 svensk politik* (Stockholm, 1994), pp.22–3; Mats Bäck and Tommy Möller, *Partier och organizationer* (1990, 2nd edition, Gothenburg, 1992), pp.231–44.
7. Bo Rothstein, *Den korporativa staten: intresseorganizationer och statsförualtning i svensk politik* (Stockholm, 1992), pp.62–71; Larsson, pp.329–31; Petersson, pp.109–12.
8. The debate can also be developed to include the sports movement's relationship with the business world which is another important source of financial support. However, this relationship will not be discussed here.
9. K. Arne Blom and Jan Lindroth, *Idrottens historia* (Farsta, 1995), p.185; Micheletti, p.46.
10. The distinction between associations and popular movements was developed in the joint Nordic research project 'Från association till massorganization – samhällsutveckling och det moderna föreningsväsendets uppkomst i ett jämförande nordiskt perspektiv'. See Torkel Jansson, *Adertonhundratalets associationer* (Uppsala, 1985). For a summary of the research project see *Scandinavian Journal of History*, 13 (1988). In research on the history of sport see: Jan Lindroth, *Idrottens väg till folkrörelse: studier i svensk idrottsrörelse till 1915*, Studia historica upsaliensia (Uppsala, 1974); Leif Yttergren, *Från skidsport till skogsmulle. Friluftsfrämjandet 1892–1992* (1992); Leif Yttergren, *Täflan är lifvet. Idrottens organizering och sportifiering 1860–1898* (Stockholm, 1995). For a discussion on the Swedish 'popular movements paradigm', see Henrik Meinander, 'Idrottshistorisk forskning i Norden: traditioner och trender 1970–1990', in *Historisk Tidskrift för Finland*, 1 (1991); Bill Sund, 'Aktuella tendenser inom svensk och internationell idrottsforskning', in *Historisk Tidskrlft*, 4 (1991).
11. Blom and Lindroth, *Idrottens historia*, pp.185–6; Yttergren, *Täflan är lifvet*, pp.11–12.
12. Jan Engberg, *Folkrörelserna: välfärdssamhället* (Umeå, 1986), pp.9–11; Blom and Lindroth, pp.186–7.
13. Lars-Arne Norborg, *Sveriges historia under 1800- och 1900talen. Svensk samhällsutveckling*

1809–1986 (Stockholm, 1988), pp.126–7; Micheletti, p.29; Bäck and Möller, pp.151–6.

14. Finn Olstad, *Norsk Idretts historie*. *Försvar, sport, klasskamp 1861–1939* (Østerås, 1987), pp.11–14, 106–7; Else Trangbæk (ed.), *Dansk idræts liv*. *Den moderne idræts gennembrud 1860–1940* (Copenhagen, 1995), p.30; Lindroth, *Idrottens väg till folkrörelse*, p.139; Yttergren, *Från skidsport till skogsmulle*, pp.19–20.

15. Yttergren, *Från skidsport till skogsmulle*, p.19; Olstad, pp.11–12; Ove Korsgaard, *Kampen om kroppen*. *Dansk idræts historie gennem 200 år* (Copenhagen, 1982), pp.62–5.

16. Sveriges centralförening för idrottens främjande exists today, but without the same influence as earlier. RF took over the society's responsibilities in 1931 after an initiative from the Crown Prince Adolf, later Gustav VI, see Jan Lindroth, *Idrott mellan krigen. organizationer, ledare och idéer 1 den svenska ldrottsrörelsen 1919–1939* (Stockholm, 1987), pp.119–27.

17. Until 1910 the Centralforeningen for Udbredelse af Legemsøvelser og Vaabenbrug (from 1893 Centralforeningen for Udbredelse af Idraet) was responsible for the co-ordination of sport. It was the disagreements between this body and the specialized leagues that led to the new arrangement of 1910, see Olstad, pp.111–15.

18. Olstad, p.188; Goksøyr, *Staten og Idretten*, pp.17–20.

19. Trangbæk, *Dansk idrætsliv*, pp.115–18; Bøje and Eichberg, pp.133–9.

20. It should, though, be mentioned that this applies at the national level. The socio-economic structure on the local level has not been studied more closely by researchers in sports history.

21. Lindroth, *Idrottens väg till folkrörelse*, pp.172–6, 193–4; Goksøyr, *Staten og idretten*, pp.75–7.

22. The Danish 'popular' sports to a certain degree diverged from this pattern because of their connection with the 'grundtvig' peasant culture.

23. Here it should be pointed out that the Finnish sports movement received its first annual state grant in 1920.

24. Goksøyr, *Staten og idretten*, pp.17–19.

25. Trangbæk, *Dansk idrætsliv*, pp.35–6, 84–6, 115–18

26. Lars-Arne Norborg and Lennart Sjbstedt, *Grannländernas historia* (1970, 4th edition Arlöv, 1987), 190–204; Petersson, pp.22–6.

27. Petersson, pp.22–6, 74–7.

28. The Swedish political scientist Bo Rothstein has shown that the corporative structures were not only the result of social democrats becoming the governing party. The 'first' example of a corporative administration model in Sweden during the 1930s occured under a Conservative government, see Bo Rothstein, 'Svenska intresseorganizationer: Från lösningar till problem', in Johan P. Olsen (ed.), *Svensk demokrati 1 förändring* (Stockholm, 1991).

29. The development of workers' sport in Sweden has been studied by Rolf Pålbrant, *Arbetarrörelsen och idrotten 1919–1939,* Studia historica upsaliensia (Uppsala, 1977). See also Mats Franzen, 'Sporten, ungdomen och folkhemmets begynnelse', in *Arkiv för studier 1 arbetarrörelsens historia*, 61–2 (1995). For Norwegian conditions see Olstad. Danish workers' sport is discussed by Korsgaard and others. It should also be added that a vigorous workers' sport movement developed in Finland and still exists. See Pålbrant, pp.107–8.

30. Johnny Wijk, Department of History, University of Stockholm, is at present studying how events during the Second World War influenced the position of the Nordic sports movements in society. See Johnny Wijk, 'Folkrörelser på marsch – om idrottsrörelsens samhällsetablering under andra världskriget', in *Svensk idrottsforskning* 3 (1996).

31. Hilding Johansson, 'Idrottens väg till massrörelse', in *Svensk idrott 1903–1953 – En ekonomisk, historisk och sociologisk undersökning utförd på uppdrag av sveriges riksidrottsförbund med anledning av dess femtioårsjubileum* (Malmö, 1953), p.84; Hans-Erik Olson, 'Idrotts- och friluftslivets politiska ekonomi', in Johnny Andersson (ed.), *Turbulens i rörelse, sju perspektiv på ldrottens framtid* (Ødeshög, 1991), pp.69–70; Blom and Lindroth, p.243; Else Trangbæk, *Dansk idrætsliv. Velfaerd og fritid 1940–1996* (Copenhagen, 1995), pp.111–30; Goksøyr, *Staten og idretten*, pp.78–9.

32. Micheletti, pp.79–83. See also Olof Ruin, *1 välfärdens tjänst. Tage Erlander 1946–1969* (Stockholm, 1986).

33. This presentation of conditions in Sweden is based on a summary of results drawn up by

Norberg.
34. Johansson, pp.68–70; Olsson, p.62
35. *Idrotten och samhället,* SOU 1957:41.
36. No report of the investigation was ever published, nor is there any material in the archives.
37. *Idrott åt alla,* SOU 1969: 29.
38. This presentation of conditions in Norway is based on Goksøyr, *Staten og Idretten;* Goksøyr (ed.), *Kropp, kultur og tippekamp;* Stein Tønnesson, *Norsk idretts historie, Folkehelse, trim, stjerner 1939–1986* (Østerås 1986), ch.4–5.
39. This presentation of conditions in Denmark is based on Trangbæk, *Dansk idrætsliv;* Bøje and Eichberg.
40. Petersson, pp.24–7.

Gender in Modern Society:
Femininity, Gymnastics and Sport

ELSE TRANGBÆK

Gymnastics and sport ... are a unique approach to being together with people. When people are in tune here, I believe that things will be much easier in other spheres.

Gymnastics has been my inner fixed point, it has given me physical strength and pleasure; here I am just me.

These quotations come from interviews with elderly women about the gymnastics of their youth and what it has meant to their lives.[1] At the same time, they tell us about women who have experienced something during physical and social activity which has taught them something about themselves and their relationships with other people. They have learned something about life and for life.

In different ways, gymnastics and sport[2] in the Nordic countries and elsewhere were important in the upbringing of 'the modern citizen' during the nineteenth century. The participants learned through action how to be such citizens. In gymnastics clubs and on sports fields a dialogue between the individual and the community could constantly be undertaken. In addition, the development and expansion of club life within sport were important for the establishment of crucial social networks. Arguably, the way gymnastics and sport socialized 'a good citizen' differed greatly. While gymnastics perhaps promoted virtues such as health, order and precision, sports perhaps produced the communal integration of the individual through the socialization that took place in the sports clubs.

Sport has often been considered as essentially masculine, symbolizing the ideals of modern industrial society and at the same time contributing significantly to its construction.[3] This was certainly true of the Nordic countries at the end of the nineteenth century. Gymnastics on the other hand with its emphasis on aesthetics, spirituality and control has been considered better suited to the creation of a proper femininity!

The school and the home had been the main arenas for upbringing until about the year 1900 when youth organizations were established and became partners and opponents in the socialization of the young. At the beginning of the twentieth century, adolescence became set apart as an independent and relatively stable period between childhood and adulthood, a phase of life that came to be dominated by formal education and adult control, and became both a process of segregation and integration.[4] Sport was seen as a sort of transitional ritual that turned the immature boy into the mature man.[5] The American anthropologist David Gilmore argues that girls, unlike boys, do not require cultural intervention in the form of statements of expectation and testing procedures in order to be able to develop from girlhood to womanhood. According to Gilmore, the transition from immaturity to maturity involves 'automatic' and 'natural' sequences for girls.[6]

Whereas gymnastics and sport have often been ascribed a certain gender exclusivity, the contention here is that neither gymnastics nor sport has a gender.[7] On the contrary, both came into existence as social constructions at a time when the lives of men and women were different.[8] History, and especially the specific behaviour of the participants, can help to show that sport is concerned with more than just rituals, and, as mentioned above, produces citizens. The modern cultural and social lives of women and men have helped in many ways to change the perception of the feminine and masculine, and have dissolved the frequently restrictive gender associations of sport and gymnastics. This study, by means of two case studies; gymnastics and handball, respectively, will show how gymnastics in the Danish tradition helped to expand the perception of femininity and facilitated access to the world of sport. The two case studies have been selected because both are what could be called success stories, but they also bring to light some fundamental features of the cultural system constituted by gymnastics and handball.[9]

This essay will begin by offering an interpretative framework for femininity and look at the body as a referent for interpretations of meanings and describe the 'constructions' of femininity, sport and gymnastics as they were made at the end of the nineteenth century. The conclusion will reflect on how the perception of sport as a masculine domain has helped to constrict the perception of masculinity, whereas sport understood as social interaction has helped to expand the perception of femininity.

As in other countries,[10] Nordic research on gender in relation to sport and gymnastics has primarily dealt with women and has been carried out by women.[11] Henrik Meinander and Hans Bonde are the only Nordic historians who have concentrated specifically on masculinity in relation to sport and physical education in school and leisure time, respectively.[12]

Understanding Femininity

A clarification of terms is necessary in order to be able to analyse gender, here exemplified particularly by femininity. The starting point here is the work of the Danish historian Bente Rosenbeck. She writes, 'I regard the term *femininity* as something different from both *woman's life* as actually lived and from the *female sex* – the biological sex.' She treats femininity as a *norm* for what women are, the female sex as a reference to *biological sex* and woman's life as an expression of all that *women do and create*. Correspondingly, one can speak about the male sex as a biological category. Consequently, men can be feminine, as this refers to the way a given culture or period expresses attitudinal and behavioural differences between the sexes which both sexes can ignore. Rosenbeck states that the categories femininity and masculinity are based on biological differences that are reinforced through ideology and social practice, so that it is difficult to decide what is determined biologically and what is determined socially.[13] This fact, of course, gives rise to certain methodological problems in connection with the cultural analyses that focus on gender. The Danish historian Birgitte Possing points out the paradox that feminist researchers on the one hand make it clear that gender as a category is a historically variable reality, but on the other hand find it impossible to define femininity. How can variability be examined in something to which it is impossible to set limits? She believes that the problem is due to the fact that 'the historical descriptive *norms* for femininity have often been mixed up with the subjective and diverging forms of *behaviour*, which women as living beings have manifested.'[14] Both norms and behaviour change, but according to Possing, the two variables should not be part of the same definition because of the inherent instability in the gender categories.[15] This analysis will use Rosenbeck's three categories (femininity, female sex, woman's life) which are useful when taking concrete historical 'snapshots' in time and space.

The Body as Referent

In the nineteenth century, attempts were made to look into the body through dissection and microscopy in order to find tangible truths about *the body*, while today there are researchers with a background in cognitive semantics who see the body as a form of referent for understanding and interpreting the significance and meaning that are hidden from the human eye.[16] This essay has been inspired by the philosopher George Lakoff and the linguist Mark Johnson and their theories concerning the formation of meaning. For them the conceptual world is organized into categories and most of our thoughts involve these categories. They regard the body as a central referent, which is the basis for the underlying metaphors that appear in language and the way we think. The categories act as systems of meaning based on the body's experiences. The central point of their theories is that meaning formation contains value judgements, and, expressed in a very simplified way, some of the things they talk about are scales consisting of *orientation metaphors,* for example, an 'up-down' scale. The value of good is 'up', bad is 'down' and so on.[17] The values can change priority, but the physical basis of value judgements is constant. They also introduce another scale about the relation between the centre and the periphery.[18]

Making the many metaphors on the scale visible offers the possibility of subtle analysis, which can help us to break a hierarchical logic that is often wrong. What factors had meanings of 'up-down' for women at the end of the nineteenth century – in society and in gymnastics and sport? And how can they lead to an understanding of the relationships between sport, gymnastics and femininity?

The 'Constructions' of Femininity, Gymnastics and Sport

In order to approach an understanding of the 'constructions' of femininity, gymnastics and sport, this study will describe, very broadly, each social construction and its agents, and look at the institutional frameworks of which the constructions were part.

Sex becomes Biological

'One is not born as a woman – one becomes one,' wrote Simone de Beauvoir in *The Second Sex* in 1943. The recognition that 'one becomes one' has since then involved many attempts to clarify the construction of femininity, on the basis of the new view of the body and gender that arose in the nineteenth century.[19] Charles Darwin's theory of evolution published in 1859 started an intellectual revolution, as human beings were included in the evolutionary laws of organic nature. Darwin's theories helped to provide biological explanations for women's subordinate position in society.[20] Likewise, the many new scientific advances in the fields of physics, chemistry and biology became significant factors in people's lives, because they were the basis for many technological and medical advances. In 1876 medical science had arrived at the knowledge that fertilization was brought about by fusion of the ovum and sperm cells, a discovery that helped to give women an active role in procreation. Women's reproductive ability was considered in conflict with their intellectual ability, with consequences for upbringing and schooling. The brains and nervous systems of girls must not be burdened to the detriment of their reproductive capacity. This argument was based on the theory of limited energy, which proposed the idea of a natural amount of total energy in the body.[21] Doctors began to learn about the body, about women's physiology and biology, the commencement of menstruation (the menarche), its sequence, and its cessation (menopause), about ovulation, pregnancy and childbirth.[22] The life and role of women came to be based on anatomy, biology and physiology. Woman was indeed perceived as a person, but as a 'mother in particular'.[23]

The theories of evolution, medical science and technology, supported by the other scientific advances, all helped to provide the polarization of the sexes with biological explanations. The new factor was not the polarization of the sexes, but the fact that the perception of sex received a scientific basis and became biology. The scientific and cognitive 'advances', which created the *norm* for masculinity and femininity were supported by changed *behaviour patterns*, associated with demographic and occupational issues which had taken place as early as the middle of the century.

In most European countries there was at that time a break with the traditional division of labour between the sexes, where the women worked in the home while the men were active in trade and industry and had public, cultural and political privileges and responsibilities. The well-known feminine cardinal virtues – piety, purity, subservience and domesticity – did not accord with the fact that, on the grounds of social, mental and intellectual needs, an increasing number of women demanded a share in the educational system, occupations and certain civil rights.[24] Before the women's movements proper gained importance and raised the 'question of women', the official name for this paradoxical problem was 'the surplus of women problem', which was a joint-European problem in the middle of the nineteenth century.[25] The 'surplus' groups of women sought such jobs as teachers and nurses. Women teachers in this context are particularly interesting as they were so important for girls' physical education in the schools. In her work about Natalie Zahle and her school empire, Birgitte Possing points out that the authorities considered it very important that the women teachers possessed what they called feminine virtues – and passed them on in classroom and gymnasium.[26]

It is important for the following analysis to look at which virtues were ascribed to the two sexes. In 1976 K. Hausen published a systematic analysis of the sex-specific virtues as they were described in German medical, pedagogical, psychological and literary encyclopaedias for the whole of the nineteenth century.[27] (See Table 1.)

Precisely the fact that more and more groups through their behaviour and habits came into conflict with the prevailing norms of what was appropriate for the two sexes helped to make femininity a subject of discussion. The polarization of the sexes became a scientific question and gave rise to knowledge about two biologically different sexes, which was

TABLE 1

Men Destined For	Women Destined For
The outer life, public life, wide horizon	The inner life, domestic life nearness
Activity (energy, strength, will-power, firmness, courage, daring)	Passivity (weakness, resignation, devotion, fickleness, modesty)
Doing (independence, ambition, goal-oriented, industrious, taking authority, power, antagonism)	Being (dependence, hard-working, eager, preserving, self-denial, impact adaptive, loving, goodness, sympathetic)
Rationality (spirit, sensible, intellect, thought, knowledge, abstract thought)	Emotionality (feeling, heartbeat sensitivity, being influenced, receptive, religious, understanding)
Virtue (dignity)	Virtues (modesty, chastity, decorum, loveable, tactful, grace, beauty)

used to structure a social order based on gender, where the *body* was 'the foundation of gender'.[28] Sport and gymnastics, because of perceptions of the gendered body, thus become a central source for the understanding of femininity and masculinity.

The 'Construction' of Sport and Gymnastics

From the end of the seventeenth century until the beginning of the nineteenth century, modern sport and gymnastics were part and parcel of the ideas of the Age of Enlightenment about the emancipation of the individual. Two works were of particular importance, John Locke's *Some thoughts concerning Education* (1693) and Jean Jacques Rousseau's *Emile* (1762). Both books stressed that physical education – indoors and outdoors – was a central element in education.

On the basis of the philanthropic ideas of the eighteenth century incorporating physical education into general education, attempts were made to systematize gymnastic exercise. This resulted in two essentially different systems, the German and the Swedish. The focus here is on the Swedish system, because of its construction based on the body and its scientific elements in relation to the construction of femininity.[29]

Historic perceptions of the difference between sport and gymnastics may be usefully illustrated with reference to the father of the modern Olympic Games, Pierre de Coubertin. He believed that sport and the Olympic Games were superior to gymnastics. Sport was a better means of developing character, because, unlike gymnastics, it developed individuality and liberated the individual.

Another Utopian notion is to imagine that Sport can be officially united with Moderation in the name of science, and constrained to live with her. It would be an unnatural marriage. It needs the freedom of excess. That is its essence, its object and the secret of its moral worth.[30]

Coubertin's ideas about the qualitative difference between gymnastics and sport reflect the differences between 'these social constructions', as they were expressed at the end of the nineteenth century. The relation between moderation and excess, and the scale between them, is important for interpreting the period relationship between gender, gymnastics and sport.[31]

About Sport

In the second half of the nineteenth century, traditional games such as football became standardized and regimented in the English public schools. The impetus was the increasingly industrialized society. On the one hand, sport, through the efforts to make it comparable and uniform, came to symbolize something static – a universal culture. On the other hand, through the promotion of personal development it came to reflect and reinforce the constant demands of modern society for growth and development.

The virtues generally linked to character formation and the 'excess' of sport in the late nineteenth century may be illustrated by Danish books on sport from that time. In a book from 1895, for example, some of the virtues mentioned were 'self-denial, stamina, resourcefulness, courage, alertness, and intensified willpower'.[32] Another writer expressed it in this way: 'The constant efforts to surpass his fellow men in the use of his eyes, nerves, brain and muscles help to develop the attributes, which, especially in men, are essential in the fight for existence, namely, physical strength, endurance, willpower and a practical sense.'[33] 'Citius – altius – fortius', the motto of the Olympic Games, was added to these virtues and expressed the athletic priorities of the time. Sport was seen, as already mentioned, as a central and formative ritual for men, because it contained, in a condensed form, the attributes needed in 'a grown man'. In the seventy-fifth anniversary publication of Denmark's first football club, Københavns Boldklub founded in 1876, priorities were formulated thus: 'KB makes men into boys and boys into men.'[34] Sport was thus primarily directed at boys in school and young men and their leisure time.

Modern sport was introduced into the Nordic countries and Denmark in the second half of the nineteenth century.[35] The Danish historian Jørn Hansen has made a study of those who were behind its introduction in Denmark, the so-called men of civilization and progress, and he has classified them according to social position and age. They represented the same social groups who participated in the general modernization of Danish society. It is interesting that while 80 per cent consisted of people from the middle classes (mainly directors in trade and industry, academics and senior civil servants), only just over 10 per cent were teachers and school principals. Unfortunately, a similar study has not been made as regards the Danish pioneers in gymnastics for the same period, but teachers, educators and school principals completely dominated the discipline.[36]

Sports leaders were mostly middle-class males. The few female leaders were mostly school mistresses, and had – at least in Denmark – great difficulty in influencing the leadership of sports organizations on account of the amateur rules.[37] The male leaders of sport were amateurs, in contrast to many of the women who gradually became leaders.

About Swedish Gymnastics

The father of Swedish gymnastics, P.H. Ling took a physiological stance.[38] From 1804 to 1813 he carried out dissections, and inspired by these he experimented with an anatomical/physiological approach to exercise. He argued that if gymnastics was to survive, it had to become scientific and be practised according to the principles of physiology. In 1808 he described the goals of gymnastics as he saw them in an article 'About the hardening of the human body', in which he asserted that gymnastics must try to create a balance between the various organs of the body in order thereby to promote strength and health. In addition, Ling stated that the educative potential of gymnastics was so obvious that it was not necessary to prove 'its contribution to the development of a manly character'.[39] The systematization of gymnastics with a physiological approach in the form of Swedish gymnastics was in marked contrast to the more pedagogical approach in German gymnastics.[40] Swedish gymnastics constructed exercises that could ensure the balanced development of the body through 'correct' exercises.[41]

In Denmark, as in other countries, the pioneers of gymnastics came largely from educational, medical and military circles. Doctors showed particular interest in women's participation in gymnastics. The Danish doctor, A.G. Drachmann, stated in his article 'About the physical education of our girl children' that gymnastics for women should 'take into account aesthetic considerations of grace and deportment'.[42] As in other countries, Swedish gymnastics in Denmark started in schools and military establishments,[43] but Swedish gymnastics clubs in Denmark came to symbolize agrarian modernization and the rural struggle for the introduction of a true parliamentary system.[44] In contrast to the clubs, Swedish gymnastics in the schools had no symbolic value. Here the gymnastic exercises were meant to 'educate the whole body ... and train all the organs and functions'.[45] The collective, scientific exercises in the schools, as in many other places in the world, were in the nature of 'scientific drill', while in the clubs they became part of a living culture.[46]

About Sport, Gymnastics and Femininity

In sport and gymnastics the aim was to educate participants through physical activity. But while sport stressed individual competitiveness, gymnastics focused on collective cohesion. Swedish gymnastics in particular stressed control and the subordination of the individual to the team and to the teacher's commands to ensure the performance of the correct exercises at the correct time. The ideals of sport, as expressed for example in 'Citius – altius – fortius', suited modern society's entrepreneurship and had implications and possibilities for male youth destined for an aggressive life in the market place, while the ideals of gymnastics were more suited to an accommodating life in the home – or so the period arguments went.

In order to be able to interpret the relationship between femininity, sport and gymnastics, Table 2 presents a schematic survey of the period virtues of sport and gymnastics in relation to men's and women's different period destinies.

TABLE 2
SURVEY OF THE VIRTUES OF SPORT AND GYMNASTICS[47]

Sport	Swedish Gymnastics
Self-denial	Hardening of the body
Stamina	Discipline
Resourcefulness:	
Courage	Rationality
Alertness	Physical education
Physical strength	Equilateral training of the body
Willpower	Control
Practical sense	Ability to adapt
Excess	Moderation

Table 1 dealt with men's and women's different destinies in public and private life. Women lived their lives in a closed environment and a private sphere. Life in the home and school were to a great extent women's only arena of experience. The emphasis in sport and gymnastics on activity, in contrast to the female destiny of 'passivity', signalled 'up' for men, just as the general category 'doing' in Table 1 does. But if we look at the words that symbolize 'doing' and 'being', the picture changes slightly. For example, self-denial and adaptation were part of women's 'being' at the same time as they were regarded as virtues in both sport and gymnastics. The 'rationality' of Swedish gymnastics was a clear destiny for men, while the demands of sport for 'excess' must be seen as being inconsistent with this and more linked to the category 'emotionality', and thereby a female destiny. Few of the female virtues in Table 1 are linked to those of gymnastics, whilst the virtue 'dignity', which is designated as the destiny of men, is linked to both sport and gymnastics. The pronounced virtues/symbols of the activities thus do not express an unequivocal connection with the gender virtues created by society, even though masculinity was closer to the centre of both gymnastics and sport than femininity.

There are different analytical relations, in different positions on the scale: centre and periphery.

1. *Swedish gymnastics and femininity* are both based on the body and science and indicate a certain harmony between gymnastics, femininity and the modernization of society, a modernization where women's emancipation was linked to qualifying to be a housewife and mother – through education and a healthy lifestyle – for life in the family and the private sphere. Many of the female teachers and head teachers of the time were in favour of Swedish gymnastics, because they regarded it as a useful means of 'inner emancipation'.[48] Swedish gymnastics was an acceptable culture for women. The move towards the centre of the activity could begin.

2. *Sport and femininity, however, present problems.* The rejection by sport of the scientific and collective as the centre of the activity meant that femininity was 'down'. The individual, the virtues and the public sphere signalled 'up' for men. With the support of 'the men of civilization and progress', sport became part of a civilizing process, which had the potential both to segregate and to integrate. Here, the young men – if they could live up to the norms of behaviour – could be integrated into sport and society and move towards the centre, where activity, power and influence were. In contrast, sport came to mean either a process of segregation for women or transgression of the norms of femininity of the time.[49]

Gymnastics and sport, with upbringing as the starting point, have different options for the qualification of young people for life in society. Thus sport at the turn of the century had become part of the collective consciousness of masculinity, and was the 'playground' for young men, in particular in their free time and in the public sphere. This is where they made themselves into 'the modern citizen'. In this way, sport helped to construct masculinity at the turn of the century. Gymnastics activities were carried on primarily in the school and home, and the closed and private space of the gymnastics hall. In addition to this, the scientific and physical aspects of gymnastics were linked to the female sex – woman as a biological being. It was precisely the collective schooling in gymnastics, the capacity for moderation and its scientific basis, which were those elements that gave women 'access' to the world of sport.

Woman's Life in Gymnastics and Sport

In spite of the fact that the period virtues at the turn of the century signalled 'down' for women in sport and, to an extent, gymnastics, many women took up the challenge. The two case studies, gymnastics and handball, each in its own way illustrate women's ability to build a bridge between sport and gymnastics and a bridge from sport and gymnastics to woman's life and life in society, as well as the capacity to move from the periphery towards the centre in the world of sport – by transgressing the norms of femininity.

The first study focuses on the Danish women's gymnastics teams which gave displays at the Olympic Festival in 1906 and the Olympic Games in 1908.[50] The second attempts to explain why handball, apparently so masculine, had equal numbers of male and female participants in Denmark.

Danish Women in the Olympic Stadium

> Physical exercise is an essential part of upbringing, and the health, joy of life and fitness for work that can be got from well-led gymnastics training are of essential importance for life. This is particularly true for women.[51]

The combination of qualities mentioned in the quotation – health, joy of life and fitness for work – demonstrates very clearly the breadth of view held by Paul Petersen[52] in 1886 on physical education for women, and the potential of sport in general. Some years previously A.G. Drachmann had devised a gymnastics system for women.[53] Although familiar with Swedish 'scientific' gymnastics, both Petersen and Drachmann endorsed a less rigid form. Petersen pointed out many times that one-sidedness in physical education should be avoided, and he therefore recommended both gymnastics and sport for women. He stressed the principle of inclination and referred to his own gymnastic system as 'rational pleasurable gymnastics', in contrast to Swedish 'compulsory gymnastics'.[54] His method of working and his ideas brought him into conflict with those who extolled Swedish gymnastics and agitated for their introduction in the schools.[55] Petersen's women's gymnastics had impressed many people for a number of years but had also been subjected to harsh criticism due to the flaws in the system and, in particular, his belief that public performance was an appropriate part of the development of women's gymnastics.

His women's gymnastics team was invited to give a display in the Olympic stadium in Athens in 1906 on the occasion of the tenth anniversary of the first modern Olympic Games. During the stay in Athens, the twelve women gymnasts, led by Petersen's daughter, Magdalene Paul Petersen, were the guests of the royal family and stayed in the palace. A few quotations indicate the enormous interest shown in the women.

> The whole female world of Athens, indeed the men too, talked all day yesterday about the Danish ladies. They talked about the grace, nobility and suppleness of their movements. They displayed all the athletic good points, but primarily, the health of body and soul. One noticed that all their movements without exception were beautifully done, that they were absolutely deliberate and seemly. The Attic women admit all this and acknowledge it. But it is not enough to acknowledge a beautiful fact; it is also necessary to imitate it in such a way that our beautiful sex can take part in the competition at the next Olympic Games.[56]

The Greek newspapers suggested 'that the Danish women gymnasts' performance will possibly be the beginning of a revolution in the Greek people's idea of what a woman can and should be occupied with'.[57]

At the Olympic Games in London in 1908, 20 Danish gymnasts and two women leaders from Kvindelige Idrætsforening participated.[58] At the opening ceremony of the Olympic Games on 15 July the Danish women were the only female team. *The Daily Telegraph* wrote:

> The very appearance of the young ladies as they stepped into the arena in their neat cream costumes and golden-brown stockings captivated every eye. In their physique there was nothing of the Amazonian. They were really under medium stature. No one of their number could have established even the remotest pretensions to 'massiveness'.[59]

The women clearly broke down prejudices about the way active women can and should present themselves. The newspapers, in total surrender to their charm, wrote that their like had not been seen in England before. Even in the difficult exercises the women never lost their grace. In addition, they performed apparatus exercises and still managed to combine 'grace and activity'.[60] It was precisely this combination of different systems and energetic activity for women that comprised the tradition of Danish women's gymnastics. In discussing the pros and cons of competition, it is interesting to note that the Danish girls' gymnastics was especially admired, because health and the exercise of the whole body, not competition, was the motivation. As the *Telegraph* article stated: 'For that reason, the competitive element being eliminated, this physical training is not carried to excess among the rising womanhood in Denmark.'[61]

In the many cuttings and the many quotations about the participation of the women in the festival in 1906, and the Olympic Games in 1908, one thing stands out: female pride in and the enthusiasm for their performances. Women expressed delight in this achievement of their own sex, and the gymnasts themselves must have been proud also of their pioneering achievement. Like 'proper' stars, they got on to the front pages of the newspapers and were applauded on their homecoming. From the newspaper reports it seems that they broke through many barriers. A cluster of words describe the cultural attributes considered appropriate for a 'proper' woman of the period: beautiful, graceful, noble, lithe, seemly, shapely. What the women should not resemble contained the barrier-breaking elements: 'nothing of the Amazonian', massiveness, too energetic activity. That the Danish gymnasts successfully and attractively combined the acceptable with the unacceptable was precisely what aroused enthusiasm – it is here that success was to be found. These gymnasts rejected the myths about women and built up a belief in their own power – through the use of the resources of the body.[62] The pride and pleasure in their own bodies by extension enhanced the quality of life for many women.

The pioneers behind the development of Danish women's gymnastics had the ability to move in the gender border area and cross the border between personal action and public activity. They possessed further ability to take up physical challenges, reject social constraints and redefine aesthetic expression and in consequence aroused excitement in participant and spectator. The qualities given priority by Danish women's gymnastics occupied the space between the captivity of gymnastics and the freedom of sport. In this space, these gymnasts mounted a platform, from which both the women of gymnastics and sport could launch themselves – the Olympic Games. Collective effort helped to strengthen the conviction of the individual woman and give her the belief that opportunity in modern society could be grasped – by women.

Handball: A Playground for Women Too

'Woman must develop into a woman and not into a man, or something in between a man and a woman,' wrote Denmark's first sports doctor Ove Bøje in 1943, in an article entitled 'Women and Sport'.[63] Norms for femininity in sport had not changed much since doctors had first offered their opinions on the subject some 50 years previously. The concern was 'the female sex functions'. It is interesting that this opinion could still be voiced considering the large following of women that gymnastics and sport had at that time. Clearly sexual stereotyping was still alive and well. Of course, gymnastics was better suited to the period norms of femininity than sport. Over the years many studies have documented the difficult path women had to tread to enter the world of sport.[64] It was only in 1944 that Danish women were allowed to compete in the Danish athletics championships.[65] The story of handball in Denmark as a sport in which women were in the majority reveals why 'sportification' for a long time had been a masculine prerogative.[66] But the story also reveals a particularly Danish factor in the Danish sports system ('idrætsystem') – its different organizations with different cultures and ideologies.[67] For example, the objectives of the Danish Gymnastics and Sports Association (DGI)[68] have their basis in the belief that activities are a means of enlightenment – a tradition with a national and rural foundation and orientation and here, therefore, called a 'popular culture'. In contrast, Denmark's Sports Federation (DIF)[69] has a global, industrialized foundation and orientation and is here called a 'sportified culture'.[70]

In Denmark, the first official statistics about sports participation appeared in 1938.[71] These 'Sports statistics', which give the average for the whole country, are not divided into the main organizations. But if the number of participants on a country-wide basis is compared with the number from the 'sportified culture' (DIF) the difference will indicate how many participants there were in the 'the popular-culture'. Table 3 shows that in 1938 women made up between 30 per cent and 35 per cent of the total number of active sports participants in Denmark . Today it is just under 40 per cent. Women were represented in all sports except boxing, football, wrestling, weight-lifting and cycling. Women were in the majority in handball, gymnastics and swimming. This has been true since the 1930s. In addition, there were many women in badminton, figure skating and rowing. According to the period norms of femininity and masculinity, the activities in which women participated included virtues from both areas. So either the norms had changed or else the sports culture had changed. By looking at the proportion of women in the 'sportfied culture' (DIF), we can perhaps come close to an answer. Here sport is still essentially a male activity.

TABLE 3

Women's proportion of the total number of active sports participants on a country-wide basis[72]		Women's proportion of the total number of active sports articipants in DIF	
1938	35 per cent	1938	?[73]
1943	33 per cent	1943	20 per cent
1948	29 per cent	1948	16 per cent
1953	30 per cent	1953	15 per cent

The proportion of women in the 'sportified culture' was somewhat smaller than that country-wide, which in itself can be simply explained by the lack of harmony between the norms of the time and the ideals of sport and by the fact that women had less interest in, or were expected to display less interest in, competition than men.[74] Are gender norms or other cultural factors the explanation? Here it is interesting to look at handball as a relatively physical game, because of the high percentage of female participants.

In Table 4 there are considerable differences between the sex distribution of performers on a country-wide basis, and in the Danish Handball Association under the DIF.

One of the major differences between the participation of the two sexes must be found in the differences between the 'popular culture' and the 'sportified culture' and between the culture of the rural and urban areas. From the middle of the 1930s the popular gymnastics organizations in Denmark began to include various sports disciplines in their programmes in addition to gymnastics and rifle-shooting. Gymnastics organizations in the country were losing members. New ways to boost recruitment were considered and there was discussion, sometimes quite fierce, about whether

TABLE 4

Year	Number of active participants, country-wide, in handball		Danish Handball Association – member of DIF	
	Men	Women	Men	Women
1938	14.016	14.074		
1943	29.149	29.94	10.828	7.361
1948	41.596	33,735*	14.03	9.732
1953	57.961	62.022	16.24	12.59

*The reason for the smaller number of women in 1948 has not been investigated.

it was desirable to incorporate sports.[75] The result was that in most gymnastics clubs in the rural areas handball was played in summertime while gymnastics was played in winter. With this arrangement members could be retained all year round.

In this way the gymnastics culture built a bridge to the sports culture. Playing handball in the rural area was not a single sex, but more a 'unisex', activity. It was not until 1970 that in the Danish Handball Federation there were as many men as women as active members. A cautious interpretation is that the more 'sportified' culture in the town clubs (with one-discipline clubs) delayed women's participation. The participation of large numbers of women in handball in Denmark today could not have occurred if it had not been for the gymnastics and/or 'the popular organizations' as bridge builders.

So when the Danish women's national handball team won the European championship in 1995 and 1997 and the gold medal in the Olympics in 1996, it was due to a long-established tradition of female participation in Denmark, in both gymnastics *and* handball. It is precisely this 'both/and' that has enabled women to move to the centre of the sports performance – but not as yet to the centre of sports administration where power and influence reside.[76] Movement towards the centre has changed feminine norms, but has not provided equal rights – as yet!

Has Sport a Gender?

In Denmark, from approximately the middle of the nineteenth century gymnastics and sport were used as a means of educating the young. They were socialization agents by which parents, school and society in different ways could exercise control, particularly over adolescents. Socially constructed gender roles made sport essentially a manifestation of masculinity at odds with manifestations of femininity. This gender confrontation cannot be explained logically in the light of stated period virtues associated with gymnastics and sport. Both ostensibly included male and female virtues. Explanations must be sought in a wider, irrational cultural context in which sport was considered unsuitable for women and sport in the public sphere was especially unacceptable. And this is precisely where the lived woman's life reconstructed the image of femininity. Women showed themselves in the public sphere and gracefully incorporated in their performances masculine elements demonstrating clearly that 'emancipated' women could still be feminine and not dangerous. In this way, they partially reconstructed, and certainly expanded the concept of femininity and thus allayed fears of threatening gender transgression. In the 1930s many women began to participate in many different sports, but when women became the majority in handball, replete with the traditional gender virtues of sport, it was due, among other things, to the fact that in Denmark the game was not part of a mono-gendered culture, but a bi-gendered culture established over time with both masculine and feminine virtues.

To be emancipated in modern society is to abandon past gender norms and traditions. What did those Danish women who dared to participate in gymnastics and eventually sport give up? Initially, they forfeited gender, certainly safety and security, and tested themselves in new arenas and in new relationships. They were poised between continuity and change, and as a result they often achieved a broader-based support. When they tilted to change rather than continuity, they certainly helped change the concept of femininity – with advantage to women and men. What past norms and traditions did men have to surrender? Virtually none. Perceptions of masculinity were not challenged in sport. And to be at the centre of sport still facilitated access to the centre of society. Of course, it could be argued that today sport, because of its continued masculine predominance in certain areas, still results in restricted concepts of both masculinity and femininity.[77]

NOTES

1. One of many interviews – from the author's project in progress – with women between 75 and 85 years old about the importance of sport in their lives. The women represent various institutes/milieus that practised gymnastics and sport. Thus the informants come from folk high-schools, associations, educational institutes and women who participated in the Olympic Games.
2. By gymnastics the reference is primarily to inspiration from Swedish gymnastics – collective exercises, just as in the case of sport the reference is to the sport inspired by England, which made its breakthrough in the Nordic countries at the end of the nineteenth century.
3. Hans Bonde, *Mandighed og sport* (Odense, 1991).
4. Steffen Kieselberg, 'En farlig alder', in *Ungdommens historie* (København, 1985), pp.26–31 An important factor in the development of modern society was the struggle for social and political rights. Those who had rights and opportunities could move towards the centre of society, while others became marginalized.
5. Hans Bonde, *Mandighed og sport* (Odense, 1991). This author would dispute that sport is a sort of transitional ritual that should turn the boy into a proper man, as a transitional ritual is something that only happens once in a lifetime, and the consequences of the action are irrevocable. In sport, the same action occurs time after time.
6. This is based on an article by Henning Bech, 'Man International I/S', in *Tidsskriftet Antropologi*, 24 (1991), which is partly a review of David Gilmore's book *Manhood in the Making: Cultural Concepts of Masculinity* (New York, 1990), pp.111–16.
7. Eva Oloffson points out, for instance, 'that there is no female sport. There are only female participants in male sport'. Eva Oloffson, *Har kvinnorna en sportslig chans? Den svensk idrottsrörelsen ock kvinnorna under 1900 tallet* (Umeå, 1989), p.185.
8. By constructions, this author is well aware that neither polarization of the sexes, nor sport, nor gymnastics must be perceived as static and narrow constructions, linked to one specific time. But 'construction' is used as an expression of a social construction that became part of the collective consciousness – and in that way is important for the relationships between people.

9. Orvar Löfgren writes that the precondition for bringing to light a basic feature in a certain mentality or a certain cultural system is a paradigmatic test, showing the great cultural impact, for example on many levels of society. O. Löfgren, 'På jakt efter den borgerlige kulturen', in C. Kvium and B. Wåhlin, *Mentalitetsforandringer* (Århus, 1987), p.118.

10. In an effort to put Nordic gender research in regard to sport into context, we have used Ann Hall, *Feminism and Sporting Bodies* (New York and London, 1996), where she identifies three different levels of gender analyses in sport as follows: (a) categoric research, with a primary focus on quantifying and empirically studying gender or race differences in athletic participation, performance, and abilities, and attempting to explain their existence in terms of biological factors and socialization; (b) distributive research, which examines the distribution of resources (e.g. competitive opportunities, coaching positions, administrators, income levels, sponsorship) and focuses on inequality in opportunities, access, and financial resources; and (c) relational analyses, which begin with the assumption that sporting practices are historically produced, socially constructed and culturally defined to serve the interests and needs of powerful groups in society. Sport, therefore, is seen as a cultural representation of social relations and here includes gender, class, and race relations. Briefly, the position of the Nordic gender research in relation to sport in the above-mentioned categories would be primarily in (a) and (c), while the sociological investigations as regards gender have been in (b).

11. In the Nordic countries, the following researchers in particular have been working with female history and female perspectives in relation to sport: Leena Laine and Henrik Meinander (Finland), Gerd von der Lippe (Norway), Eva Olofsson and Claes Annerstedt (Sweden), Laila Ottesen and Else Trangbæk (Denmark) and with male history and male perspectives in relation to sport: Hans Bonde (Denmark) and Henrik Meinander (Finland).

12. Henrik Meinander, *Towards a Bourgeois Manhood: Boys' Physical Education in Nordic Secondary Schools 1880–1920* (Helsinki,1994), and Hans Bonde, *Mandighed og Sport* (Odense, 1991).

13. Bente Rosenbeck, *Kroppens politik. Om køn, kultur og videnskab* (København, 1992), p.75.

14. Birgitte Possing, *Viljens styrke. Natalie Zahle. En biografi.* Bd. 1 (København, 1992), pp.171–2.

15. Birgitte Possing, *Viljens styrke*, pp.171–2, points out that 'the subjective gender is so complicated that it cannot be reduced to a theoretical or historical category. With an inter-disciplinary approach, we know today that it is impossible to differentiate between 1. Biological sex (girl-boy, woman-man), 2. The sexual gender (hetero-, homo-, bi-, trans-sexual), 3. The psychological gender (identity), 4. The historical gender (the social role) and 5. The fictional gender (the literary game or utopia).'

16. Marianne Raakilde Jespersen, 'Kroppens renaissance' in *Kvinder, Køn & Forskning*, Årg. 2 (1996), 65–80. The article touches on how the current humanistic interest in the body has parallels in the preoccupation with the human body in the nineteenth century. It is formulated thus: 'Again the body is put forward as the locus of truth.'

17. George Lakoff and Mark Johnson, *Metaphors we live by* (Chicago, 1980), pp.14–21.

18. Mark Johnson, *The Body in the Mind: The bodily basis of meaning, imagination and reason* (Chicago, 1987), pp.124–5. Else Trangbæk, 'Gender and Skating – about understanding meaningfulness for women', in *Winter Games Warm Traditions, Selected papers from the 2. international ISHPES seminar* Lillehammer 1994 (Oslo,) pp.240–9.

19. From the 1960s, historians' analyses of women's conditions over time rejected gender as a universal category and instead regard it as a historical and cultural category, which, like class and race, was a precondition for understanding the important issues in life.

20. Jennifer Hargreaves, *Sporting Females: Critical issues in the history and sociology of women's sports* (London, 1994), pp.44–6, and Patricia Vertinsky, *The Eternally Wounded Woman: Women, exercise and doctors in the late nineteenth century* (Manchester, 1990), p.21.

21. Herbert Spencer transferred the German physicist Hermann Helmholtz' theory of preservation to the development of the human being. According to this theory, people had only access to a limited supply of energy. Bente Rosenbeck, *Kroppens politik*, p.15.

22. Vertinsky, *The Eternally Wounded Woman*, pp.39–108. Vertinsky records doctors' views on

the problematic period in a woman's life – the period from puberty to menopause.

23. Bente Rosenbeck, Bente, *Kvindekøn*, pp.54ff.
24. Theodore Stanton (ed.), *The Woman Question in Europe* (London, 1884) contains a survey of women's education, jobs, civil rights etc. in most European countries. The various contributions which were collected in 1880–81 contain central and useful information enabling comparison between the different countries – and, in particular, they contain the views of contemporary women about the 'woman question'.
25. It is probably not coincidental that this female surplus problem cropped up at the same time as occupational female emancipation.
26. Birgitte Possing, *Viljens styrke*, pp.170–83.
27. The table is made on the basis of K. Hausen, 'Die Polarisierung der "Geschlechts-charaktere" – Eine Spiegelung der Dissozation von Erwerbs- und Familieleben', in W. Conze: *Socialgeschichte der Familie in der Neuzeit Europas* (Stuttgart, 1976), p.368.
28. Thomas Laquer, *Making Sex: Body and Gender from the Greeks to Freud* (Harvard University Press, 1990), p.125 here quoted from Marianne Raakilde Jespersen, 'Kroppens Renaissance', p.76.
29. German gymnastics are not set rigid systems, but on the contrary, systems that changed character throughout the nineteenth century through the effort of such men as Jahn, Massmann, Werner, Spiess Maul and others. The educational emphasis remained to the fore. This can particularly be seen in the *Barrenstreit,* when parliament decided that the German system was 'better' than the Swedish.
30. Pierre de Coubertin, Address delivered at the opening of the Olympic Congress in the town hall in Prague, May 1925, published by Imprimerie d'Etat à Prague, here quoted from Pierre de Coubertin, *The Olympic Idea, Discourses and Essays* (Køln, 1967), p.96.
31. Coubertin opposed women's participation in the Olympic Games competitions all his life. In his vision of the Olympic Games there was no room for women.
32. A. Lobedanz, *Efterskrift til Fressel* (København, 1895), p.59.
33. W.Hovgaard, *Sport* (København, 1888).
34. Here quoted from Hans Bonde, *Mandighed og sport*, p.182.
35. Else Trangbæk (ed.), *Den engelske sports gennembrud i Norden* (København, 1989).
36. Jørn Hansen registered the names and occupations of a total of 464 pioneers born before 1900. The selection was made on the basis of the visibility of the people in books and journals as active and as organizers. In all, 183 of the 464 were born before 1880 and had thus helped to establish modern sport in Denmark. The Danish Sports Federation was founded in 1896. Jørn Hansen, 'Den moderne idræt', in Else Trangbæk, Jørn Hansen, Niels Kayser Nielsen *et al., Dansk Idrætsliv*, Bd. 1 (København, 1995), pp.24–6.
37. In the years around 1920 there was a discussion in DIF about whether female gymnastics teachers could be admitted to the leadership, because according to the DIF rules they were regarded as professional, since they 'exclusively or to a great degree support themselves by teaching sport and gymnastics'. Herbert Sander *et al., Dansk Idræt gennem 50 Aar* (København, 1946) p.279. However, in 1921 an addition was made to this rule, in the following words: 'An exception from this until further notice is female teachers of women's gymnastics without competitive purposes'. DIF archive, pakke 3–4, 3/10 1921 (Record Office).
38. P.H. Ling (1776–1839), Swedish gymnastics teacher and poet.
39. This change occurred when compulsory military service was introduced in Sweden in 1812, and Ling pointed out the potential of gymnastics in national upbringing. Signe Prytz, *P.H.Ling og hans gymnastikpædagogiske indsats* (København, 1941), pp.111–13.
40. Else Trangbæk, *Mellem leg og disciplin. Gymnastikken i Danmark i 1800-tallet* (Auning, 1987), pp.25–47 and 197–200.
41. Else Trangbæk, *Mellem leg og disciplin,* pp.25–48.
42. A.G. Drachmann, *Om Vore Pigebørns fysiske Opdragelse* (København, 1867), p.1.
43. In 1814 German pedagogical gymnastics was the basis for the introduction of gymnastics in Danish schools, as a compulsory subject for both boys and girls. In 1828, the subject was restricted to boys only, but with the Handbook of 1899, which was based on Swedish gymnastics, the subject was again made compulsory for girls. Swedish gymnastics was

introduced in Danish military training in 1905.

44. Else Trangbæk, 'Danish Gymnastics: What's so Danish about the Danes?' in *International Journal of the History of Sport*, 13, 2 (Aug. 1996), 203–14.

45. Else Trangbæk, *Mellem leg og disciplin*, p.137.

46. A. Guttmann, *Women's Sports: A History* (New York, 1991), pp.110–11, and Jennifer Hargreaves, *Sporting Females*, pp.69–79.

47. Both gymnastics and sport had, in general, some idea of hygiene, control and discipline – but the virtues mentioned in the table are especially those that were linked to the actual activity/movements. The virtues mentioned refer only to those mentioned in quotations about sport in the article – for gymnastics, other virtues have been added, which are from quotations from around 1900.

48. There were two types of women's emancipation at the time. Both were based on education and the acquisition of civil rights. But the one (inner emancipation) still regarded the role of housewife and mother as the central role in women's lives, and education was meant to qualify the woman to life 'within the framework of the home', and for this purpose knowledge about health and hygiene were of great importance. The other (outer emancipation) was based on the struggle for equal conditions – outside the home too.

49. For a deeper understanding of the relationship between femininity, sport and power, see Jennifer Hargreaves, *Sporting Females*.

50. Danish women's gymnastics teams gave displays at the Olympic Festival in 1906, and at the Olympic Games in 1908, 1912 and 1920. In the written history of the Olympic Games there is little mention of these women who participated 'on the sidelines' of the 'proper Olympic Games'. The purpose of the gymnastics displays was to present gymnastics at a time when there was an ideological struggle between gymnastics and sport. The collective and health-oriented ideas of gymnastics with lack of specialization were in opposition to Coubertin's ideas about the Olympic Games and sport. Coubertin was also against women's participation in the Games. In spite of this, women have participated in the games since 1900. But participation went slowly – upto and including the Olympic Games in Antwerp in 1920, only a total of 202 women (from all countries) had taken part in Olympic competition, exactly the same number as the Danish women gymnasts in the displays of 1906 (12), 1908 (20), 1912 (150) and 1920 (20). The participation in displays helped women into participation in sport – at least in Denmark.

51. *Meddelelser fra Paul Petersens Institutter 1886* (Det kongelige Bibliotek).

52. Paul Petersen (1845–1906) was trained as a sergeant in the Army. After taking a two-year course at the Army Gymnastics School, he applied for a position as a teacher in a private school. In 1871 he was employed at the 'Ny Realskole' in Nörrebro in Copenhagen, and here he began to develop gymnastics, to the delight of the boys in the school. It was here that Petersen started 'the core troop' a group.of boys who came to form the nucleus of one of the first gymnastics clubs in Denmark, Hermes, in 1874 – in which, among other things, he introduced the German Turn-gymnastics. In 1878 Petersen opened 'The Institute for Danish Women's Gymnastics' and afterwards he started both a gymnastics club and a rowing club for women.

53. A.G. Drachmann (1810–1892), physician, is one of the Danish pioneers in women's sports history in Denmark. As early as 1859 he founded an institute of physical training.

54. Petersen was a practical man, who based his work on experience, inspired by his belief in Greek philosophy, and supplemented it with scientific rationality when it did not conflict with his pedagogical ideas about variation, tempo and plurality in his teaching. Else Trangbæk, *Mellem leg og disciplin*, pp.189–95.

55. Else Trangbæk, 'Danish gymnastics', 207–11.

56. *Nationaltidende*, 3 May 1906.

57. Quoted from a Greek newspaper in *Vort Land*, 29 April 1906.

58. Kvindelig Idrætsforening was a new club started by a group of women, who in 1906 broke away from the Copenhagen Women Gymnastics Club in protest against the club's enforcement of its right to choose the leader of the team. The gymnasts wanted influence over their own circumstances, took the consequences and started a new club. See Else Trangbæk, 'Discipline and Emancipation through Sport. The pioneers of Women's Sport in

Denmark', in *Scandinavian Journal of History of Sport*, 21 (1996), 130–1.
59. *Daily Mail*, 21 July 1908.
60. *The Queen – The Lady's Newspaper*, 18 July 1908.
61. Ibid.
62. Else Trangbæk, 'Discipline and Emancipation', 126–8.
63. *Dansk Idræts-Forbunds Officielle Meddelelser* 1943.
64. In her book *Sporting Females*, Jennifer Hargreaves gives a very good account – theoretical and empirical – of discrimination, limitations, struggles, power relations etc. within women's sport.
65. It was especially in relation to athletics that a lot of discussion arose for and against women's participation in the activities and competitions. In 1920 German national women's athletics championships were started, in Sweden 1927, and in England 1927. Else Trangbæk, *Health, Elite Sport and the Female Body– from a historical point of view* (forthcoming in ISHPES Studies, Vol. 6: *Body and Health, Science and Sport from a Historical Perspective*).
66. Gerd von der Lippe, 'Handball Gender and Sportification of Body-Culture: 1900–40', *International Review for Sociology of Sport*, 29 (1994) discusses why handball in Norway had most followers among women, while in Germany, most of the followers were men. The story of women's handball in Denmark follows on from Gerd von der Lippe, but statistical material from the two different Danish organizations enables further specification as regards gender and sportification.
67. Else Trangbæk, 'Danish Gymnastics', 203–14, and Henning Eichberg, 'Body Culture and Democratic Nationalism: Popular Gymnastic in Nineteenth-Century Denmark', *International Journal of the History of Sport*, 12, 2 (Aug. 1995), 108–24.
68. The popular sports organizations in Denmark started in 1861 with the foundation of The Danish Rifle Club Associations; in 1929 the Danish Gymnastics Associations broke away from the rifle club association and in 1992 they merged to form the Danish Gymnastics and Sport Associations (1.5 million members).
69. The Danish Sports Association was founded in 1896 and represents today Olympic and popular sport (1.5 million members).
70. Else Trangbæk, 'What so Danish about the Danes?'.
71. In the years 1938, 1943, 1948 and 1952, the Statistical Department published figures for all sport in Denmark. Information about members and sports disciplines were collected via the central organizations and DIF's specialist associations. The summary of the members covers the age group 14–40. The statistics are not divided according to organization, but show the average for the country as a whole. The statistical material is very comprehensive about sport in Denmark as regards facilities (premises – outdoor and indoor, hygiene, bathing facilities, etc.) – and categorized into sports disciplines and local areas. In addition there is information about municipal grants to sport.
72. The following statistical summaries have been made by Else Trangbæk on the basis of *Danmarks Statistik. Statistiske Efterretninger*, No. 45 Aargang 30 1938, No. 60 1943, No. 26 Årgang 41 1949 og No. 46 Årgang 46 1954, København 1938, 1944, 1949 og 1954.
73. In 1938 DIF did not categorize its members by sex.
74. Helge Andersen *et al.*, *Sporten i Danmark i sociologisk belysning* (København, 1957).
75. At the annual meetings in De Danske Gymnastikforeninger (the Danish Gymnastics Associations – one of the popular associations) at the end of the 1930s, the decline in the numbers who participated in gymnastics was frequently discussed. In 1938, a gymnastics leader Th. Larsen says that gymnastics had become co-ordinated with handball. He amplifies the statement by saying 'handball must be taught just as gymnastics is taught. The tone in the ball arena should be the same as in gymnastics, otherwise the game of handball cannot be used in educational youth work.' *Ungdom og Idræt*, 42, 11, 18 March 1938.
76. In spite of the fact that women now make up 53 per cent of the active participants in the Danish Handball Association, there are almost no women in the leadership of the Handball Association.
77. In spite of many active women in the world of sport there are still very few in leading administrative and decision-making positions.

Maintaining a Military Capability: The Finnish Home Guard, European Fashion and Sport for War

ERKKI VASARA

One of the most important tasks facing the government of Finland during the spring of 1918 was the organization of national defence. The civil war between the bourgeois and the workers' movements, the whites and the reds, had ended in victory for the whites at the same time as Finland's liberation from Russia occurred, to which it had belonged since 1809. The white troops had included a hard core of Home Guards recruited throughout 1917 and led by officers who had been trained secretly in Germany. Their opponents were revolutionaries who formed themselves into the Finnish Red Guard in 1917 and whose leaders looked to a future socialist republic. The victory of the whites ensured a bourgeois society and led to Finland's breakaway from Lenin's Bolshevik Russia.

In those areas controlled by the whites during the civil war there was continual mobilization. Those called up became the first recruits to the regular army created in the summer of 1918. However, men from both the red and white forces were conscripted into the regular army. Simultaneously various Home Guards were merged into one organization. The new Home Guard took men only from the white side. During the entire inter-war period the organization had about 100,000 members at a time when Finland had a population of three and a half million. The task of the Home Guard was twofold: to be a voluntary armed defence organization in support of the regular army and to confront communist activity in Finland.

Sport played an important complementary role to military training in the Home Guard. It was seen both as a way of training men to be fit front-line soldiers and a way of enticing men into the force. Finland has long winters with heavy snow falls in most parts of the country and training for winter warfare was given priority. Skiing, therefore, became a major military sport. Both the General Staff and the Sports Organizers of the Home Guard in the regions were quick to advocate increased skiing practice and better skiing skills. The overall Sports Organizer from 1920 to 1931, Lieutenant-Colonel Kustaa Eemil Levälahti, for example, in the organization's mouthpiece *Suojeluskuntalaisen Lehti* (the Home Guard's' .newspaper) provided continual advice on skiing from 1921 onwards. On one occasion he wrote that 'it is shameful if you do not ski at least once during the winter!'[1]

Levälahti's remark was a clear indication that Finns – including the Home Guard – in the early 1920s were not really a skiing nation. It is not surprising, therefore, that Yrjö Nykänen, the Sports Organizer from the Viipuri Home Guard district, stated in 1923 that in the Carelian Isthmus 'only in a few Home Guard units did they practise skiing with any real enthusiasm'. A year later, under the signature 'Skier', a correspondent complained to the district magazine *Kymenlaakson Vartio* (Kymenlaakso Guard) that the spectators in his district generally came to the skiing competitions and festivities 'in every way, except on skis' and that even participants came to the starting point by other means. 'Skier' stated that the practice of skiing was 'very rare'. He thought it wrong to call Finland a great skiing nation: 'it is as idiotic as if a Russian were to claim that Russians are highly civilized because among them there are some great writers'.[2] To change matters, the Sports Organizers of the Home Guard did all in their power to get their districts onto ski tracks, especially the young. In an issue of the *Hakkapeliitta*, the Home Guard magazine, on skiing for January 1926, Levälahti specifically made the point that children would inject new vitality into the sport.

There were three levels in skiing as in other sports: national, district and village! The best of the village competitors represented their Home Guard at district level. The best of the district represented it at national level. Competitions at the lowest level naturally formed the major part of the organization's competitive activities, and in them lay the real strength of Home Guard sport. In 1930 there were about 630 Home Guard units in all, and each one was divided into as many as ten village divisions. The magnitude of the competition organizers' task can thus be appreciated. The number of those participating could add up to many thousands. In the early 1920s skiing competitions were restricted to a 10 kilometre track, but very soon the General Staff saw fit to lengthen the distance to 20 kilometres. Väinö Teivaala called for talks between the district sports organizers on the proposed change in April, 1921. From a military point of view the change seemed necessary and was accepted. A soldier certainly had to be able to ski easily for at least some 20 kilometres. The new competitions helped make this possible.[3]

The district and national Home Guards events attracted hundreds of participants and were major sports festivals. The Home Guard complemented the work of the civilian sports organization SVUL. The organization was completely 'White' having expelled all members who had belonged to the Red Guard in 1918. It organized a wide range of skiing competitions. SVUL reviewed its selection of distances for its national championships during the 1920s, and by the end of the 1920s championship distances were finally set at 10 and 50 kilometres for the general event and 10 x 5 kilometres for the team event. The 18–21-year-olds and over 35-year-olds skied 20 kilometres, and women and girls skied 5 kilometres. The district championships involved 20 kilometres for the general event, 10 kilometres for the young and the older men's events and 5 kilometres for the women's and girls' event. The programme for the district championship was clearly similar to the Home Guard's skiing competitions.[4]

Sensibly, as a military organization, the Home Guard also considered, the biathlon important. The distance of the biathlon in both the Home Guard national skiing championships and district and village competitions was 8 kilometres. Following a suggestion made by K. E. Levälahti in 1922 both team, individual and senior biathlon events were included in the championships from 1923 in the interest of maximum military fitness. Incidentally the fact that the Soviet Union was seen as Finland's likely enemy could be seen in the targets used in the mid-1920s during the Home Guard biathlon competitions. They were half-size caricatures of Russians. New, neutral targets were eventually used, but as late as the autumn of 1926 the General Staff told the district leaders that 'the targets featuring Russians will still remain in use this winter'. They were also used in the winter of 1927.[5]

The Home Guard biathlon was introduced for very practical reasons. As B. Grannas, the Sports Organizer for the Turku Home Guard district, pointed out in 1925, 'As good skiers are often mediocre marksmen, this forces them to concentrate even more on their shooting skills if they want to succeed in the competitions.' He also considered, however, that many senior Home Guardsmen were far too easily carried away by their marksmanship skills and should concentrate more on skiing. Thus skiing practice was increased.[6] Grannas's attitude was sensible and represented the ambitions of the organization's sports leaders, but it must be admitted that there was a good deal of wishful thinking in these ambitions. Performances in skiing and shooting were to remain far from perfect.

Military patrol skiing was another important Home Guard activity. At a meeting of national sports organizers in December 1922 Levälahti reported that participation in the two preceding years in military patrol skiing competitions had been 'unexpectedly slack'. As Levälahti pointed out, interest in the event should be stimulated 'in every way' because 'military patrol skiing was the most essential form of competition in the Home Guard'. It was also necessary, he stated, to improve the men's map-reading capability and recruit more local Home Guard officers to train patrols for the competitions. Levälahti suggested changes in the competitions, so that the event 'concentrated more on reconnoitring skills and map-reading than on skiing ability and endurance'. While military patrol skiing was considered a vital military attribute by the Home Guard sports organizers, in general performance changed little despite the attempted reforms.

After skiing athletics was the most prominent sport in the Home Guard. Following Finnish successes in the Olympic Games of 1912 and 1920 in Stockholm and Antwerp, athletics were popular. On the advice given by Väinö Teivaala at a Home Guard meeting in 1921 in his role of assistant to K.E. Levälahti, the athletics programme consisted of a 4 x 100 m. relay, a 3,000 m. race and the pentathlon, which included 100 m. and 1,500 m. races and shot put, javelin and pole vault. At the national championships each district was to have a five-man team for the 3,000 metre race in which the three best results were to be taken into account, and one representative for each thousand members in the pentathlon.[7]

The favoured position of athletics in Finnish sporting life meant that the Home Guard national championships were popular events. Hundreds of competitors of a high standard understandably gave both spectators and public, through press reports, the impression of a vibrant athletic culture in the Home Guard. Large numbers of competitors in the district championships gave the same impression, especially in Viipuri and Varsinais-Suomi (Finland Proper). But this impression was misleading because in a number of districts throughout the country Home Guard athletics was rather weak. In most Home Guard units there was only one meeting in the summer. There were some village competitions, but they were not especially well supported. In addition, there was a further meeting linked to the Home Guards' Summer Festival.

The General Staff encouraged cross-country running as well as skiing for obvious military reasons. Each year the Home Guard newspaper exhorted its men to train for this event in the spring and published guidelines on preparation for competition.[8] Local Home Guards held their own cross-country running competitions at the summer sports in May, to select representatives for the district competitions a few weeks later. Despite frequent exhortations and short courses (3 kilometres) cross country running was not popular in the 1920s. It was a similar story in orienteering, introduced in the second half of the 1920s as a summer athletic event, and like the winter biathlon, with an added military component – grenade throwing. At first, then, there was little interest in cross-country competitions but as the 1920s progressed they became somewhat more popular. Nevertheless, by the end of the decade, many Home Guards still did not organize any competitions. The worst districts in this respect were Satakunta, Turunmaa, Sortavala, Mikkeli, Northern Carelia, Jyväskylä and Vaasa. Most noticeable for their competitions were the Northern Uusimaa, Northern Häme, Kuopio and Kainuu districts. Oddly, although cross country competitions were not as numerous as athletics competitions, they attracted more spectators.

Interestingly, skiing eventually became more popular than athletics. There were good reasons for this. Skiing was constantly stressed as militarily the most important activity and the men themselves found it easier to practise as the ski tracks were on their doorsteps while sports grounds might be up to 10 kilometres away especially in the North and East of the country. Skiing also came more naturally to them, for in many places it was a normal means of transport. The relatively greater popularity of skiing together with a lack of suitable summer facilities impeded the development of athletics well into the 1920s. Interest in athletics remained mostly concentrated in the civilian sports societies. Only the most enthusiastic summer sportsmen from the Home Guards participated in their own athletic competitions and these men also took part in any SVUL events in their area.

Skiing in various forms and athletics were not the only Home Guard physical activities. From its inception the Home Guard included gymnastics in its sports programmes. K.E. Levälahti was a committed gymnast and considered gymnastics the basis of all other sports. He greatly admired the Czech national Sokol gymnastics movement in which team gymnastics, military training and patriotism were combined. He thought Finnish gymnastics inflexible and unsuitable for the Home Guards and developed a gymnastics programme which combined speed and flexibility based on the ideas of the Dane, Niels Bukh. Levälahti's aim was to make his Home Guard's gymnastics a Finnish variation of Sokol.

Specific gymnastics training schedules were distributed through the districts to every Home Guard. Every year numerous articles were written in the organization's newspapers by sports organizers on the importance of gymnastics. The conviction that gymnastics were essential was underlined by both Home Guard and SVUL gymnastics festivals during the 1920s. Home Guards participated in both. The success of Home Guard gymnastics throughout the country as a whole was dependent, however, on local conditions and leadership. Facilities were few and skilled leadership thin on the ground despite annual training programmes for local gymnastics and sport advisers of General Staff. Most advisers were more interested in skiing, pesäpallo (the Finnish form of baseball) and athletics than in gymnastics. Participation in the Home Guard gymnastics competitions therefore was quite modest.

Nevertheless the popularity of gymnastics did gradually increase, especially in the Viipuri, Southern Häme, Finland Proper and Northern Uusimaa districts. On the other hand, Northern Häme was one of the country's weakest districts for gymnastics though successful and active in other sports. It is clear that this district simply did not bother with gymnastics. Gymnastics in the Turunmaa, Satakunta, Jyväskylä, Raahe and Pohjola districts was also completely neglected and the necessary facilities were non-existent in other districts. However, there were Home Guard gymnasts who could attract large crowds to their performances at gymnastics festivals. This was recognised by the gymnastics section of SVUL which allowed the Home Guard to award medals to Home Guard gymnasts who had reached SVUL medal standards at the gymnastics festival in Turku in 1928.[9]

Where the Home Guard gymnastics failed for lack of facilities, pesäpallo prospered. Lauri Pihkala spent many years developing rules for the game based on American baseball. In a passionate series of articles in 1921 he maintained that pesäpallo was an excellent training for war. Hitting the pesäpallo ball was the same as firing in the front-line, throwing it the same as hand-grenade lobbing and the rush to a 'base' the same as the rush to cover in battle. In his history of Finnish pesäpallo Erkki Laitinen emphasizes the part played by the Home Guard in the game's infancy. In his opinion, 'pesäpallo's favoured position in the Home Guard sports was fundamental to the introduction and dissemination of the game. The Home Guards spread the game on a broad front and in many different ways: through competitions, courses, information and equipment.' He was convinced, however, that the most effective way of spreading pesäpallo was the Home Guard pesäpallo matches: 'they gave the event the most publicity, and excited and drew people to them'.[10]

According to Laitinen, the pesäpallo finals of the Home Guard attracted more spectators in the 1920s than pesäpallo at the Finnish SVUL championships. Laitinen also credits the Home Guard with making improvements in the actual game. For example, in the finals of 1927 the catcher Pasi Harvela from Kymenlaakso Home Guard district destroyed the opposition by pitching the ball in a new way. And in November, 1927 the Home Guard sports organizers revised the rules of pesäpallo and decided upon a number of changes. Frans Manty,[15] a Home Guard officer who was a member of SVUL's pesäpallo section, then proposed these changes at a SVUL meeting! This made sense. Pesäpallo players were often members of both Home Guard and SVUL teams.[11]

Other Home Guard sports were swimming, rowing, cycling and wrestling. In the 1920s swimming was rarely included due to a shortage of swimming pools. The sports courses organized by the district staff every summer listed swimming as a form of training, but it was not a competitive sport. Rowing was on the programme of some Home Guards in the coastal districts of Turunmaa and Vaasa. There was cycling in Ostrobothnia. Wrestling was also dependent on local interest. The champion wrestler, V.J. Penttala, recalls wrestling in the Southern Ostrobothnia and Sortavala districts, 'where they had wrestlers as military leaders' in the 1930s.

The Finnish Home Guard had its counterparts in Europe in the 1920s and 1930s. There were a number of similar forces mainly in the eastern and central European countries whose *raison d'être* was also defence against Russia and prevention of internal revolution. They were to be found in Estonia, Latvia and Lithuania and as far away as Romania and Bulgaria. Right-wing as well as left-wing Guards were established in Germany and Austria where their function, were both military and political. Even in England during the 1920s and 1930s there were defence organizations. In Sweden, Denmark and Norway national defence organizations were closely linked to higher education from which they drew their reserve officers. Jarmo Matikainen is correct when he states that 'much attention was paid to defence in Europe during the inter-war years, and the Home Guard organization was in no way special'.[12]

The Estonian Kaitseliit (Home Guard) arose out of the country's struggle for independence between 1917 and 1918 and was established at the end of 1918 in similar circumstances to those of Finland. Some time afterwards the organization merged with the Estonian regular army. But after an attempted communist coup in 1924 the Kaitseliit reappeared and continued to function until June, 1940 when the Soviet Union occupied Estonia.

Administratively, Kaitseliit came under the defence ministry which appointed its leaders at all levels except for the lowest units where administrators were elected. The middle level, according to the statutes of the Kaitseliit was for national defence but was required also to help in accidents, to promote the military training of members and to further physical education in the Estonian Republic. 'Kodukaitse' (Home Safety) was the women's wing of the organization and concentrated on economic support for the Kaitseliit and like the 'Lotta-Svärd' organization in Finland, on canteen and nursing tasks. The boys' organization 'Noored Kotkad' (the Young Eagles) and the girls' equivalent, 'Kodutytred' (the Daughters of the Home), were created in the 1920s. The Kaitseliit had about 30,000 members in 1931 and about 42,600 in 1939. Kodukaitse had between 8,000 and 16,000 members. In the late thirties the boys' organization had about 20,000 members and girls' organization about 8,000 members. There were about one million inhabitants in Estonia in 1939. Of all the European defence organizations Kaitseliit was the nearest equivalent to the Finnish Home Guard. By 1924 Kaitseliit was politically to the right – the central league of Estonian freedom fighters had a foothold in the organization. Anders Larke, leader of the freedom fighters, was one of the founders of Kaitseliit.[13]

An armed defence organization was founded in 1908 in Poland as a marksmen's league, Zwiatzek Strzelecki. It had about 300,000 members by the late 1930s. Originally it was a marksmen's secret society and although primarily for shooting, included other sports, for example, cross-country skiing. It had activities for boys over 14 years. The 14–16-year-olds belonged to the 'Eagles', 17–18-year-olds to the 'Audacious' and the 19–21-year-olds to the 'Marksmen'. There was also the Sokol gymnastics movement with 50,000 members in 1939, and there was also a scout movement of 200,000 boys and 80,000 girls.[14]

The Scandinavian countries' defence organizations were different in character, activities and size to those of the Baltic States and Central Europe. The Swedish 'Landstorm' movement was founded at the beginning of the twentieth century for the training of officers of the militia. Its base was the local defence organizations, whose central body was set up in 1912. In Denmark, the 'Kongens Livjaeger' (the King's Personal Guards) was founded in 1801, languished somewhat in the nineteenth century, but had picked up by the time the First World War broke out. It was 3,000–4,000 strong. Its programme consisted mostly of organized marksmanship practice and competitions. It was funded by private donation and had close ties with the army. During the 1930s the number of 'Personal Guards' decreased to about 2,000 and in 1937 the organization was disbanded much to the disapproval of 'White Negro', a commentator in the Finnish Home Guard newspaper *Hakkapeliitta*. In Norway, the 'Leidangs lag' used some conscription areas for army infantry regiments. The state supported the organization financially and additional income came from membership subscriptions.[15]

There was some co-operation and exchange of ideas between Finnish and Estonian Guards;[16] for example, in biathlon scoring, ski-making, and skiing courses, and the Finnish Guards sent members to Estonia at its own expense.[17] Athletes crossed the Baltic to take part in competitions. All in all, the Finns were able to give their Estonian 'brothers' a great deal of help. In the late 1930s the team and relay skiing competitions of the Finnish, Estonian, Latvian and Polish Protection Guards were the most important international competitions in which the Home Guard's top skiers participated expressly as Home Guards. The first competitions were held in 1936 in Zakopane in Poland, where the Zwiazek Strzelecki organization acted as hosts and inaugurated a special challenge cup competition. Zwiazek Strzelecki also introduced military marching competitions in which teams from both army and sports organizations could participate and these continued until the Second World War.[18] Zwiazek Strzelecki also stressed cross-country skiing and hired a visiting skiing instructor, the Finn, Ilmari Vartiainen.[19] In 1937 the Finnish Home Guard was host for the international Guard championships in Kuopio and the winter championships at Puijo. In 1938 the winter competition was to have been held in Viljandi in Estonia but was cancelled at the last minute because of a surprising lack of snow.[20] However, even prior to 1938 and the cancelled championship at Viljandi the Home Guard's General Staff were questioning the value of participation in the international skiing competitions. Lauri Pihkala was strongly against it. He complained of the expense and inconvenience. In his view only the team biathlon was worthwhile. He was fully aware, however, of the benefit of friendly ties between the 'brother' organizations and therefore suggested more military activities like a team marksman match to be held outside the skiing season. He also proposed orienteering. Ideally, he would have liked to have limited foreign competition to Estonia because he was doubtful about Polish motives: the Poles seemed to consider beating the Estonians more important than fraternal contact with the other countries. He did consider, however, that a team biathlon competition with the Swedish would be beneficial. Although the chairman of the competition committee, N.V. Hersalo, was receptive to Pihkala's ideas, the Second World War broke out before anything could be done.[21] The Finnish Home Guard, incidentally, introduced pesäpallo to the Kaitseliit with assistance from SVUL and pesäpallo league. In the early 1930s the game was very popular in Estonia, but by 1939 was rarely played. Understandably, marksmanship had a high priority in all the defence organizations. International marksmanship competitions included those between Helsinki and Tallinn, those against Riga and the Danish Kongens Livjaeger.

Through a variety of sports, therefore, the Finnish Home Guard had close contacts with their counterparts in other countries. District sports organizers made numerous tours abroad and, as mentioned already, leading Home Guard sportsmen took part in competitions both in Finland and as guests of brother organizations. Foreign visits were organised by the Home Guard General Staff Sports Division and led, during the 1920s mostly by K.E. Levälahti whose main interest, as also mentioned above, was gymnastics. Consequently, most visits were to well-known gymnastics colleges in Denmark, the other Nordic countries and Germany. There were also visits to Sokol gymnastics festivals in Czechoslovakia. Levälahti was convinced of the importance of gymnastics to the Home Guard and the foreign visits in furthering them.[22] This view was misguided since Finnish sports traditions and a lack of gymnastics facilities were the real reason why gymnastics were not popular in the Home Guard. The General Staff had no power to change this. The core of Home Guard sport was made up of skiing, biathlon, athletics and pesäpallo during the 1920s. These required no foreign support.

The educational journeys abroad were seen as opportunities for broadening the horizons of those who made them. Commenting on the foreign visits Matikainen explained that help from abroad was needed because Finland was a young nation without experience in physical and military training. This is difficult to accept with regards to physical training. The structure of the Home Guard, and the Home Guard sports established in 1918–21, provides clear evidence of an efficient organization covering the whole country. There was little practical benefit from the district leaders' foreign journeys. Most visits were to gymnastics [or sports] colleges which did not offer training for work in national organizations. Furthermore, Home Guard sport built on Finnish sporting life of earlier decades in SVUL clubs and societies for the young. A national tradition of sport that reached far back into the nineteenth century provided the vitality from which the active sportsmen of the Home Guards drew inspiration and experience. Then again professional abilities were enhanced by courses organized by the General Staff and district staff. Any deficiencies in these could not be remedied from abroad. Finally, by 1921 the basic sports programme was already 'a condensed programme on a broad front' which successfully promoted national and military unity. The basic irrelevance of foreign visits was evident from the fact that the changes that were made in the sports programme in the 1930s were based on national suggestions. There was no need for foreign guidance at any stage. With respect to competition and co-operation with, for example, Estonian and Polish 'brother' organizations, the reality was that the Finnish Home Guard was then clearly the donor, training, for example, the Kaitseliit in both summer and winter sports.

The Baltic States and the Central European countries had, like Finland, one Home Guard per country, but there were a number of different Home Guard organizations in Germany in the aftermath of the First World War. Germany in the 1920s was internally fragmented under the Weimar constitution, political passions ran wild and democratic organizations had many enemies, right-wing factions from the days of the old empire, communists who dreamt of a proletarian dictatorship and the burgeoning national socialists. Moderate bourgeois and the social democrats who supported the Republic of 1918 faced an increasingly difficult task. There were numerous organizations interested in military matters which drew members from right-wing university and college students. Like the right-wing Home Guards, they hankered after the great days of the former Empire with its military code of honour. Home Guards were an overt threat to the new democracy because they did not believe in it. They were made up mainly of officers and soldiers from the former Imperial army, bitter at the destruction of the old system, the shame of the Versailles Peace Treaty, the appearance of communists on the political scene and the high number of unemployed officers. In accordance with the Peace Treaty, the German army had had to be considerably reduced and about a thousand officers lost their jobs.[23]

The Versailles Peace Treaty forbade military exercises in national German organizations, but not sports. The Home Guards, therefore, used sport as a means of military training. The sports of the Guards differed slightly depending on the preferences of national and local leaders. Prominent among the guards organizations were the 'Freikorps' led by former officers. Of these organizations the strongest was the veterans' organization 'Stahlhelm' (Steel Helmet). It had about 100,000 members in 1924. Later, when other than front-line soldiers were allowed to join the organization, its numbers increased sharply and in 1932, 340,000 Germans belonged to Stahlhelm. In 1923 Stahlhelm started a young people's section which included physical training in its programme. Sportkamp Hage (Competitions) began in 1925 and in the late 1920s sport was common in Stahlhelm and other right wing Guards.[24]

It is neither necessary nor relevant to this study to attempt an examination of the sports of the numerous German organizations. One example is enough. The Freikorps organization, 'Bund Oberland', functioned in different parts of Germany and had an active sports programme comparable with that of the Finnish Home Guard. It tied its sports activities to military training and concentrated on shooting, skiing, team competitions and athletics. Both training and competitions were organized and took place both at division and national level. An emphasis on skiing demonstrated a preoccupation with preparation for warfare in all conditions. Members unused to skiing on tracks and slopes attended special courses. Those who took up skiing could participate in time in the different skiing competitions arranged by the organization. Marksmanship and competitions were also a part of the Bund Oberland programme. Shooting competitions were organized from the divisional level upwards. The divisions also arranged annually special 'Wehrsportfest' (military sports festivities). At the Kelheim division of Bavaria the 1928 festival included marksmen's competitions, where the participants shot three times, from lying, kneeling and standing positions. In addition to the marksmanship competition there was the long jump, 'Keulenwerfen' (hammer throwing) and hurdles. All the events were to be carried out with a 10 kg rucksack on the back. The final event was for a special shooting prize.[25]

Training for 'Wehrsport' military sports took place at different times of the year. For example, there was an autumn 'Wehrtreffe' (military sports meeting) in the Franken province of Hohenecke in 1928, in which 200 men took part. The programme consisted mainly of military exercises. The sport events began at 2.30 a.m. with a bugle call after which a 1½ hour practise night march followed. At 7.00 a.m. participants were woken up for a run to the nearby Bühl hill, where they had morning gymnastics. After this followed more military-type sports such as climbing practice on special climbing walls, hammer throwing and the playing of 'medizinball'[26] into the afternoon. 'Deutscher Schutzen und Wanderbund' (Germany's Marksmen and Hikers' League) was a parallel organization to Bund Oberland and included *inter alia*, shooting, terrain practices and several forms of sport.[27]

The organizations that offered military training and military sports unconnected with the German army were socially anchored in the Weimar Republic. The 'Finanzorganization' (Financial Organization) in Coburg was by the mid-1920s a specialist organization to raise financial support for these activities, and various reservist organizations of the FO was supported by industrial and banking circles as well as wholesale and retail businessmen and farmers, FO's supporters considered the organization particularly important. By spreading the burden of financial support they were able to encourage a large membership to train by means of sport for the restoration of Germany's defence capability.[28]

The German state too had its national plans for sports of a military and educational nature for young people. A plan to co-ordinate 'Wehrsportorganization' (military sports training) was put forward at the end of the Weimar Republic in 1932 by Edwin von Stulpnagel, a retired infantry general. Soldiers played an important part in the scheme because the organization was meant to work with the 'Reichswehr' (army). Fifty infantry officers, captains and first lieutenants were to teach for three months at a time. What still remained unclear was whether they would wear their own uniform and use the army's training grounds.[29]

Reichswehr also had its own direct claims on the organization. The long term aim was to get all German 6 to 21-year-old male citizens into good physical condition and to give them pre-military training, as in France. The short-term goal was to give pre-military training including terrain practice to the 16 to 26-year-olds. Initially courses were only available for participants training for service in the army, navy and frontier guard units. Therefore, the training included basic infantry training according to the Ministry of the Interior's programme: training in marksmanship with small calibre weapons, in the use of gas masks and basic training for infantry training. Drilling could only be undertaken for disciplinary reasons, and otherwise military practice was theoretically to be avoided.[30]

Germany's Ministry of the Interior reminded General von Stulpnagel when he was preparing the training programme for the organization, that the Versailles Peace Treaty forbade military training for young German men, but not fitness training. Emphasis, therefore, was placed on 'terrain sports' with the aim of training for military readiness. The men were supposed to acquire physical and mental fitness 'conquering the terrain' in special 'Geländesportschulen' (terrain sports schools). They also learnt subordination and hygiene and the simple life toughened them up. The training for those under 18 was divided into physical and mental training which were the foundation of 'terrain sports'. Training was in the 'Körperschule' (fitness school) and 'Leistungsschule' (performance school). The former aimed at physical strength, tenacity and toughness through gymnastics, handball, 'medizinball', running and practice in close combat or boxing. The goals of the performance school were mental determination, strength and aggression. Its activities were athletics, boxing, battle games and if possible swimming in which everyone had to pass an examination (reichswimmerprüfung). Examinations were compulsory for training in discipline, application and motivation.[31]

The emphasis on the military purpose of the training could not have been clearer. There was a noticeable stress on terrain sports in the programme. There was hiking with 12.5 or 7.5 kg. rucksacks over distances of 25 or 15 kilometres at a speed of 12 minutes per kilometre. The hikes were also used for camping practice and the use of map and compass. The terrain sports camps provided weekly hikes (marches). The distance was gradually increased over three weeks – starting with 10 km. hikes and finishing with 25 km. hikes. The training included survival techniques, movement observation in daylight, in mist or in the dark of night. Orienteering and small calibre shooting were also included because of their military value.[32]

The sports programme for the training of the 19 to 26-year-olds also clearly served military purposes. Athletics was used to develop speed as in 100 and 400 metres running where the desired time was respectively 13.5 and 68 seconds. In long and high jump the standards were respectively 460 and 125 cm. In the throwing events participants could choose between a javelin or discus and the standards were 30 or 25 metres respectively. Strength events were either shot-putting with a 7.25 kg shot to be thrown 7 metres, or carrying a 37½ kg. load in both hands for 20 metres or six pulls of the body upwards to the bar. Endurance events consisted of an eight man team carrying out a 20 kilometre march in 4 hours and 10 kilometres running to be completed in 50 minutes. There was also small calibre shooting: 3 × 5 shots from a 50 metre distance from a lying, kneeling and standing positions. Two minutes were allowed for each 5 shot series. The result required was 75 points from a ten-ringed target. When the target had 12 rings the trainees were supposed to get at least 100 points. There were terrain practices, map reading and if conditions permitted the German league's examination for life-saving and riding tests.[33]

The Ministry of the Interior's instructions were detailed and informative as to the German government's views on the physical education of the young. It wanted strong, hard and fit soldiers. Self-evidently the use of sport as pre-military training of the young and those of the age for military service was not only practised by the Nazi regime. During the Weimar Republic right-wing private organizations *and* state military organizations used sport to train young men to be soldiers who, in time, would be able to defend Germany in a future war.

In the Germany of the Weimar Republic the connection between sports and military capability was well understood. Through sport the right wing trained future soldiers to defend Germany in a future European war, the social democrats to defend democratic society and the rights of the workers' movement, the Communists for a revolution, whose cadres would need to use force in the struggle against the bourgeois defenders of the *status quo*. In practice, sports training for all these groups was similar.

In the spring of 1933 the National Socialists came to power, crushed the left-wing organizations and merged in one way or another the bourgeois organizations with their own party apparatus. The idea of combining sport and fighting fitness was valued more than ever and military sports increased during the Nazi era. The National Socialist government quickly repudiated the limits placed on the German military forces by the Versailles Treaty, restrictions that the Nazi Party itself had, with other far right-wingers, used for whipping up German chauvinism during the 1920s. Rearmament was begun at a rapid pace and the Nazi organizations expanded the military training of the young and the use of sport in military training. Sport was an important factor in shaping Germans 'as racially clean Aryans'. In the summer of 1936 the Nazi regime, as is well known, used the Olympic Games in Berlin as a showcase for the new German sports culture.

In summary, the use of sport for military readiness was widespread in much of Europe in the inter-war years. The Finnish Home Guard was only one of many European defence organizations. Simultaneous with various peace movements in Europe political groupings connected to the right began to prepare the young for a possible new war. While the horrors of the First World War stimulated pacifism in Europe and there were disarmament negotiations and discussions between governments to ensure peace, a number of factors militated against it. The Versailles Peace Treaty had humbled Germany which infuriated the nationalist and revanchist right-wingers, while the small nations sandwiched between Russia and Western Europe considered the new Soviet Union a constant military threat. And in all these countries there existed dangerous internal forces against which they had to protect themselves. In these conditions defence organizations were inevitable.

The organizations, of course, had their own national and traditional views about sport as a excellent way of training boys and men to be soldiers, but the activities were to a great extent the same. The sports of the Finnish Home Guard organization was part and parcel of a European phenomenon: sport as a preparation for war.

NOTES

1. K. E. Levälahti, *'Suksille' Suojeluskuntalaisen Lehti*, 1 (1921), 6 and 7. See also sports leader Nykdnen, 'Hiihtotaitoa edistämään', *Kannaksen Vartio*, 1 (1923), 7; Sportsleader Nykänen, 'Murtomaahiihdon harjoittelu', *Kannaksen Vartio*, 2 (1923), 25 and 26; Ranne Roni, 'Murtomaahiihdon harrastustavoista', *Kannaksen Vartio*, 3 (1926), 75 and 76.

2. Sports leader Nykänen, 'Hiihtotaitoa edistämään!', *Kannaksen Vartio*, 1 (1923), 7; sports leader Nykänen, 'Talven hiihtotoiminnasta', *Kannaksen Vartio*, 4 (1923), 11 and 12; Hiihtäjä, i.e. skier, 'Suksille, suksille!', *Kymenlaakson Vartio*, 2 (1924), 32 and 33.

3. Meeting of the district sports leaders 29–30 April 1921. *Sota-arkisto* (Military Archives of Finland, Helsinki, hereafter *SArk*) *Suojeluskuntain yliesikunnan kokoelma* (Collection of the High Command of the Civil Guard Organization, hereafter *SkY*) *Urheiluosasto* (Sports Section, hereafter *Urheiluos*), Volume Dbl.

4. Aimo Halila and Paul Sirmeikkö, *Suomen Voimistelu-ja Urheiluliitto SVUL 1900–1960* (Vammala, 1960), p.410.

5. Ibid., pp.408–10; Meeting of the district sports leaders 9 Dec.1922. *SArk*, *SkY*, *Urheiluos*. Volume Dbl; *SkY* letter no. 5937.26.1d to all district leaders 25 Oct.1926. *SArk*, *SkY*, *Urheiluos*, Volume Db2.

6. Meeting of the district sports leaders 10–12 Feb. 1925. *SArk*, *SkY*, *Urheiluos*. Volume Db27.

7. Meeting of the district sports leaders in 29.–30 April 1921 and SkY letter no. 2403.21.VI to all district leaders 30 July 1921. *SArk*, *SkY*, *Urheiluos*. Volume Dbl.

8. See for example 'Murtomaajuoksu', *Sarkatakki*, 4 (1924), 77 and 78.

9. SVUL: n voimistelujaoston (SVUL, Finnish Sports Federation, Gymnastics Section) letter no.464 to *SkY* , 7 May 1928. *SArk*. *SkY Urheiluos*. Volume Fbl.

10. Erkki Laitinen, *Pesäpallo – kansallispeli 60 vuotta* (Saarijärvi, 1983), p.86.

11. Ibid., p.134; *SkY* letter 625.27.1d to SVUL's 'pesäpallo' section 19 Nov. 1927. *SArk*. *SkY Urheiluos*. Volume Fbl.

12. Jarmo Matikainen, 'Suojeluskuntajärjestön yhteydet Euroopan muihin sotilasjärjestöihin ja ulkovaltoihin vuosina 1920–1934' (unpublished Master's thesis, University of Helsinki, 1989), 1, see also 13. In the study Matikainen gives a time limit, because 'we cannot talk of independent foreign co-operation, however after 1934 when the Civil Guards were moved over to the organization's divisional mobilization duties' and 'the Civil Guards tried even more to integrate themselves with the country's regular armed forces'. Ibid., 51.

13. 'Eestin suojeluskuntajärjestö', *Kannaksen Vartio*, 7–8 (1937), 229–33; Matikainen, 17–20.

14. 'Sotilaallinen nuorisokasvatus Puolassa', *Hakkapeliitta*, 34 (1939), 1059; see also Matikainen, 30–3.

15. Valkoinen neekeri i.e. the white negro, ' "Viides rengas" rakoilee', *Hakkapeliitta*, 31 (1937), 96; Matikainen, 37–40.

16. Estonia Kaitseliit headquarters' letter no. 2201.27 to Colonel Lauri Malmberg 7.1.1928 and *SkY*'s letter 3395.30.1d to Estonia Kaitseliit headquarters 20.5.1930. *SArk*. *SkY Urheiluos*. Volume Fb2.

17. Estonia Kaitseliit headquarters' letter no. 2201.27 to Colonel Lauri Malmberg 7 Jan. 1928 and *SkY*'s letter no. 746.28.1d to Colonel Roska (Kaitseliit headquarters) 4.2.1929. Estonia Kaitseliit headquarters' letter no. 2701.28 to Colonel Lauri Malmberg 19 Jan.1929 and *SkY*'s letter 559.29.1d to Kaitseliit headquarters in Tallinn 4 Feb. 1929. *SArk*. *SkY Urheiluos*. Volume Fb I; *SkY*'s letter no. 972.29.1d to the Civil Guard district leaders of Viipuri, Mikkeli, Jyväskylä and Southern Häme. *SArk*. *SkY Urheiluos*. Volume Db3.

18. Wladyslaw Los, 'Puolan suojeluskuntain marssikilpailut', *Hakkapeliitta*, 45 (1938), 1400 and 1401.

19. Ilmari Vartiainen, 'Puolan suojeluskunnat ja armeija suksilla', *Hakkapeliitta*, 17 (1938), 520–2.

20. *SArk*. *SkY Urheiluos*. Volume Fb2: Wettkampfbestimmungen für die internationalen Skiwettbewerbe die im Jahre 1937 von Suomen Suojeluskuntajärjestö angeordnet werden; SkY's letter no. 7617.36. Id to all district leaders 14 Dec. 1936, SkY's letters (Finnish copies without filing numbers) to Estonia Kaitseliit leader 30 Dec.1936 and to Latvia's and Poland's civil guard leaders 31 Dec.1936; Kaitseliit headquarter's letter no. 418.R to Colonel Lauri

Malmberg 8 Dec.1937; Programm des Aufenthaltes der Skimannschaften in Eesti Bestimmungen der Skiwettbewerbe zwischen freiwilligen Selbstschutzorganizationen Finnlands, Lettlands, Polens und Estlands, die seitens des Eesti Kaitseliit von 18.–20. Februar 1938 in Wiljandi veranstaltet werden; SkY's letter no. 1195.38.ld to the district leaders Southern Häme, Northern Savo, Kymenlaakso and Northern Karelia 7 Feb. 1938 and Estonia Kaitseliit headquarters' letter no. 418.R to SkY 8 Feb. 1938.

21. The suggestion of the Civil Guard Organization's standpoint on the question of continuing the international civil guard skiing, written by Lauri Pihkala, the leader of the sports section of the High Command of the Civil Guard Organization. *SArk. SkY Urheiluos.* Volume Fb2,

22. Matikainen, 81 and 97.

23. *Der grosse Brockhaus, Volume 5,* 16. völlig neuarbeitete Aufiage (Oldenburg, 1954), p.330.

24. About the Stahlhelm's membership development see for example Dieter Fricke, Werner Fritsch, Herbert Gottwald, Siegfried Schmidt and Manfred Weissbecker (eds.), *Lexikon zur Parteiengeschichte: Die bürgerlichen und kleinbürgerlichen Parteien und Verbände in Deutschland 1789–1945,* ibn vier Bänden, Band I (Leipzig, 1983), p.145. Generally on the organization see ibid, pp.145–58; Seppo Hentilä, 'Proletarische Wehrertüchtigung' durch den Sport?' (unpublished manuscript, Helsinki, 1995). The manuscript used by the present author is a part of Hentilä's research on Europe's workers' sports and cultural movements; Hans Jürgen Kuron, *Freikorps und Bund Oberland* (dissertation, Erlangen, 1960), 134.

25. Traditionsgemeinschaft der Freikorps und Bundes Oberland (ed.), *Bildchronik zur Geschichte des Freikorps und Bundes Oberland.* Edited by (hereafter *Bildchronik*) (Munich, 1974), pp.177 and 200.

26. Medizinball, 'a ball used for medical purposes'. It was bigger and heavier than a basket ball, and if used correctly could be used in gymnastics exercises for stretching and so forth.

27. *Bildchronik,* p.222.

28. Finanzorganization F. O. Vortrag 29 Oct.1925 (speaker's name cut off). *Bundesarchiv-Militärarchiv* (German Federal Archives – Military Archives, Freiburg im Breisgau, hereafter BA-M). Sammlung (Collection) Reichsheer Volume 8/v. 923.

29. Germany's Reichswehr's headquarters'(Chef der Heeresleitung) leader's letter no. T.A.Nr. 570/3 geh.Kdos T 2 IH A to the German Reichswehrminister (i.e. national minister of defence) 15 July 1932. BA-M. Sammlung Reichswehr Volume 8/v. 896 B 1. 154–5.

30. Militärische Forderungen an eine Organisation zur Errichtung der deutschen Jugend. Encl. in the former. BA-M. Sammlung Reichsheer Volume 8/v.

31. *Richtlinien für die Ausbildung im Geländesport: Als Manuskript gedruckt im Auftrage des Reichsministers des Innern* (Berlin, 1932).

32. Ibid.

33. Ibid.

Sport in Society: The Nordic World and Other Worlds

J.A. MANGAN

There are Ibsenian images of the 'Nordic World' in western culture that lend themselves to pantheistic romanticism; silver birch trees fringing the lonely lake, a white church reflected in a glassy fiord, snow-tipped firs shimmering in the cold sunshine. Likewise there is an Aryan romanticism associated with the blue-eyed, blond-haired 'Norsemen' from Nordic fiords and forests, an image cultivated, it sometimes seems, by almost every elementary school teacher – at least in Britain!

And if at least one British historian of sport is correct in his assertion regarding the gullibility of those who once viewed British pre-industrial sport through heavily rose-tinted spectacles, then such *ingénus*, if they existed and still exist, would surely find it hard to resist extending their romantic imagination to pre-industrial Nordic sport![1]

Mats Hellspong, whose main interest is the contrast between traditional and contemporary Swedish sport, therefore, serves realists and history well by making it clear, in passing, that Swedish traditional sports have their roots, at least in part, in pre-industrial duelling with sword and dagger. His brief, description of the grotesque 'sport' of 'bältesspänning' or knife-fighting, presents a firmly unromantic image of writhing and struggling protagonists, bound together by a single belt, stabbing and thrusting at each other watched by their anxious women clutching large sheets to bind up the cuts and slashes and stem the flow of blood.

However, perhaps even more to the historical point, he states emphatically in his conclusion that in the recent evolution of sport in Sweden there was an absolute hiatus, with the single exception of the island of Gotland, between 'traditional' sport and 'modern' sport: 'The break in continuity *was* clear cut ... at the end of the nineteenth century a number of new sports appeared which had no predecessors in traditional culture. Sport became newly cosmopolitan and unambiguously modern.'[2] Traditional sports in mainland Sweden, states Hellspong, withered away with the coming of the modern sports of Cotton, Coubertin and their Nordic proselytizers, enthusiasts and camp-followers.[3]

Hellspong takes issue with Richard Holt in his assumption, in a British context, of a nineteenth-century situation of some change and some continuity of differing speeds in different places, observing that such a model of evolution has no relevance for Sweden.[4]

Interestingly, Roger Hutchinson, in his recent book confidently entitled *Empire Games: The British Invention of Twentieth Century Sport*, implicitly makes much the same point about the Outer Hebrides. Hutchinson describes the arrival of Frederic Rea in December 1889 at Lochboisdale on the Hebridean island of South Uist – the first Catholic, albeit English, headmaster since the Reformation.[5] South Uist was well off any beaten track: 'although part of the United Kingdom, [it] was more alien to most of the people of England and lowland Scotland than many parts of Asia, Africa, Australia and America. Far more British civil servants spoke Urdu than the language of the Hebrides, Scottish Gaelic.'[6]

South Uist, claims Hutchinson, was 'an alien land, an incomprehensible place, a district almost unrecognisable as part of Britain',[7] and it shared with the rest of the Hebrides and mainland Gaidhealtached 'an antique repertoire of sports and recreations':[8] 'cluich an tighe' (a form of rounders), 'speilean' (known in various forms in Britain and North America as cat and bat, bat and trap and trap and ball), 'spidean' (a form of pitch and toss), 'propataireachd' (a form of quoits, and 'leagail sheaghdair' (a form of skittles). The boys wrestled ('carachd') and the girls danced ('iomart fhaochag'). And for as long as both spoken and written records could be recalled, over some 500 years the islanders had played 'iomain' or 'camanachd', literally 'the bent-stick game' known more widely as shinty.

Within two decades, if Hutchinson is to be believed, 'shinty was no longer played there ... One thousand four hundred years of deeply ingrained sporting tradition were wiped like chalk from the face of the island.'[9] And so it was with 'speilean' and 'cluich an tighe'. Custom was abandoned, neither maliciously nor necessarily calculatedly but remarkably swiftly and finally, by a game 'almost as young and innocent as ... Rea himself; a game that was travelling like some benevolent virus across the shrinking world in the kitbags and carpet-bags and Gladstone bags of British soldiers, merchants, labourers, ministers of religion, and schoolmasters.'[10] Such happenings occurred not only in South Uist and the Outer Hebrides, of course, but across the world. 'They were imperial ... repeated on ... Indian *maidans* and ... across the high veldts of Victoria's possessions.'[11]

Homo Ludens Imperiosus, 'in his imperial role of man of firm duty, confident ambitious moral intention *and* applied athletics' was abroad on his civilizing mission.[12] This was as true of the Catholic schoolmaster, Frederic Rea, in Lochboisdale, South Uist as it was of the Anglican schoolmaster, Cecil Earle Tyndale-Biscoe, in Srinagar, Kashmir.[13] For Rea, cast in the moralistic mould of English elementary schoolteachers of the period,[14] ancient shinty, says Hutchinson, would have seemed 'more of a barbaric route than a sport, possessing no civilised or civilising attributes at all'.[15] For Tyndale-Biscoe, modern (British) sport created 'the muscle and the skill to fight evil and to promote good', the essential virtues of Christian civilization.[16] And for both Rea and Tyndale-Biscoe soccer was a main means of moral persuasion.[17]

The two islands, South Uist and Gotland,[18] in their polarised cultural responses to the emergence of modern sport, offer an opportunity to reflect on the possibility of a cultural model of transition from pre-industrial to industrial sport in Europe, and very probably many other parts of the world, that goes beyond the somewhat nebulous and certainly incomplete explanatory model contained in the rather vague statement, 'the early nineteenth century was less unambiguously "traditional" and the late nineteenth century less "modern" than appearance might suggest'.[19] There is irony, too, in the statement by the same author that the interplay of change and continuity, persistence in some things and innovation in others, is too complex to be slotted neatly into a simple 'modernization' model.[20] A simple modernization model, in appropriate circumstances, may well be entirely appropriate. The paradox of complexity is occasional simplicity! That much is clear from the research of Hellspong and Hutchinson.

The issue, of course, is one of ensuring a sufficiently comprehensive and precise explanatory model of change and continuity to capture, as far as possible, 'reality'.[21] Any consideration of the evolution of modern sport in Europe must embrace a constellation of credible concepts. It is more than likely, it is suggested here, that in both Britain and the rest of western Europe in the late nineteenth and early twentieth centuries there could be found in different places at different times partial and total continuity of custom, change of custom that was slow, gradual and fast, termination of custom that was also slow, gradual and fast and parallelism – continuity and change existing side by side – extensive, moderate and limited. There also was, most certainly, assimilation, adaptation and rejection associated with diffusion at differing speeds, in various forms and in differing intensities for a multiplicity of reasons. In short, the matter of degree of continuity and change merits the closest consideration. And as a corollary, there is segmentation – the attitudes and actions of different groups *and* individuals in society which determine the extent of change, continuity, termination and parallelism.

With regard to the diffusion of British sport as a cohesive force throughout its empire,[22] it has been argued that it is sensible to appreciate that

> there was no culturally monolithic response to attempts to utilise sport as an imperial bond. A major problem that the analyst of ideological

proselytism and its cultural consequences should confront is the nature of interpretation, assimilation and adaptation and the extent of resistance and rejection by the proselytised – in a phrase, the extent and form of ideological implementation. Any analyst worth his salt should be aware of cultural discontinuities as well as continuities. The unanticipated consequences of stated intentions are neither unusual nor unreal.[23]

It is an argument that applies *equally* to the diffusion of modern sport in Europe (and Britain) in the late nineteenth and early twentieth centuries.

It is rather obvious, then, and not necessarily particularly illuminating, to observe that one part of the nineteenth century was less than wholly traditional in its sport and one part less than wholly modern. A greater sensitivity to conceptual possibilities and the use of a wider conceptual vocabulary clearly offers the opportunity for more subtle interpretations of evolutionary progress. As has been observed in another context 'the task of analysing the nature of the purposes, processes and significance of sport as a form of cultural association is a complex one'.[24] It requires sophistication of concept and contemplation. An attempt at precisely this sophistication of concept and contemplation along the lines set out above as an antidote to earlier analytical simplification, in the specific setting of a micro-cultural case-study – Winchester College, an institutional repository of both continuity and change in sport covering some four hundred years of British cultural evolution, is at present underway.[25] The usefulness of this approach in due course can be considered by others. The hope is that it will serve as an explanatory device offering more profound insights into the complicated and changing relationship between sport, culture and society than the somewhat unsubtle approach referred to earlier. Hellspong's assertion has resonances for other worlds beyond the Nordic world.

It may be helpful, however, to offer an immediate illustration of how those who argue partially for some measure, but certainly not enough, of analytical complexity associated with continuity and change can overlook essential steps in the process. The illustration deals with the much applauded, much trumpeted, much admired concept of 'fair play',[26] an 'Anglo-Saxon' concept as enthusiastically praised in the Nordic nations, as Per Jørgensen makes clear in this volume, as anywhere else – and which at least regarding its early moments, is widely misunderstood. Nowhere more clearly than in this statement:

> The Victorians would never have subscribed to the contemporary orthodoxy that 'winning isn't the most important thing, it's the only thing'. Their philosophy of competition was altogether more subtle, emphasizing the value of victory much less than the utility of failure.

> The downgrading the mere 'winning' of games in favour of simply 'taking part' lay in the impetus this gave to widespread participation and to the idea of life as a constant struggle. By teaching boys how to lose well and how to win with dignity, the wider competitive principle was strengthened. For to succeed in any competition – sporting, academic, or economic – the odds were very much that you would lose before you would win. It was vital that boys should not be discouraged by initial set-backs and that they should persevere until success finally came.[27]

The emphasis in the latter part of the above passage is modern, liberal and 'therapeutic'! The *period* emphasis was less concerned with the creation of 'positive self-image' and the avoidance of low esteem than with control, order and containment.[28] Even when 'fair play' had served its initial purpose of transforming middle- and upper-class hooligans into heroes, it was utilized as a symbol of moral superiority rather than an instrument of pastoral therapy.[29]

Furthermore, any historian who has taken the trouble to read thoroughly the detailed studies of late Victorian and Edwardian public school life and the numerous biographies and autobiographies available dealing with school life, cannot fail to be aware of its ruthless system of winners and losers – 'bloods' (athletic heroes) and others, athletes and 'remnants', 'hearties' and 'aesthetes'.[30]

This system produced numerous bitter recollections. To take but one notable example, Anthony Blunt, aesthete and intellectual, was so scarred by his harsh experiences at the hands of the 'bloods' at Marlborough in the 1920s[31] that it is quite reasonable to suggest that his later loathing of the British Establishment and his career as a spy for the Soviet Union was, in part, the product of his schooldays. His lack of success at games and his consequent low institutional status brought ridicule, mockery and harassment. He was savagely discouraged!

Blunt became a distinguished art critic; C.R. Nevinson became a famous painter. He described his days at Uppingham, a public school in the Midlands, as follows:

> I had no wish to go to any such school at all, but nevertheless Uppingham did seem to be the best. Since then I have often wondered what the worst was like. No qualms of mine gave me an inkling of the horrors I was to undergo … the brutality and bestiality in the dormitories made life a hell on earth. An apathy settled on me. I withered. I learned nothing: I did nothing. I was kicked, hounded, caned, flogged, hairbrushed, morning, noon and night. The more I suffered, the less I cared. The longer I stayed, the harder I grew.[32]

In this extract there is not a shred of evidence of gradual inclusion through encouragement. Nevinson's was not the experience of all, but it was without question the experience of many. He was far from untypical.

It flies in the face of endless evidence to write of 'fair play' as the late nineteenth- and early twentieth-century equivalent of a modern school guidance and counselling system attempting to ensure self-respect. To coin a phrase: 'Tell that to the pre-Great War public schoolboy'! Plainly put, it is a travesty of the historic truth. It is quite possible that it is not only antiquarians peddling a *Lucky Jim* world of 'Merrie England' who can be gullible.[33]

As it has been clearly stated, but equally clearly not understood by some sports historians, in the public schools there was more often than not 'an ideology for public consumption and an ideology for personal practice: in a phrase Muscular Christianity for the consumer, Social Darwinism for the constrained.'[34] It has also been stated that 'various ideologies *co-existed* in the public schools. They overlapped, even fused on occasion, but certain of their elements were discrete even contradictory. To fail to recognise this is to neglect a real complexity in favour of an unreal simplicity.'[35]

Apart from some recent historians of sport,[36] among those who have wholly failed to appreciate the genesis of the concept of 'fair play', incidentally, was Pierre de Coubertin.[37] Coubertin was a man of aristocratic prejudice, historical misconception and utopian idealism: in his view 'fair play' was an inherent quality of the English gentleman and sport as played by the English gentleman was a means of promoting international harmony. Here the intention is to describe in some detail the *real* origins of the concept of English 'fair play' so dear to his heart and so largely misunderstood by him and some recent and current sports historians, and to argue that the concept in its genesis was a utilitarian rather than an idealistic instrument in the past – and, incidentally, should be an equally utilitarian concept in the present and the future.

In the nineteenth century the term 'fair play' became closely linked to the games field. Why was this? To answer this question a brief history of nineteenth-century middle- and upper-class education in Britain is necessary. Between approximately 1850 and 1900 the members of the private boarding schools and universities of the English middle and upper classes 'invented' several major games in a modernized form.[38] For reasons too lengthy and complicated to go into here, team games became the centre of public school life.[39]

In the schools these games were instruments of reform. Prior to 1850 life in the schools, to adapt the classic Hobbesian expression, was nasty, brutish and certainly for some, not short enough. These schools were often godless, cold and brutal places.[40] Eton, arguably the most famous of these schools, was a microcosm of a macrocosm – the external upper-class world beyond the schools' walls; a world of hard-drinking, horse-racing, gambling, blood sports, prize fighting and sexual indulgence.[41] Internal entertainments in the evenings were boy-made – sometimes esoteric, idiosyncratic, and both bloody and bloodthirsty:

> In Long Chamber, Collegers, locked up for the night in their quarters, would engage periodically in a traditional domestic sport of their own ... When lights went out, in the darkness each night the rats came in troops, ... On the night of a grande chasse traps were baited and set
>
> ...
>
> When a sufficient host was judged to have been lured on to the killing ground, the longed-for order to attack was given; the boys leapt out of bed, and silence and darkness were changed into the cries of hunters and the glare of torches. The rats stampeded. But all known holes and escape routes had been blocked. Fugitives took refuge under beds and bureaux and were pursued and bludgeoned to death in half an hour's good run of the grande chasse ... the rats were stripped of their skins, which were carefully stretched and dried, and the trophies nailed in rows over the broad fireplaces from the ceilings downwards.[42]

While at Harrow, certainly one of the more famous of the schools:

> The wildness, brutality and irresponsibility of [the] boys of the times is extensively recorded. Torre recalled that in the years before Vaughan many boys kept a dog and cats, the one to kill the others. He mentioned another popular activity – stone-throwing – and described fights between the Harrow boys and the navvies building the London and North-Western railway. [43]

Before the middle of the nineteenth century rebellions within the schools were not uncommon events. Bored, starving and brutalized boys occasionally turned on their official tormentors with explosive resentment. There were rebellions and uprisings in the schools throughout the eighteenth and nineteenth centuries. Among the most notorious were Eton (1768), Westminster (1793), Rugby (1797), Winchester (1818) and Marlborough (1850).

However, after 1850 there were no more major rebellions or uprisings. The transformation of English upper-middle class masculinity from well-bred hooligan to well-bred hero had begun. And the centre of this process was the public school House System.[44] The last notable rebellion, at a school in the West Country called Marlborough, occurred in 1850.[45] The date is significant. This last rebellion brought about an educational revolution in

the schools – the coming of compulsory team games, the creation of
extensive and expensive playing fields and the establishment of cups and
cup-ties, leagues and league tables as an *antidote* to revolt.

In 1852, when George Edward Lynch Cotton became head master of
Marlborough, then a rather seedy public school mostly for the sons of
Church of England ministers of modest means, he arrived hard on the heels
of 'The Great Rebellion' of 1850. He gave careful thought to both reform
and renaissance. Another revolution would be bad for the school – and bad
for his career. By a brilliant piece of social engineering he ended rebellions
for ever and inadvertently laid the foundations of a *social* revolution – the
Games Cult of the English Public School that in time serendipitously swept
the world – and, to a large extent, 'taught it to play' in the modern idiom
initiating, as this volume bears part witness, a 'Global Sporting Revolution'
that has yet to run its course.[46]

Arguably, in the history of world sport Cotton is as, if not probably more,
important than Coubertin. However, be that as it may, both Cotton, the
realist, and Coubertin, the idealist, were major 'agents of change' who had
considerable influence both directly and indirectly, on the sport of the
twentieth century. Cotton used team games as instruments of social control.
He divided his boarding school into Houses, each with some fifty boys and
a master chosen for his enthusiasm for games, he made successful athletes
into house prefects (leaders) and he introduced house leagues and cups to
maintain interest in games-playing.[47] Games, of course, need games fields,
and he persuaded the parents of his boys to devote funds for their creation.[48]
This 'house-system' in its immediate post-1850 form was adopted
throughout the public school system: extensive playing fields, compulsory
games, cups and cup-ties, leagues and championships became commonplace
throughout the public school world – and later throughout the whole world.

A transformation now came about in upper-middle class masculinity and
morality, in adolescent manners and mores. Not least of the innovations
which followed closely in the wake of the facilities and arrangements, was
a set of values to ensure constructive rather than destructive involvement on
the now extensive and expensive public school playing fields. In the words
of one famous public school headmaster:

> A game is to be played for the game's sake ... no unfair advantage of
> any sort can ever be taken ... within the rules no mercy is to be
> expected, or accepted or shown by either side; the lesson to be learnt
> by each individual is the subordination of self in order that he may
> render his best service as the member of a team in which he relies
> upon all the rest; and all the rest rely upon him ... Finally, never on
> any occasion must he show the white feather.[49]

There is little evidence here of concern for individual self-image or anxiety over loss of self-esteem!

Cotton's house system and the subsequent public school house system operated functionally at several levels. It ensured that sizeable numbers of boys 'could be herded together away from home and its comforts and be adequately controlled and emotionally sustained', but it also served as a crucible, in which under the most extreme 'heat' individuality was moulded into conformity.[50] Control rather than concern was the catchword.

Innovation, of course, contained the seeds of a problem – the possibility of anarchic, undisciplined brutality on the new formal games fields as a continuation of a similar and earlier behaviour on earlier informal school gamesfields, in school yards, in streets, lanes and the countryside. Clearly a new code of conduct has to be sharply defined, implemented and enforced by the new athletic masters recruited to the schools. The generic name of that code was 'fair play'.

The genesis of 'fair play' lay, therefore, not in nobility but in savagery, and not in pastoral concern but in pupil control. And 'fair play' was not the instinctive behaviour of gentlemen but the acquired behaviour of roughnecks, albeit of some social standing. It was cultivated carefully as a practical tool. It was a means of ensuring *controlled confrontation* in the physical struggles on the new playing fields. Eventually around the concept of 'fair play' a mythology grew. It was required. The image of the schools had to be redeemed. Evangelicalism had sobered some of the middle and upper classes: survival now demanded the same of the middle- and upper-class schools.

Necessity became Morality – and then Mythology!

The term 'fair play' is to be found in the sixteenth century but had no association with sport. By the end of the nineteenth century it had come to mean 'upright conduct in a game' and was closely associated with games and games fields! How did this come about? The answer is set out above. A transformation from unlicensed hooliganism to licensed heartiness was needed. The purpose of 'fair play', as a utilitarian instrument of social engineering, was to promote social integration and avoid social disintegration. The public school sector rose to the challenge. In the Social Darwinian climate of the second half of the nineteenth century individuals simply made the best of it.

'Manliness, a substantive widely favoured by prelates on speech days and headmasters on Sundays, embraced antithetical values – success, aggression and ruthlessness, yet victory within the rules, courtesy in triumph, compassion for the defeated.'[51] This image of the integrated, 'cloned', controlled and confident winner took the Western World by storm. Private necessity became a public virtue.

> 'Fair Play' is a great conception, ... in these two words are summed up all that English education and ethics hold most dear ... Fair play means ... seeing the man and fellow-player in one's opponent ... The youngest English child learns that it is wrong to take advantage of the weak, and unmanly to ill-treat a beaten adversary ... In brief, sport is England's greatest teacher.[52]

And team games became a means of moral inculcation:

> By virtue of their play-sense the English have acquired certain qualities which are as precious to themselves as they are pleasing to others ... remarkable social and moral gifts, the result of team work, that is to say manly rivalry under the aegis of fair play.[53]

And 'Anglo-Saxon' qualities encapsulated in the expression 'fair play', which many came to consider *inherent* rather than inculcated, became emblems of moral superiority in victory and defeat. In the words of one imperial moralist, Rev. Dr S. P. P. Slater:

> We would rather lose a game than win it unfairly. We would rather respect the spirit of the law than its letter. We would exact a spirit of absolute obedience to the authorities set over us, never questioning the umpire. We would desire in a race or a game [to] go on if we can till we drop dead. We would hope that the spirit would be developed amongst us which is not so very greatly concerned for itself, so long as the side on which we are is successful.[54]

A myth of extraordinary potency and longevity thus came into being: the manly decency of the English gentleman.

The late Victorian and Edwardian Games Cult of the English Public School and the Myth of the English Gentleman were greatly admired by certain influential continental Europeans including the Swede, Viktor Balck, and certainly not least Coubertin.[55] Their endorsement aided their ascendancy and created within the schools themselves a complacent and confident ethnocentricity. As Jeffrey Richards has remarked

> 'Fair Play' became the motto of a nation whose ideology and religious faith were subsumed under Imperialism, with its belief in the British as the elect who had a God-given duty to govern and civilise the world. In the wake of imperialism the public schools in particular their games fields became 'mints for turning out Empire-builders'.[56]

In short, a seldom appreciated consequence of ethnocentricity was the transformation of the famous concept of 'fair play' from a utilitarian instrument of private control into a moralistic public virtue largely 'peculiar' to the upper- and middle-class English schoolboy. In turn, this concept became for numerous Englishmen, for some continental Europeans and for many around the globe a symbol of the superiority of the English Gentleman. 'Fair play' was seen as both his largely exclusive property and, to an extent, one source of his imperial success.

After the Great War public school moral priorities were widely challenged by British and other critics and the games cult was increasingly derided and eventually became defunct.[57] However, the ideal of 'fair play' was above suspicion and beyond criticism. It remained a source of admiration and envy in Continental Europe and around the globe. Merely one indication of the longevity of its appeal was its adoption as a hopeful exhortation in the European Nations Cup of 1990. Clearly its origins were never scrutinized, its original purpose never understood and its adoption as a symbol of ebullient chauvinism generally insufficiently appreciated. Coubertin in his time was caught up in this wider European eulogistic euphoria – and the rest, as they say, is Olympic history!

Above a historical reality is reconstructed. What of its modern relevance? Does the past have a message for the present? Unquestionably. This is the irony. Modern sport is replete with destructive elements – amoral commercialism, professional cheating, drug abuse. The origins of 'fair play' as a *means of calculated control* should be understood, and the practical value of the concept – in a modern workable form – should be appreciated. The past is ignored at our peril. Cotton and his innovations contain a message for our time. Among others, Coubertin's successors have need of him.

And what of John Major's *Raising the Game*?[58] History revisited. Forward into the past. Once again games are to be used as a form of control, distraction and discipline. Off the streets and onto the sports fields. And athlete 'super stars', the 'bloods' of the post-millennium, are role models. Games for nineteenth-century advantaged and bored adolescents are to become games for twentieth- century disadvantaged and bored adolescents. Tradition reinvented!

In passing, incidentally, it should be stressed that the debt of modern sport to past middle- and upper-class public schoolboys (and masters) is considerable and as yet not fully explored.[59] Of course, it is not total. However, public schoolboys and staff at school and in later life in Britain, Empire and elsewhere, did systematize, re-organize and regulate, in its early moments, a good deal of what is now considered modern sport, especially modern team games. The schools *were* responsible for a 'revolution' and their members were 'revolutionaries' by accident, by calculation and by chance in varying measures.

The middle and upper middle classes, as the contributors to *The Nordic World* make abundantly clear, made a disproportionate contribution to the early evolution of modern sport. Their individual and collective contributions have not so much been overestimated as underestimated. Much research in the Nordic nations, and all around the world, remains to be done to locate the middle and upper class, as well as the working class, inspirationalists and innovators of what has been called 'the Global Sporting Revolution' of the modern age.[60]

Other contributors to *The Nordic World* also raise issues, directly and indirectly, that advance our knowledge of the significance of sport in society. Erkki Vasara, in his discussion of selected European 'voluntary defence forces' between the wars, provides a reasonable, detailed outline of the structural arrangements put in place in Finland and in a selection of other European nations to ensure a military capability of body *and* mind. This is useful in as far as it goes but it contains shortcomings revealed elsewhere by those who make perhaps too much of obvious national structural arrangements such as conscription, and certainly make too little of rhetorical agents of indoctrination such as popular literature.[61]

Vasara, therefore, advances the discussion of the relationship between sport and war, and sport as a training for war, both directly by offering evidence of appropriate and effective structural agents and indirectly by virtually ignoring the agencies creating, sustaining and propagating an appropriate militaristic mind set. He is certainly not alone.

The significance of this omission can be illustrated by means or reference to another world In recent years in British historiography a revisionist school of historians, too little known, it would appear, to sports historians to their disadvantage, which includes Geoffrey Best, Jeffrey Richards, John MacKenzie, Anne Summers and others,[62] has revealed an intense militaristic indoctrination, predominantly but *not* exclusively, of the young of the middle and upper-middle classes in late Victorian society by linking playing-field and battlefield, militarism, patriotism and imperialism. However, it is important to be clear that this was not restricted to the public school system!

> In the early years of the twentieth century, the public school ... 'tradition' of duty, discipline and self-sacrifice was given wider social sanction, visibility and expression. As MacKenzie has made clear this 'tradition' inspired a host of associations and organisations in an effort to give it wider focus, stimulus and momentum. These included the Boy Scouts, the Boys' Brigade, Empire Youth Movement and lesser groups such as the Navy League, the Legion of Frontiersmen, the National Service League, the Girls' Patriotic League, the League of Empire, and the British Empire Union. The 'tradition' was promoted

with special determination by the tireless efforts of Reginald Brabazon, twelfth Earl of Meath (1841–1928) through three social movements – the Lads' Drill Association, the Duty and Discipline Movement and the Empire Day Movement.[63]

This indoctrination was potent in its impact, profound in its effect and militaristic in its nature.

When reflecting on militarism in Britain, at least on one occasion, the sports historian appears to have dipped his smallest toe into the available pool of literature.[64] It is hardly surprising that the full extent of and *the particular nature of* British Victorian and Edwardian militarism seems to have escaped his notice. As Anne Summers put it so pertinently, the fact that Britain produced 1.5 million volunteers in the first two years of the Great War suggests that the nation must have developed, over a long period, a very wide and pervasive range of military or militaristic modes of thinking.[65] Exactly. Dipping quickly into the 'pool', or to change the metaphor, trawling a shallow catch of sources instead of hauling out a deep catch of books and articles, has clear dangers. These dangers are increased if even structural dimensions such as educational innovations in both private and state education across Britain are insufficiently understood.

Speaking of Britain, Corelli Barnett, the distinguished military historian, once wrote that 'to hear politicians and constitutional historians holding forth on the virtues of parliamentary democracy, it is easy to forget that ours is a civilisation largely born out of war and devoted to it'.[66] These are bold but true words, and no truer in their application than to the late nineteenth century when training for sport and war in Britain went hand in hand.

The historian John Gooch is in no doubt. By the turn of the century, he states, *virtually everyone* seemed to be interested in war.[67] How was this interest achieved? Certainly not by conscription. There was none. Certainly not by the soldiers of a large standing army on the Prussian or French model marching up and down like a parade of peacocks exciting young and old with their martial beauty, precision and virility. There was no such army. Certainly not by state endorsement of sport across the whole nation. Of course, there was some state endorsement of exercise for military purposes and there was extensive private endorsement of sport as a training for war. Nevertheless there was no lack of 'jingoism' (the British coined the word!) due to a lack of national sporting bodies across Britain. There was a network of remarkably effective military inspirationalists and activists across the nation that went well beyond the public school system. None of this is to suggest that there were no differences between Continental Europe and Great Britain, but there were more similarities than have been understood, recognized and appreciated.

The myth of Britain in the late nineteenth and early twentieth centuries as an anti-militaristic society can no longer be sustained. The reverse was true: 'emphasis on military matters was intense. It amounted to the worship of war as a sacred path to moral purity, ascendancy and domination. In the second half of the nineteenth century war came to be seen as a moral mandate.'[68] Extraordinary claims were made for it. John Ruskin, as an aged aesthete, was moved to declaim to an audience of young philistine officers at the Royal Military Academy, Woolwich: 'All great nations were nourished in war and wasted in peace, taught by war and deceived by peace, trained in war and betrayed by peace – in a word, they were born in war and expired in peace.'[69]

Others were no less eulogistic about the merits of war.[70] This fact, its links with the playing field and its considerable significance for socialization through art and literature seems largely to have escaped the notice of sports historians despite the ample academic evidence and analysis available. Yet, in the Age of the New Imperialism, towards the end of the nineteenth century, 'a rhetoric of jingoistic conceit in poetry, prose and painting ... coalesced into a triadic instrument of propaganda in which ... the *self-sacrificial subaltern* [junior officer] – was celebrated'.[71] Just why 'colonial battlefields [*and the later Great War battlefields*][72] were exotic versions of the playing fields of Eton and elsewhere'[73] can be indicated, by merely two of many available quotations.

Esmé Wingfield-Stratford wrote in his autobiography *Before the Lamps Went Out*:

> ... the whole atmosphere of the time seemed to be faintly redolent of gunpowder ... among those who professed and called themselves gentlefolk in the *fin de siècle* – and I think this would apply to an *even wider circle* [emphasis added] – everybody seemed to be talking about those two linked attractions of war and empire.[74]

and later in his book he made it abundantly clear that war for many public school subalterns was a game:

> It would be a mistake to imagine that this light-hearted playing with fire had anything in common with the grim blood lust of Continental militarism. Nations with open frontiers, and every fit man a soldier, did not think of war as a game, played between professional teams for the entertainment of the ordinary civilian. But that was just how we, in those roaring 'nineties, did think of it. And though the best, it was only one of many games.[75]

The rhetoric of indoctrination was astonishing in its efficacy. Geoffrey Best has referred to an epidemic of martial enthusiasm in British society and especially in its public schools, the schools for the privileged, and sought its source. In his view, location could lead to an understanding of the nation's attitude to war (not simply imperial wars) , and even more importantly, it might allow detection of the sources of the militarism he considered responsible for the Great War to a far greater degree than 'incidents', assassinations, telegrams and ultimata[76] – and, it should be added, Continental conscription and national sporting bodies. The search of Best and others is sensitive and subtle. It recognizes the power of the forces of ideological rhetoric and the associated instrument of conditioning into militaristic conformity – the school playing field.

It is naïve to divorce imperial militarism from a wider militarism,[77] particularly in association with a widely anticipated European confrontation.[78] An awareness of the threat of a coming war with Germany characterized the last decade of the nineteenth and the first decade of the twentieth centuries.[79] A 'war paranoia gripped the Britain of the late Victorian-Edwardian period'.[80] One result was 'that Vigilance was the key word in boy's literature during the years which preceded the Great War, and readers must have realised that they were being exhorted to prepare for the defence of Great Britain – not for the expansion of Greater Britain.'[81]

It is equally naïve to consider that anti-German propaganda on the part of bitter Continental enemies of Germany was an exclusive outcome of their militarism and was exclusive in its vitriol.[82] *The War Illustrated*, early in the Great War, wrote of the German soldier: 'His face is fully expressive of all the savagery and "frightfulness" associated with the exponents of higher civilisation, so-called … compare his physiognomy with the frank, open countenance of the British.'[83] And more than this, as Colin Veitch has observed, 'sport allowed an athletic distinction to be drawn between the two nations who shared the same racial and linguistic heritage … sports and games were [means] through which the Englishman could be shown to have acquired his national character, and without which the German nation had lapsed into military barbarism'.[84] As Veitch records, sport was used persistently in the propaganda of English physical, moral and military superiority and German inferiority.[85]

> Full sixty yards I've seen them throw
> With all that nicety of aim
> They learn on British cricket fields.
> Ah, bombing is a Briton's game!
> Shell-hole to shell-hole, trench to trench,
> 'Lobbing them over' with an eye
> As true as though it were a game
> And friends were having tea close by.[86]

The extent of the impact of the highly influential forces of indoctrination, prose, poetry and painting, has been exhaustively analysed and examples extensively presented,[87] but seemingly insufficiently absorbed and appreciated by the sports historians.[88]

And yet as Michael Howard has stated:

> one of the explicit criteria of national education after 1870 in most Western European countries was to produce a generation physically fit for and *psychologically attuned to war* [emphasis added]. It was a necessary part of citizenship. The history of one's country was depicted by writers both of school text-books and of popular works as the history of its military triumphs.[89]

And this was as true for Britain as it was for several other European countries.

In contrasting nationalism in Europe it is clear that the sports historian has been absorbed in institutional, structural and chronological happenings. However the consideration of structural phenomena sometimes gives cause for concern. The statement that before the Great War, while in France gymnastics were military in purpose, in contrast the 'main role of gymnastics in Britain was to provide a little rudimentary exercise for school children – 'Drill', as it was called, was brief, basic and by no means uniformly practised', for example, certainly needs amendment.[90] It demonstrates a surprising ignorance of the extent to which a military emphasis characterized elementary school gymnastics and the desire of many in society to maximize its provision, that went far beyond the mere provision of basic physical activity. The reality was considerably more complicated.

It is instructive to consider the arguments and evidence contained in Alan Penn's study of drill in the elementary school entitled *Targeting the Schools: Militarism, Elementary School and Drill 1870–1914*:

> The period 1870–75 was one in which the teaching of drill and, in particular, military drill, became an accepted practice in the nation's elementary schools. It was sanctioned by the Education Department and encouraged by members of Her Majesty's Inspectorate. It was at that time, too, that the Society for the Encouragement of Arts, Commerce and Manufactures in Great Britain (hereafter referred to as the Society of Arts) involved itself in the issue. Drill, whether 'military' or 'ordinary' was accorded a place in the curriculum of most elementary schools. Whilst the subject itself found few to criticise its inclusion there was to be sustained discussion and argument as to the form it should take.[91]

And when a gradual shift from 'military' to 'ordinary' drill gradually took place, it was not always easy to distinguish between the two.[92] The inspector for the South East Division reported in 1890, for example, that 'military drill has become less prominent, but the increasing vigour and accuracy with which the present exercises are done make this the less to be regretted'.[93] As Penn remarks, these qualities were precisely the virtues required of military drill![94]

Military drill was supported by the War Office which recommended a number of useful training manuals including the *Field Exercise Book*, and the *Manual of Elementary Military Exercise and Drill* used in army schools. In addition, there were commercially produced aids such as *School Drill, Brownes Position Drill: a Practical Guide to Squad and Setting up Drill* and *The Schoolmaster's Drill Assistant, a manual for Elementary Schools* to be used 'in boys', girls' or mixed departments'.[95]

Penn discusses at length the various subsequent actions, debates and developments:

> During the period from 1875 to 1899 parliamentary debates swung to and fro with the contest to determine what form of physical training should be provided for elementary school children. The Trades Union Congress powerfully expressed its anxiety over the looming threat of conscription and the inherent dangers of military training when imposed on children. Her Majesty's inspectors reported favourably on one kind of drill or critically on another, or drew attention to the lack of proper facilities for any form of physical exercise to be practised effectively. The introduction of variable grants for discipline and organisation and changes in the annual Codes accelerated the process by which physical training or military drill gained a permanent place in the curriculum.[96]

As in the case of the teaching of reading, writing and arithmetic, if for somewhat different reasons, there were certainly difficulties implementing both kinds of drill for both town and country schools: in towns there was a serious lack of playground space and it was not always easy to find sufficient and suitable instructors. In rural areas small schools, few available male teachers and insufficient funding posed problems. In addition, there was some opposition to drill, especially military drill. Nevertheless, Penn concludes that:

> Throughout the period 1890 to 1914 there was an active lobby in favour of securing an honoured place for the teaching of military drill within the elementary school curriculum. At times successes were dramatic, as when the powerful and influential London School Board

was persuaded to adopt the programme proposed by the Society of Arts in 1875. Influential individuals such as Lord Roberts emerged on the national stage to raise the expectations and hopes of militarists; at other times local initiatives gave evidence of practices which, if generally applied, could advance the cause significantly.[97]

The motive of the committed was far more than to provide 'a little rudimentary exercise'.[98] One school inspector of the 1880s, for example, the Rev. D.J. Stewart, an advocate of military drill, spoke of it as 'highly intelligent exercise',[99] while more typically, the Duke of Wellington in 1902 wrote, 'we must train the whole youth of the nation to arms … only thus can we maintain our position in the world. Thus, too, we can give a sense of duty, discipline, obedience and responsibility to hundreds of thousands who are without it, and improve the deteriorating physique of our large and growing urban population.' At the turn of the century: 'there were many Members of Parliament and others, who, while denying their militarism, were resolute in claiming that Britain needed to address the issue of universal military training, and were insistent that such training should commence in the elementary schools'.[100]

Of course, towards the end of the first decade of the twentieth century it was recognized by some, and perhaps surprisingly by the Board of Education, that 'elementary schoolboys could … play the game'.[101] The Department of the Board of Education for 1905–6 contained the following obeisance to 'the games ethic':

> Victory or defeat, their individual success or failure, will be far less important than 'playing the game', and from their pride in 'the school' and its good name will spring a stronger love of fair play, the power to give and take which counts for so much in the rough and tumble of life.[102]

As Penn states, 'These sentiments written in respect of elementary school children show how far the Board had moved from the earlier championing of military drill *in the interests of discipline, control, and obedience,* to instruction' [emphasis added].[103] The controlling role of drill has long been known to historians of sport. As long ago as the 1970s it was observed that:

> At the other end of the social spectrum, the Elementary School, physical training programmes reflected expected behavioural norms. Drill in this establishment was a ritualistic response to social categorization. During these activities the proles were … training for the mechanistic occupations of later life', for which, it was considered at the time, 'they were by virtue of their low condition particularly well suited.[104]

A careful and thorough analysis of the role of drill in pre-1914 elementary education offers a rather different picture of its purpose than the initial, misleading brief remark!

There is much of relevance in recent British research on the propaganda of the playing fields that Nordic analysts can read with advantage. Jørn Hansen, in his contribution to *The Nordic World*, provides a too brief glimpse of the force of nationalistic rhetoric in stiffening patriotic resolve, in perpetuating a sense of national identity and in resisting military occupation, in his moving description of the second annual meeting of 'Nordslesvigs Fælles Idrætsforening' at Sønderborg in 1907:

> During the procession others joined in and the procession grew larger and larger on its way through the village and the triumphal arch of the festival field. After the sports there were songs and speeches. These were supposed to be politically neutral, but the symbolic meanings in the songs 'Se, det lyser for vort Øje' (See how it Shines for our Eyes) and 'Loft dit Hoved' (Raise your Head) could not be misunderstood by the initiated.[105]

And again when he describes the patriotic passions aroused by the later joint Sonderberg and Hensborg pro-Danish march to the symbolic Dybbol Earthworks, scene of the heroic resistance to the Germans in 1864:

> The pro-Germans, however, organized a counter march and met them with the 'Schleswig-Holstein' song. The pro-Danes sang 'Vift stolt pa kodans bolger' (The Proud Waves of the Baltic). At Dybbol roughly 300 pro-Danes were met by nearly 1,500 pro-Germans who disturbed the Danish meeting, according to Meyer, by howling the German song. The pro-Danes withdrew, singing the national patriotic Danish song from 1848, 'De gang jeg drog af sted' (The Time I Left That Place). In Sonderborg the German navy could not guarantee the safety of the pro-Danes and they returned to the steamer in some disarray. When the steamer left the quay it was to the sound of their singing of the Danish national anthem 'Det er et yngdigt land' (It is a Lovely Country).[106]

It is precisely these ritualistic, symbolic and mythical elements of patriotism in sport that Goksøyr also briefly, and too briefly, explores in his chapter. It is to be hoped that he takes his inquiries further. A detailed examination of footballing rituals, symbols and myths of 'the people's'' nationalism in the inter-war years in Norway could throw a bright light on the relationship between nationalism, sport and the emotions of those who, unlike, for example, many English public schoolboys, were mostly unaccustomed by habit, largely unaided by education and generally unassisted by contacts from putting pen to paper to record feelings, events and moments, those whom Goksøyr calls 'the people'. It is, of course, in this area of inquiry that oral history comes into its own. Patriotic 'popular resonance' is insufficiently investigated in many others worlds than the Nordic World: 'Large sports gatherings [have] now acquired acute symbolic significance as new manifestations of old impulses.'[107] Goksøyr points the way to innovative research well beyond Norway's frontiers.

Henrik Meinander in his chapter, the 'Power of Public Pronouncement', reveals a delicate appreciation of the efficacy of the rhetoric of sport. He is also sensibly alert to the tension between rhetoric and action[108] – and to the fact that acceptance of rhetoric depends on its capacity to relate meaningfully to reality as it is interpreted at a specific moment in time by means of compelling allusion. Meinander's example of the impact of Freudian rhetoric on the European middle classes is an apt illustration of this. Similarly, the stanzas of English versifiers drawing graphic comparisons of the similar realities of the struggles on playingfields and battlefields made an equally powerful impression on the receptive minds of middle and upper-middle class public schoolboys:

> All night before the brink of death
> In fitful sleep the army lay,
> For through the dream that stilled their breath
> Too gauntly glared the coming day.
>
> We played again the immortal games,
> And grappled with the fierce old friends,
> And cheered the dead undying names,
> And sang the song that never ends.[109]

They too, like the young described by Meinander, were conditioned 'to discuss and plan the future with the help of myths and messages from the past'.[110] Meinander is another who can usefully take his investigations of the relationship between sport and rhetoric further.

Hellspong, Vasara, Hansen, Goksøyr and Meinander in their different ways raise issues of general relevance to cultural historians, military historians and sports historians. The value of *The Nordic World* lies both in its world and in wider worlds.

NOTES

1. See Richard Holt, *Sport and the British: A Modern History* (Oxford, 1989), p.12. No gullible antiquarians are actually mentioned by name.

2. See above, M. Hellspong, 'A Timeless Excitement ...', p.11
3. For Cotton's unsung contribution to modern sport, see J.A. Mangan, *Athleticism in the Victorian and Edwardian Public School: the emergence and consolidation of an educational ideology*, pp.22–8 and p.42. See also 'Cotton and Coubertin: European Realism and Idealism in the Making of Modern European Masculinity', in the Proceedings of the First CESH (European Seminar for Sports History) Rome, Autumn 1996, forthcoming. An updated and adapted version of this paper is incorporated into the later part of this chapter but the original contains more detailed information.
4. Hellspong, 'Timeless Excitement ...'
5. Roger Hutchinson, *Empire Games: The British Invention of Twentieth Century Sport* (Edinburgh, 1996), see Chapter One, *passim.*
6. Hutchinson, *Empire Games*, p.8.
7. Ibid., p.9.
8. Ibid., p.9.
9. Ibid., p.10.
10. Ibid., pp.10–11.
11. Ibid., p.15.
12. See J.A. Mangan, 'Prologue: Britain's Chief Spiritual Export: Imperial Sport as Moral Metaphor, Political Symbol and Cultural Bond', in J.A. Mangan, *The Cultural Bond: Sport, Empire, Society* (London, 1992), p.1.
13. Tyndale-Biscoe was an extraordinary educationist. For details of his time in Kashmir, see J.A. Mangan, 'Christ and the Imperial Gamesfields: evangelical athletes of the Empire', in J.A. Mangan, *The Games Ethic and Imperialism: Aspects of the Diffusion of an Ideal* (Harmondsworth, 1986), pp.168–92. *The Games Ethic* is to be reissued shortly by Frank Cass, London in the same Cass series as *The Nordic World*, namely Sport in the Global Society.
14. For a valuable and original contribution to studies in English elementary education which discusses the borrowed morality (from the public schools) of a selection of training colleges for elementary school teachers, see Colm Hickey, 'Athleticism and the London Training Colleges' (doctoral thesis, IRCSSS, University of Strathclyde, to be completed in 1998).
15. Hutchinson, *Empire Games*, p.16.
16. Mangan, 'Christ and the Imperial Gamesfields', p.187.
17. Hutchinson (*Empire Games.*) provides a highly amusing description of the introduction of soccer to South Uist (pp.12–13) while Mangan (*The Games Ethic*) has an even more hilarious description of the coming of soccer to Srinigar (p.184).
18. See Hellspong, 'A Timeless Excitement', *passim.*
19. Quoted by Hellspong from Holt, *Sport and the British* (p.12), p.23.
20. Holt, *Sport and the British*, p.12.
21. For an interesting description of 'reality' in history, see Keith Jenkins, *Re-thinking History* (London, 1991), pp.11–20.
22. See Mangan, 'Prologue', in *The Cultural Bond, passim.*
23. Ibid., p.4.
24. Ibid., p.8.
25. As Hellspong mentions in his chapter, this is being done by J.A. Mangan and Stephen Bailey. Winchester is the oldest public school in Britain and dates from the fourteenth century.
26. There are numerous considerations of 'fair play' in the literature of sport. One extended study is Peter McIntosh, *Fair Play: Ethics and Sport in Education* (London, 1979).
27. See Holt, *Sport and the British*, p.97. Most curiously, at least one commentator on British sport and society omits the term completely, see Dennis Brailsford, *British Sport: A Social History* (Cambridge, 1992), and similarly, at least one commentator on the British public school system fails to mention it, see Christine Heward, *Making a Man of Him* (London, 1988).
28. See below, pp.180–3.
29. Ibid.

30. For an exhaustive bibliography, see Mangan, *Athleticism in the Victorian and Edwardian Public School*, pp.309–36.
31. See Mangan, *Athleticism*, p.176 and p.300.
32. See J.A. Mangan, 'Social Darwinism and upper class education in late Victorian and Edwardian England' in J.A. Mangan and James Walvin (eds.), *Manliness and Morality: Middle-class Masculinity in Britain and America, 1800–1940* (Manchester, 1987), p.143.
33. In Kingsley Amis' novel *Lucky Jim*, Professor Welch, to the exasperation of his subordinate Jim Dixon, was taken up with an image of a medieval 'Merrie England' of pure fantasy.
34. Mangan, 'Social Darwinism', p.139.
35. Ibid., p.142.
36. Apart from Richard Holt, *Sport and the British*, see Chapter Two of Peter C. McIntosh's *Fair Play*, pp.20–36 (London, 1979). McIntosh has a wholly one-sided view of the origins of 'fair play' ascribing them to the motives of muscular Christians. For a rather different view, embracing a more complicated reality in the schools, see Mangan, 'Social Darwinism', *passim*.
37. See note 3 above. The following pages (up to p.183) include adapted, extended, and updated material from the paper 'Coubertin and Cotton: European Realism and Idealism in the Making of Modern Masculinity', Proceedings of the First CESH Seminar, Rome, Autumn, 1996, forthcoming.
38. See Mangan, *Athleticism, passim*.
39. However incredible this statement may appear to modern eyes, there can be little doubt as to its accuracy. For extensive evidence of this state of affairs, see Mangan, *Athleticism, passim*.
40. The most graphic description of the state of the schools at this time is certainly to be found in John Chandos, *Boys Together: English Public Schools 1800–1864* (London, 1984).
41. Chandos, p.131.
42. Chandos, *Boys Together*, pp.131–2.
43. Mangan, *Athleticism*, p.31.
44. This system was crucial to the transformation. For a description of the innovatory house system of George Edward Lynch Cotton at Marlborough, see Mangan *Athleticism*, pp.146–50.
45. This rebellion is known at Marlborough as the 'Great rebellion'. There is some controversy over its full extent but it certainly was a significant uprising by the boys and in all probability led to the resignation of the headmaster, M. Wilkinson, and thus to the subsequent appointment of his radical successor, G.E.C. Cotton.
46. The term is, of course, an adaptation of the well-known title of an article by Charles Tennyson, 'They Taught the World to Play', in *Victorian Studies* (March, 1959).
47. His main objective was to ensure, in his own words in a letter to parents on his arrival, that the pupils were kept 'as much as possible together in one body in the college itself, and in the playground'. Games were a means, literally, of social control.
48. A copy of the letter he sent to parents is to be found in Mangan, *Athleticism*, Appendix 1 (pp.228–30).
49. Mangan, *Athleticism*, p.7.
50. Ibid., p.150.
51. Ibid., p.135.
52. Price Collier, *England and the English from an American Point of View* (London, 1913), p.41.
53. Rudolf Kirchev, *Fair Play: The Games of Merrie England* (London, 1928), p.74.
54. I am indebted to David Brown for the quotation from his personal archives on the Canadian public schools.
55. See Pierre de Coubertin, 'Are the public schools a failure?' *Fortnightly Review*, Vol. LXXIII, No.432 (1902), pp.976–86.
56. Jeffrey Richards, 'Passing the love of Women: Manly love and Victorian Society', in Mangan and Walvin, *Manliness and Morality*, p.104.
57. See Mangan, *Athleticism*, 'Epilogue', pp.207–19.

58. *Raising the Game* was published in 1995. It was a British Government document 'putting forward ideas to rebuild the strength of every level of British sport' ('Introduction' by John Major, p.1). Due to the intense commitment of the Prime Minister to the document, it became known widely as 'Major's Raising the Game'. In it, among things, Major remarked, 'My ambition is simply stated. It is to put sport back at the heart of weekly life in *every* school' ('Introduction', p.2).

59. Only a small number of the schools of the public school system, the matrix of much of modern world sport, have been investigated. Much remains to be discovered, for example, about innovators, inspirationalists, antagonists and organisational variations. In addition the rhetoric of indoctrination has been only skimmed. Ideological apologists remain to be comprehensively located and researched. Significant vehicles of indoctrination such as school magazines remain to be thoroughly scrutinized.

60. A term the author uses in lecture, seminar and discussion to describe the growth of world sport in the twentieth century.

61. For an example of this rather too narrow preoccupation note the importance Richard Holt has attached to the presence of gymnastics and conscription as symbols of militarism in pre-Great War France and the consequent absence of militarism in pre-Great War Britain, due to an absence of conscription and a national system of state supported gymnastics. See, Richard Holt, 'Contrasting Nationalisms: sport, militarism and the unitary state in Britain and France before 1914', in J.A. Mangan (ed.), *Tribal Identities: Sport, Nationalism, Identity* (London, 1996), pp.38–54. As this chapter of *The Nordic World* and a number of other chapters and papers by its author makes clear (see note 62 below) this is a myopic approach to militarism. Britain was heavily obsessed by military matters prior to the Great War. The manifestations were in part different and in part similar to those in France. It is important to recognize that there was more than one form of militarism and more than one symbol. The definition of militarism adopted here is taken from the *The Oxford Dictionary* (Oxford, 1989, 2nd Ed.), Vol.IX, p.766: 'the prevalence of military sentiment or ideals among a people'.

62. For a substantial bibliography which includes references to these and the other authors on the subject, see J.A. Mangan, 'Duty Unto Death', in Mangan, *Tribal Identities*, pp.34–8.

63. See J.A. Mangan, '"The grit of our forefathers": invented traditions, propaganda and imperialism', in John M. MacKenzie (ed.), *Imperialism and Popular Culture* (Manchester, 1986), p.127. The research of Alan Penn (note 91) and Colm Hickey (note 14) provides further support for this point. See also Anne Bloomfield, 'Sport and dance as symbols of imperialism', in Mangan, *Making Imperial Mentalities*, pp.74–95.

64. See Holt, 'Contrasting Nationalisms', Notes, for exceedingly sparse references to British militarism.

65. Mangan, 'Duty unto Death', p.14.

66. Ibid., p.12.

67. Ibid., p.14.

68. Ibid., p.13.

69. Ibid.

70. Ibid., pp.13–14.

71. Ibid., p.15.

72. Ibid., pp.26–31 provide clear evidence of the 'conceit' in its extension to the Great War. See also J.A.Mangan, 'Gamefield and Battlefield: A Romantic Alliance in Verse and the Creation of Militaristic Masculinity', in John Nauright and T. Chandler (eds.), *Making Men: Rugby and Masculine Identity* (London, 1996), pp.146–52.

73. Ibid., p.17.

74. Ibid., p.15.

75. Ibid., p.17

76. See Mangan, 'Gamesfield and Battlefield', p.141.

77. For an excellent example linking sport and imperial and anti-German militaristic propaganda, see John Astley Cooper, 'The British Imperial Spirit of Sport and War', *United Empire*, VIII, 9 (Sept. 1916).

78. Ibid., pp.26–7.

79. Ibid., p.26.
80. Ibid.
81. Ibid., p.27.
82. For an analysis of the role of sport in anti-German vitriolic propaganda, see Colin Veitch, 'Sport and War in the British Literature of the First World War, 1914–1918' (unpublished MA thesis, University of Alberta, Edmonton, 1983). In particular, see Chapter VI, 'Gallant Britons and Barbaric Huns: Sport and British Propaganda in the First World War', pp. 88–110. Veitch states that the British press characterized the German race as war-mongering barbarians and added, 'it was common for accusations against German brutality and inhumanity to be traced back to their preoccupation with duelling as opposed to team Games' (p.96). The German student fencing bout, the *Mensur* was described by one commentator of the time as 'a *Fest* of physical brutality, of voluntarily inflicted and voluntarily endured physical torture The type of courage ... developed is debased, immoral and anti-social' (F.H. Swift quoted in Veitch, p.97).
83. *The War Illustrated*, Vol.2 (1915), p.1
84. Veitch, 'Sport and War', pp.98–9.
85. Ibid.
86. George Herbert Clarke (ed.), *A Treasury of War Poetry* (London, 1919), p.286.
87. See for example, J.A. Mangan, *Athleticism,* 'Play up and play the game: the rhetoric of cohesion, identity, patriotism and morality', pp.179–203, J.A. Mangan, 'Concepts of Duty and Prospects of Adventure: Images of Empire for Public Schoolboys', in J.A. Mangan, *The Games Ethic and Imperialism*, pp.44–70, J.A. Mangan, 'Moralists, Metaphysicians and Mythologists: The "Signifiers" of a Victorian and Edwardian sub-culture', in Susan J-Bandy, *Coroebus Triumphs: The Alliance of Sport and the Arts* (San Diego, 1988), pp.141–62, J.A. Mangan, 'Noble Specimens of Manhood: schoolboy literature and the creation of a colonial chivalric code', in Jeffrey Richards, *Imperialism and Juvenile Literature* (Manchester, 1989), pp.173–94, J.A. Mangan, 'The Grit of our Forefathers: Invented Traditions, Propaganda and Imperialism', in John M. MacKenzie (ed.), *Imperialism and Popular Culture* (Manchester, 1986), pp.113–39, J.A. Mangan, 'Duty unto Death', pp, 10–38, J.A. Mangan,'Muscular, Militaristic and Manly : The British Middle Class Hero as Moral Messenger', in Richard Holt, J.A. Mangan and Pierre Lanfranchi (eds.), *European Heroes: Myth, Identity Sport* (London, 1996), pp.28–47, J.A. Mangan, 'Gamesfield and Battlefield : A Romantic Alliance in Verse and the Creation of Militaristic Masculinity', in Nauright and Chandler (eds.), *Making Men,* pp.141–57. For the wider cultural and educational context in which these articles and chapters are set, see: Mangan, *Athleticism*; Mangan, *The Games Ethic*; but also J.A. Mangan (ed.), *Benefits Bestowed?: Education and British Imperialism* (Manchester, 1988); J.A. Mangan (ed.), *Making Imperial Mentalities: Socialisation and British Imperialism* (Manchester, 1990); and J.A. Mangan (ed.), *The Imperial Curriculum: Racial Images and Education in the British Colonial Experience* (London, 1993).
88. M.J.Cronin is one sports historian who shows himself intelligently aware of this significance in his review of *Tribal Identities* in *Contemporary British History*, 10, 2 (1996), 256–8. While W. Vamplew, for example, wholly fails to perceive the significance of the relationship between sport, patriotic socialization and poetry, prose and painting and equally fails to locate weaknesses in the comparative structural approach in the volume in his review in *The International History Review*, XIX, 2 (May 1997), 483–4.
89. Michael Howard, 'War and the Nation State', Inaugural Lecture, University of Oxford, November, 1977. See also Michael Howard, 'Empire, Race and War in pre 1914 Britain', in Hugh Lloyd Jones *et al.* (eds.), *History and Imagination Essays in Honour of H.R. Trevor Roper* (London, 1981).
90. Holt, 'Contrasting Nationalisms', p.44.
91. Alan Penn, *Targeting the Schools: Militarism, Elementary School and Drill, 1870–1914* (London, forthcoming), p.1.
92. Ibid., p.26.
93. Ibid.
94. Ibid., p.27.

95. Ibid., pp.6–7.
96. Ibid., p.32.
97. Ibid., p.219.
98. Ibid., see Introduction, pp.ii–x and Chapter One, *passim*.
99. Ibid., p.221.
100. Quoted in Penn, p.125.
101. Ibid., p.230.
102. Ibid.
103. Ibid.
104. J.A. Mangan, 'Physical Education as a Ritual Process', in J.A. Mangan, *Physical Education and Sport: Sociological and Cultural Perspectives* (Oxford, 1973), p.95.
105. Hansen, 'Politics and Gymnastics', above, p.38.
106. Ibid., p.43.
107. Goksøyr, 'The Popular Sounding Board ', above, p.109.
108. Meinander, 'The Power of Public Pronouncement', above, p.52.
109. Sir Henry Newbolt, 'The School at War', *Poems: New and Old* (London, 1912), p.103. There are many hundreds, perhaps thousands when fuller investigation is made, of such examples of 'verse socialization'.
110. Meinander, 'The Power of Public Pronouncement', above, p.68.

Epilogue: Nordic World and Global Village

J. A. MANGAN

'These Norsemen are excellent persons in the main, with good sense, steadiness, wise speech and prompt action', wrote Ralph Waldo Emerson, of the heroes of the Nordic Sagas. He added, however, that

> they have a singular turn for homicide; their chief end of man is to murder or to be murdered; oars, scythe, harpoons, crowbars, peat-knives and hay-forks are tools valued by them all the more for their charming aptitude for assassinations. A pair of kings, after dinner, will divert themselves by thrusting each his sword through the other's body, as did Yngve and Alf. Another pair ride out on a morning for a frolic, and finding no weapon near, will take the bits out of their horses' mouths and crush each other's heads with them, as did Alric and Eric.[1]

These essays deal with gentler descendants in mostly gentler times and with very different 'amusements', but perhaps with equally intense passions associated with nationalism, secularism, democracy and emancipation.

Much of the volume, in one form or another, deals with modern nationalism in its relationship to sport. 'Religion', Napoleon Bonaparte once asserted, ruminating on the profound and indestructible force of religion as a means of political control in the empires of Turk and Tsar, 'is a part of destiny', adding that, 'With the soil, the laws, the manners, it forms that sacred whole which is called *La Patrie* and which one must never desert,' and concluding, that 'the principal charm of a religion consists in its memories'.[2]

It could be argued, with some plausibility, that replacement of 'religion' with the term 'sport' would carry greater conviction in the substantially secular age of late twentieth-century Europe. Sport has now become that important! The gradual emergence of modern sport as a cultural substitute for religion in the Nordic nations, implicitly if not explicitly, is also a continuous theme in this volume.

Another Napoleonic axiom that has echoed down the years, 'The strength of a people depends upon its history',[3] has been liberally interpreted by the eminent historian H.A.L. Fisher to mean that a nation cannot be successfully governed unless 'political contrivances' are carefully suited to the peculiar temperament of the governed, which in turn has been fashioned by historic forces.[4] Again, as several of the contributors to this volume make clear, in recent Nordic history in the right circumstances at the right moments, sport has been a powerful 'political contrivance' not only forging links of close patriotic allegiance between past, present and future but through state involvement, improving health, fitness and the quality of life.

Not every distinguished Frenchman's axiom is necessarily wise. The famous dictum of Bonaparte's compatriot the Compte de Sieyès that 'confidence must come from below, power from above' is scarcely acceptable to the proudly democratic Nordic nations of the modern age.[5] Sport, as the volume makes plain, can be a democratic instrument of the political certainty of 'the people' in the face of the intellectuals and politicians. Stadiums can be forums for nationalistic assertion, and players can be icons of patriotic purpose.

Some 250 years after Bonaparte and Sieyès, another Frenchman, Pierre Teilhard de Chardin, observed: 'Nowadays, over and above the bread which to simple Neolithic man symbolised food, each man demands his daily ration of iron, copper and cotton, of electricity, oil and radium, of discoveries, of the cinema and of international news.'[6] If he had been writing closer to the moment of the Millennium it is likely that he would have included sport on his list – both for men *and* women. There may be something in the remark of the nineteenth-century novelist George Eliot that 'the happiest women, like the happiest nations, have no history', but women everywhere in Europe, including the Nordic World, as this volume also makes clear, in the twentieth century have challenged history rather than ignored it, to their ultimate advantage. In this challenge, sport has played its part in their physical, psychological, educational, social and political emancipation.[7]

In short, this volume, although concerned with only a part, deals with the relationship of sport to some of the great issues of the whole 'modern global village' – nationalism, secularism, democracy and emancipation.

It is also a catalyst for a consideration of the extent of the adequacies and inadequacies of recent attempts to deal with continuity and change in the history of sport and for a demonstration of the need for greater subtlety in the analysis of patriotic militarism and the purpose and power of rhetoric – in and beyond the Nordic world.

Essentially, however, it has been its purpose, within the wider Series in which it appears, to offer a forum to Nordic scholars to reflect on sport in the context of their culture. This policy will involve other academics and other regions in the future. Fittingly, it will next embrace Australasia in the year of the Millennium Olympics in Sydney.

NOTES

1. Carl Bode and Malcolm Cowley (eds.), *The Portable Emerson* (Harmondsworth, 1981), pp.413–15.
2. Quoted in H.A.L. Fisher, *Bonapartism* (Oxford, 1957), p.45.
3. Ibid., p.77
4. Ibid., pp.77–8.
5. Emmanuel Joseph Sieyès (1748–1836) was an indestructible and at times, influential, politician of the French Revolution.
6. Pierre Teilhard de Chardin, *The Phenomenon of Man* (London, 1967, 5th ed.), p.270.
7. See George Eliot, *The Mill on the Floss* (London, 1975), p.374.

Selected Bibliography

A Timeless Excitement: Swedish Agrarian Society and Sport in the Pre-Industrial Era
Mats Hellspong

Heiner Gilmeister, *Kulturgeschichgte des Tennis* (München, 1990).

Mats Hellspong, *Idrott som folklig leg* (Rig, 1991).

Mats Hellspong, *Slå trilla. En lek pa gransen mellan folklig och modern idrott* (Rig, 1990).

Richard Holt, *Sport and the British: A Modern History* (Oxford, 1989).

Magnus Olaus, *Historia om de nordiska folken* (Stockholm, 1976).

Henrik Sandblad, *Olympia och Valhalla. Idéhistoriska aspekter av den moderna idrottsrörelsens framväxt* (Stockholm, 1976).

Per Arvid Säve, *Gotländska lekar. Utg. Av Herbert Gustavsson* (Uppsala, 1948).

Politics and Gymnastics in a Frontier Area post-1848
Jørn Hansen

Inge Adriansen, *Fædrelandet, folkeminderne og modersmaalet, Skrifter fra Museumsradet for Sønderjyllands Amt* (Sønderborg, 1990).

Jens Peter Ægidius: *Christian Flor. Paedagogen, politikeren, folkeoplyseren* (Odense Universitetsforiag, 1994).

Hans Schultz Hansen, *Danskheden i Sydslesvig 1840–1918 som folkelig og national bevægelse*. Studieafdelingen ved Dansk Centralbibliotek for Sydslesvig (Flensborg, 1990).

Uwe Heldt, '125 Jahre Turn- und Sportbund Flensburg. Ein Beitrag zur Entwicklung von Turnen und Sport in Flensburg', *Kleine reihe der Gesellschaft für Flensburg Stadtgeschichte. Bd. 1–2* (Flensburg, 1991).

Gottlieb Japsen (ed.), *Dansk og tysk i Sønderjylland* (København, 1979).

Adler Lund, *Sønderjydsk Idrætsforening. Et Bidrag til Skildring af Dansk Ungdomsliv i Sønderjylland* (Haderslev, 1932).

Chr. Pedersen (ed.), *Dansk Idræt i Grænselandet* (Haderslev, 1957).

Lorens Rerup, *Slesvig og Holsten efter 1830* (København: Politikens Forlag, 1982).

Johan Runge, *Sønderjyden, Christian Paulsen, Et slesvigsk levnedsforløb*, Udgivet af Studieafdelingen ved Dansk Centralbibliotek for Sydslesvig

(Flensborg, 1981).

Franz Winginder og Sig. Kristensen (ed,), *Dansk Ungdom i Sydslesvig 1923–1948. Sydslesvigske Danske Ungdomsforeningers Jubilæumsskrift* (Tønder, 1948).

The Power of Public Pronouncement: The Rhetoric of Nordic Sport in the Early Twentieth Century
Henrik Meinander

Henrik Berggren, *Seklets ungdom: Retorik, politik och modernitet 1900–1939* (Stockholm, 1995).

Marjatta Hietala, *Services and Urbanization at the Turn of the Century: The Diffusion of Innovations* (Helsinki, 1987).

Stephen Kern, *The Culture of Time and Space 1880–1918* (Cambridge, MA, 1994).

Tim Knudsen, *Storbyen støbes: København mellem kaos och byplan* (København, 1988).

Jan Lindroth, *Idrottens våg till folkrörelse. Studier i svensk idrottsrörelse till 1915* (Stockholm, 1974).

Henrik Meinander, *Towards a Bourgeois Manhood: Boys' Physical Education in Nordic Secondary Schools 1880–1940* (Helsinki, 1994).

Henrik Meinander, 'Den nordistiska kroppen', *Internationale idestrømninger og nordisk kultur 1850–1914: Den 22. nordiske historikermote: Oslo 13.–18. August 1994* (Oslo, 1997).

Heikki Paunonen, *Suomen kieli Helsingissä: Huomioita Helsingin puhekielen historiallisesta ja nykyvariaatosta* (Helsinki, 1995).

Henrik Sandblad, *Olympia och Valhalia: Idéhistoriska aspekter av den moderna idrottsrörelsens framväxt* (Stockholm, 1985).

Bodil Stenseth, *En norske elite: Nasjonsbyggerne på Lysaker 1890–1940* (Oslo, 1993).

Laurence Veysey, 'Intellectual History and the New Social History', John Higham and Paul K. Conkin (eds.), *New Directions in American Intellectual History* (Baltimore, 1979).

From Balck to Nurmi: The Early Olympic Movement and the Nordic Nations
Per Jørgensen

Pierre de Coubertin, *Olympic Memoirs* (Lausanne, 1979).

Per Jørgensen, 'Order, Discipline and Self-Control: The Breakthrough for the Danish Sport Federation and Sport, 1896–1916', *International Journal of the History of Sport*, 13, 3 (Dec.1996).

Allen Guttmann, *The Olympics: A History of the Modern Games* (Campaign, Illinois, 1982).

John Hoberman, *The Olympic Crisis: Sports, Politics and the Moral Order* (New York, 1986).

Per Jørgensen, *Ro, Renlighed, Regelmæssighed – Dansk Idræts-Forbund og sportens gennembrud ca. 1896 – 1918* (Odense, 1997).

David B. Kanin, *A Political History of the Olympic Games* (Boulder, Colorado 1981).

Jan Lindroth, *Idrottens våg till folkrörelse – Studier i svensk idrottsrörelse till 1915* (Uppsala, 1974).

John J. MacAloon, *This Great Symbol: Pierre de Coubertin and the Origins of the Modern Olympic Games* (Chicago, 1981).

Jeffrey O. Segrave and Donald Chu (eds.), *The Olympic Games in Transition* (Campaign, Illinois, 1988).

Jeffrey O. Segrave and Donald Chu (eds.), *Olympism* (Campaign, Illinois, 1981).

The Popular Sounding Board: Nationalism, 'the People' and Sport in Norway in the Inter-war Years
Matti Goksøyr

Benedict Andersson, *Imagined Communities* (London 1991).

Eric Hobsbawm, *Nations and Nationalisms since 1789* (Cambridge, 1991).

Eric Hobsbawm and Terence Ranger (eds.), *The Invention of Tradition* (Cambridge, 1984).

Matti Goksøyr, *Kropp, kultur og tippekamp: Statens idrettskontor, STUI og Idrettsavdelingen* (Oslo, 1996).

Matti Goksøyr, *Vi gir alt for Norge: Om nasjonal reisning og kulturell tilhørighet* (Oslo, 1996).

Halvdan Koht, *Norsk vilje* (Oslo, 1933).

Finn Olstad, *Norsk idrettshistorie 1861–1939: 'Forsvar, sport, klassekamp'* (vol.1) Oslo, 1987.

Anthony D. Smith, *National Identity* (London, 1991).

Bodil Stenseth, *En norsk elite: nasjonsbyggerne på Lysaker 1890–1940* (Oslo, 1993).

Øystein Sørensen (ed.), *Nasjonal identitet – et kunstprodukt?* (Oslo, 1994).

Stein Tønnesson, *Norden speiler seg: Identitetsdebaten 1986 – 1993* (Norsk Historisk Tidssskrift 3, 1993).

Øyvind Østerud, *Hva er nasjonalisme?* (Oslo, 1994).

A Mutual Dependency: Nordic Sports Organizations and the State
Johan R. Norberg

Claus Boje and Henning Eichberg, *Idraetens tredje vej – Om idraetten i kulturpolitikken* (Aarhus, 1994).

Matti Goksøyr, *Staten og Idretten 1861–1991* (Oslo, 1992).

Jan Lindroth, *Idrottens väg till folkrörelse – studier i Svensk idrottsrörelse till 1915,* Studia Historica Upsallensia 60 (Uppsala, 1974).

Jan Lindroth, *Idrott mellan krigen. Organisationer, ledare och ideer I den svenska idrottsrörelsen 1919–1939* (Stockholm, 1987).

Johan R. Norberg, '"I myndighets ställe": en analys av Sveriges Riksidrottsförbunds utveckling till partiell myndighet 1955–1970' (unpublished essay, Stockholm University, 1996).

Finn Olstad, *Norsk idretts historie, Forsvar, sport, klasskamp 1861–1939* (Østeras, 1986).

Else Trangbæk (ed.), *Dansk idrætsliv. Den moderne idrætsgennembrud 1860–1940* (Copenhagen, 1995).

Else Trangbæk (ed.)., *Dansk idrætsliv. Velfaerd og fritid 1940–1996* (Copenhagen, 1995).

Stein Tønnesson, *Norsk idretts historie, Folkehelse, trim, stjerner 1939–1986* (Østeras, 1986).

Gender in Modern Society: Femininity, Gymnastics and Sport
Else Trangbæk

Allen Guttmann, *Women's Sports: A History* (New York, 1991).

Ann Hall, *Feminism and Sporting Bodies* (New York and London, 1996).

Jennifer Hargreaves, *Sporting Females. Critical Issues in the History and Sociology in Women's Sports* (London, 1994).

George Lakoff and Mark Johnson, *Metaphors We Live by* (Chicago, 1980).

Birgitte Possing, *Viljens styrke. Natalie Zahle. En biografi,* Bd. I og B.II (København, 1992).

Bente Rosenbeck, *Kroppens Politik, Om kon, kultur og videnskab* (København, 1992).

Else Trangbæk, *Mellem leg og disciplin, Gymnastikken i Danmarks i 1800-tallet* (København, 1987)

Else Trangbæk, 'Discipline and Emancipation through Sport: The Pioneers of Women's Sport in Denmark', *Scandinavian Journal of History,* 2 (1996), 130–1.

Patricia Vertinsky, *The Eternally Wounded Woman: Women, Exercise and Doctors in the Late Nineteenth Century* (Manchester, 1990).

Maintaining a Military Capability: The Finnish Home Guard, European Fashion and Sport for War
Erkki Vasara

Bildchronik zur Geschichte des Freikorps und Bundes Oberland, edited by Traditionsgemeinschaft des Friekorps und Bundes Oberland (Munich, 1974).

Seppo Hentilä, ' "Proletarische Wehrertuchtigung" durch den Sport?' unpublished paper from November, 1995, Helsinki.

Niilo V. Hersalo, *Suojeluskuntain historia 1–2* (Vaasa, 1955 ja 1962).

Hans Jürgen Kuron, *Freikorps und Bund Oberland,* Dissertation (Erlangen, 1960).

Erkki Laitinen, *Pesäpallo – kansallispeli 60 vuotta* (Saarijärvi, 1983).

Jarmo Matikainen, 'Suojeluskuntajarjeston yhteydet Euroopan muihin sotilasjärjestöihin ja ulkovaltoihin vuosina 1920–1934' (unpublished MA thesis, University of Helsinki, 1989).

Hannes Raikkala, *Suojeluskuntain historia 3* (Vaasa, 1964).

Sport in Society: The Nordic World and Other Worlds
J.A. Mangan

John Chandos, *Boys Together: English Public Schools 1800–1864* (London, 1984).

Peter C. McIntosh, *Fair Play* (London, 1979).

J.A. Mangan, *Athleticism in the Victorian and Edwardian Public School: The Emergence and Consolidation of an Educational Ideology* (Cambridge, 1981).

J.A. Mangan, *The Games Ethic and Imperialism: Aspects of the Diffusion of an Ideal* (Harmondsworth, 1986).

J.A. Mangan, 'Prologue: Britain's Chief Spiritual Export: Imperial Sport as Moral Metaphor, Political Symbol and Cultural Bond', in J.A. Mangan (ed.), *The Cultural Bond: Sport, Empire, Society* (London, 1992).

J.A. Mangan, 'Gamefield and Battlefield: A Romantic Alliance in Verse and the Creation of Militaristic Masculinity', in John Nauright and T. Chandler (eds.), *Making Men: Rugby and Masculine Identity* (London, 1996).

'Social Darwinism and upper class education in late Victorian and Edwardian England', in J.A. Mangan and James Walvin (eds.), *Manliness and Morality: Middle Class Masculinity in Britain and America 1800–1940* (Manchester, 1987).

'Duty unto Death: English Masculinity and Militarism in the Age of the

New Imperialism', in J.A. Mangan (ed.), *Tribal Identities: Nationalism, Europe, Sport* (London, 1996).

Alan Penn, *Targeting the Schools: Militarism, Elementary School and Drill, 1870–1914* (London, forthcoming).

For the wider cultural and educational context in which these books, articles and chapters are set, see J.A. Mangan (ed.), *Benefits Bestowed?: Education and British Imperialism* (Manchester, 1988), J.A. Mangan (ed.), *Making Imperial Mentalities: Socialisation and British Imperialism* (Manchester, 1990) and J.A. Mangan (ed.), *The Imperial Curriculum: Racial Images and Education in the British Colonial Experience* (London, 1993).

Notes about the Contributors

Matti Goksøyr is Associate Professor in Sports History at the Norwegian University of Sport and Physical Education, Oslo, Norway. His research covers sport, cultural and national identity, sport and state policies, sports and local history and sports history theory. Publications include *Idrettsliv i borgerskapets by* (Oslo, 1991), *Staten og idretten 1861–1991* (Oslo, 1992), *Kropp, kultur og tippekamp* (Oslo, 1996), *Vi gir alt for Norge* (Oslo, 1996), as well as articles in international and national journals.

Jørn Hansen is Associate Professor (History) Department of Physical Education, Odense University, Denmark, and Head of the Danish Sports History Association. Research interests include sport in modern Danish society, sport on the Danish/German border and sport, health and humanism.

Mats Hellspong is Assistant Professor in Ethnology at Stockholm University. He was Head of the Department of Ethnology from 1983 to 1995. He has written books and articles on traditional and modern sport including *Boxningssporten I Sverige. En studie I idrottens kulturmiljo* (1982) [Boxing in Sweden: A study of the cultural environment of sport] and *Korset, fanan och fotbollen. En jamforande studie av folkorelsernas kulturmiljo* (1990) [The Cross, the Standard and the Football: a comparative study of the culture of popular movements].

Per Jørgensen is Associate Professor of History at the Institute of Exercise and Sport Sciences, University of Copenhagen, and a member of the Board of the Danish Sports History Association. His research interests include the history and sociology of sport in Denmark and the history of physical education. He has written several monographs and articles on these subjects.

J. A. Mangan is a Professor in the Faculty of Education, Strathclyde University and Director of its International Research Centre for Sport, Socialisation and Society. He is the author and editor of many books on these themes. His research interests include sport and socialization, imperialism and socialization and masculinity and socialization. He edits two Cass journals, *The International Journal of The History of Sport* and *Culture, Sport, Society*, and the new Cass Series 'Sport in the Global Society'.

Henrik Meinander is Associate Professor, Department of Education, University of Helsinki, Finland. His research interests include Finnish political and intellectual history, Nordic educational history and the history of sport. Numerous articles and three monographs published on these subjects include the internationally well-received *Towards a Bourgeois Manhood: Boys' Physical Education in Nordic Secondary Schools*, 1880–1940 (Helsinki, 1994).

Johan R. Norberg is a doctoral student in the Department of History, University of Stockholm, Sweden. He is currently working on a dissertation concerning the relationship between the Swedish sports movement and the state.

Else Trangbæk is Associate Professor, Institute of Exercise and Sport Sciences, University of Copenhagen, founder of the Danish Sports History Association and Chairwoman, 1984–96, and Chairwoman of the Danish Sports Research Council. Her research interests include gender and sport, gymnastics and sport in the process of Danish modernity, and sport, socialization and life history. She has written seven monographs and numerous articles on these subjects.

Erkki Vasara is the author of four books and several articles on the Finnish history of sport. His doctoral thesis (University of Helsinki) on sports and educational activities of the Finnish Civil Guard Organization (1918–39) was published in 1997.

Index

Books of Related Interest

Rugby's Great Split
Class, Culture and the Origins of Rugby League Football

Tony Collins

This book looks at rugby in the context of late Victorian and Edwardian England and examines how class conflict tore rugby apart in 1895 and led to the creation of the new sport of rugby league. At its heart is an explanation of how a game which was initially exclusive to public school boys was transformed into a sport which became entirely identified with the working classes of northern England. Although class conflict is seen as the motor force which ultimately drove rugby to split, the relationship between rugby, masculinity and English nationalism, England's North–South divide and the rise of the entertainment industry are also examined.

256 pages 1998   07146 4867 1 cloth   07146 4424 2 paper
Sport in the Global Society

European Heroes
Myth, Identity, Sport

J A Mangan, *University of Strathclyde*, Richard Holt, *University of Leuven, Belgium* and Pierre Lanfranchi, *De Montfort University* (Eds)

Historians of popular culture have recently been addressing the role of myth, and now it is time that social historians of sport also examined it. The contributors to this collection of essays explore the symbolic meanings that have been attached to sport in Europe by considering some of the mythic heroes who have dominated the sporting landscapes of their own countries. The ambition is to understand what these icons stood for in the eyes of those who watched or read about these vessels into which poured all manner of gender class and patriotic expectations.

184 pages   1996   0 7146 4578 8 cloth   0 7146 4125 1 paper
A special issue of the The International Journal of the History of Sport

The Games Ethic And Imperialism
Aspects of the Diffusion of an Ideal

J A Mangan, *University of Strathclyde*
New Preface and Foreword

'...not only injects fresh vigour into the old, old story but
emphasises the very peculiar nature, both of those institutions
where characters was elevated above intellect by the
encouragement of team games, and of the formidable
headmasters who held sway over them.'
The Daily Telegraph

This book is more than a description of the imperial spread of
public school games: it is a consideration of hegemony and
patronage, ideals and idealism, educational values and
aspirations, cultural assimilation and adaptation, and perhaps
most fascinating of all, the dissemination throughout the empire
of the hugely influential moralistic ideology of athleticism.

240 pages 1985; new impression, 2nd edition 1998
0 7146 4399 8 paper
Sport in the Global Society

The Global Sports Arena
Athletic Talent Migration in an Interdependent World

John Bale, *Keele University* and Joseph Maguire,
Loughborough University (Eds)

Athletes are on the move. In some sports this involves sport
labour movement from one country to another within or between
continents. In other sports, athletes assume an almost nomadic
migratory lifestyle, constantly on the move from one sport
festival to another. In addition, it appears that sport migration is
gaining momentum and that it is closely interwoven with the
broader process of global sport development taking place in the
late twentieth century.

304 pages   1994   0 7146 3489 1 cloth   0 7146 4116 2 paper

Footbinding, Feminism and Freedom
The Liberation of Women's Bodies in Modern China

Fan Hong, *De Montfort University*

This original book brings Chinese women to the centre of the Chinese cultural stage by examining the role which exercise and, subsequently, sport played in their liberation. Through the medium of womens bodies, Fan Hong explores the significance of religious beliefs, cultural codes and political dogmas for gender relations, gender concepts and the human body in an Asian setting.

352 pages   1997   0 7146 4633 4 cloth   0 7146 4334 3 paper
Sport in the Global Society

The Race Game
Sport and Politics in South Africa

Douglas Booth, *University of Otago, New Zealand*

In this book Douglas Booth takes a fresh look at the role of sport · in fostering a new national identity in South Africa. It looks at the thirty-year course and the changes in the objectives of the sports boycott of South Africa.

272 pages   1998   0 7146 4799 3 cloth   0 7146 4354 8 paper
Sport in the Global Society

The Cultural Bond
Sport, Empire, Society

J A Mangan, *University of Strathclyde* (Ed)

For Britain's Empire-builders sport was much more than merely an agreeable recreation. It became elevated to the status of a moral discipline, a symbol of imperial solidarity and superiority, even a salve for conscience. The contributors to this volume examine the aspects of the cultural associations, symbolic interpretations and emotional significance of the idea of empire and, to some extent, with the post-imperial consequences.

228 pages   1993   0 7146 3398 4 cloth   0 7146 4075 1 paper